Praise for Allan Ferguson and  Golf in Scotland

"Allan Ferguson has paved the way . . . . Take an iron or two out of your bag and carry this book instead."—**Michael Bamberger**, *Sports Illustrated;* author of *To the Linksland*

"*Golf in Scotland* is an excellent guide to the Scottish links, their inns, and many other amenities of the Scottish game."— **Michael Murphy**, author of *Golf in the Kingdom* and *The Kingdom of Shivas Irons*

"If you're inclined to travel to . . . Scottish courses, your best guide is Allan McAllister Ferguson's *Golf in Scotland*."—**Lorne Rubenstein**, Toronto *Globe and Mail*, author of *A Season in Dornoch*

"Laced with history and local lore as well as the nitty-gritty of modern golf travel, *Golf in Scotland* may prove an indispensable guide for the wise golf traveler."—**James Dodson**, author of *The Dewsweepers, Final Rounds*, and *A Golfer's Life*

"Valuable insider information . . . the book gives the skinny on planning a trip to the Auld Sod."—*Golf Magazine*

"The best inside track on how to do golf in Scotland." —**Michael Tobert**, author of *Pilgrims in the Rough: St. Andrews Beyond the 19th Hole*

"Two essentials for your golf holiday in Scotland—a knockdown shot into the wind and Allan Ferguson's book, *Golf in Scotland*. The best and most comprehensive guide available."—**Graeme Lennie**, *Head Professional, Crail Golfing Society, Fife, Scotland*

"There's simply no substitute for 'on-the-ground' knowledge and, when it comes to golf trips to Scotland—in knowing where to play, where to stay, and how much you ought to pay—there's no substitute for Allan Ferguson's *Golf in Scotland*." —**Curtis Gillespie**, author *of Playing Through: A Year of Life and Links Along the Scottish Coast*

"A must for those headed for the old country." —**Tom Kensler**, The Denver *Post*

"Allan McAllister Ferguson won't make many friends in the tour guide industry . . . but he'll compensate for that with a big boost in popularity with the individual traveler."—**Jeff Barr**, *Golfweek*

"*Golf in Scotland* is about the most sensible Scottish golf book I have read. It's nice to know that what we have over here is getting known throughout the world . . . ."—**Les Starkings**, author of *The Wee Yellow Book* and resident of Balerno near Edinburgh

And the Travelers Write

"We just returned from Scotland. The information and advice provided in *Golf in Scotland* was a great help and made the planning almost as enjoyable as the actual trip."—**Bob Patterson**, Kingwood TX

"I read your book from cover to cover several times. All the tips and recommendations you made were on target."
—**Bradford Hathaway**, Newburyport MA

"I have made twenty trips to Scotland over the past fifteen years and I found your book to be absolutely the most informative book on the subject."—**Dennis Tosh**, Oxford MS

"Kudos to your book, which convinced me I could go it alone in the planning process."—**Roger Thornton**, Simpsonville SC

"My son and I just returned from our golf trip to Scotland and it was GREAT! Your book was priceless. Everything went exactly as you said it would."
—**Todd Early**, Acworth GA

"A note of thanks for your outstanding book . . . . Was able to book eight players on both St. Andrews and Muirfield with your advice."—**Josh Weller**, Greenland NH

"This book not only describes how the tour operators overcharge, but offers clear alternatives for planning a trip. Allan knows Scotland inside out. He's a pro."
—**Howard Ganz**, Toronto, Canada

"Thanks for writing your book and sharing your wisdom."
—**Joe Burns**, Easton MD

GOLF IN SCOTLAND:

A Travel-Planning Guide

with

Profiles of **68** Great Courses

by

Allan McAllister Ferguson

New Revised Edition

WFPublishing
a division of WF Enterprises, Inc.
Denver • Colorado

Published by:
WFPublishing
a division of WF Enterprises, Inc.
1743 S. Marion St.
Denver CO 80210 USA
303-722-3441; 800-835-6692 (toll free in USA)
fax: 303-722-3441
Email: aferguson@fergusongolf.com
Web: http://www.fergusongolf.com

Cover photograph by Allan Ferguson
Cover design and graphics by Rust Graphics
Photographs by Allan Ferguson
Index by Lisa Probasco

ISBN 0-9710326-2-9

Dedication and Acknowledgements

This revised and expanded edition of *Golf in Scotland* is dedicated to all my Scottish friends in the travel trade and at the golf clubs who work so hard to make visitors to Scotland feel welcome. You know who you are.

There's another group, equally important, and those are all my clients—whether they go once or many times. They keep in touch with me and I learn from every one of their trips. They are the reason I continue to do what I do.

Special thanks to Sandy Howie, a member at Western Gailes Golf Club, and Ian Sproule, secretary of that same club, for vetting the manuscript of *Golf in Scotland*. These fine fellows have kept me from making a complete fool of myself in the discerning eyes of Scottish readers. On this side of the water, Ruth Wimmer serves much the same function. In addition to being a good proofreader, she reins me in on occasion, keeps the books, tends the garden, and fixes a mighty fine meal. I'd be in deep rough without her.

Finally, there's Kenn & Vi Rust at Rust Graphics—late of Denver, now of Tucson, Arizona. We have worked together for some fifteen years on the graphics end of various business projects. The revolution in cyberspace has allowed us to continue that collaboration over a stretch of 1,000 miles.

I'm pretty much a one-man band and, therefore, am responsible for all the rest—the advice and opinions that are "spot on" (as they say in Scotland) as well as the wrong-headed assertions. Errors of fact are another matter and I stand ready to apologize for and correct any factual errors brought to my attention.

As I say to my clients in welcome: "Off we go to Scotland!".

Allan McAllister Ferguson
President, Ferguson Golf
Denver CO USA
May 2005

TABLE OF CONTENTS

Preface to the Third Edition

A book like this is only as useful as it is current. In the space of two years one might think not much would change with an age-old topic like golf in Scotland. And one could be wrong. Given persistent price increases at the golf courses and the severe decline of the US dollar against European currencies since 2003, the circumstances surrounding golf in Scotland have changed dramatically.

In the first edition of *Golf in Scotland* I used a currency exchange rate of £1 = $1.50 to summarize prices. For the second edition, I revised all prices upward using an exchange rate of £1 = $1.55, thinking this a conservative estimate possibly erring on the "weak" side. That estimate, of course, was dead wrong. In this volume I am using an exchange rate of £1 = $1.90. Let's hope I'm wrong again—but on the high side.

To put the currency debacle in concrete terms, the typical high-end, seven-day trip that cost $3,000 in 2001 now weighs in at about $3,800. A mid-priced $2,000 trip now looks more like $2,540. And, even if you followed one of my budget itineraries at $1,400, today the tab is still going to run to about $1,800—a cost increase of over twenty-five percent!

Despite this bleak cost picture, many golfers remain willing and able to make that long-awaited trip to play golf in Scotland. This book is for you. I encourage you to go and try to forget about the dollar. If you avoid the tours you will save the biggest part of your dollar anyway.

This book stems from my work as a travel planner. The premise here is simple: *Most first-time golf travelers to Scotland need a helping hand; they don't need to have their hand held.* If you picked up this book because the title intrigued you, you are already half way toward booking your trip directly and saving hundreds, even thousands, of dollars. With this book you truly can *do it yourself without doing it alone.*

Getting to Scotland is easy. You just get on a plane and go. The problems come at the end of the plane ride. This is not just a book about Scottish golf. It's a book about *smart traveling* and, specifically, how to plan a trip on your own and thus avoid the overpriced package tours sold by tour operators and commissioned travel agencies. It's a book about how to get comfortable with the idea of doing it on your own and, consequently, not only saving a lot of money, but having a superior trip as well. *Golf in Scotland* is pitched at the North American market, but golfers everywhere, even in the UK, can benefit from the my perspective and attention to detail.

Organization of the book

Readers of my previous volumes will note that this edition has been reorganized to emphasize overall trip-planning and cost-cutting strategies.

In the Prologue, I make and rest my case for avoiding the tour operators. With this book, a computer, and a telephone in hand, there is no reason to even consider using a tour operator.

Part I, Chapter 1, "Decisions, Decisions, Decisions," is intended to serve as a rough guide to the rest of the book. Summaries of two overarching issues and eight key planning decisions include references to parts of the book where each of these important topics is discussed in greater detail.

Part I, Chapter 2, "Moneysaver Opportunities," describes a host of promotional programs that can take some of the sting out of the cost of golf in Scotland. My intent here is to get this information up front so that the value of these programs might weigh into itinerary planning.

Part II is the detailed planning part of the book. Chapter 1 addresses the most frequently-asked question I get: "What is the best time to go?" Inferentially, this is, in part, a question about weather. The rest of it has to do with possible schedule conflicts and the flow of events in Scottish tourism.

Part II, Chapter 2, presents ten itineraries to address the question, "Where should I go?". These itineraries are designed to appeal to golfers with different goals and different levels of experience with Scotland. Each gives me opportunity to address attractions of the various golf regions as well as different approaches to itinerary planning.

Part II, Chapter 3, is devoted to St. Andrews and the Old Course simply because, "Everyone Wants to Go—and Why Not?". Featured here are *eight* ways to get a tee time on the Old Course. It's not that hard.

Part II, Chapter 4, presents the real nitty-gritty—the four elements common to every golf trip: *air travel, vehicle rental, tee times,* and *lodging.* Careful study of this chapter will pay big dividends.

In Part III we come to the critical detail—the main course, if you will, or rather *sixty-eight courses,* fully described and profiled so that any golfer can write, make a call, send a fax, or email to get a tee time. Everything you need to know is here: *addresses - phone numbers - websites - key contacts - visitor policies - prices and deposit requirements.*

In the introduction to "The Directory of Courses," I've added a new index— a ranking of all sixty-eight courses by cost. I hope this raises questions like, "Why does Western Gailes cost £95 when Cruden Bay is only £55?" The answer: location - location - location. Certainly it has nothing to do with a difference in quality. This index should help golfers identify value golf. In this case, if you want a good golf course, go to Western Gailes; if you want a good golf course *and* good value, go to Cruden Bay.

Along with the objective data in "The Directory of Courses," you'll find my subjective evaluations of the courses and their locales. This is where I try to answer the question, "Why should I want to play this course?".

With photos, graphics and sidebars we've tried to make all the information more accessible and more visually appealing. Highlighted travel tips dot "The Directory of Courses" and other sections as well. All the routine work of editing has been re-visited for accuracy and currency. Several dozen lodging recommendations have been added; others have been dropped for one reason or another—usually because they are no longer in business.

Appendices include a list of useful internet sites (now more than 170) and an annotated bibliography. Together, these can help you learn more about Scotland and Scottish golf—a rewarding journey for all who love golf and the land of its origin.

Even with all the information between these covers, if you still think you'd like to engage a travel planner, you can learn more about how I work by visiting my website *www.fergusongolf.com*. Whether through this book or in person, I want you to experience a golf trip to Scotland that is *more fun*, *more rewarding*, and *less expensive* than anything offered in a pre-packaged tour.

Yours for great golf (and travel) in Scotland,

Allan McAllister Ferguson
President, Ferguson Golf
Denver CO USA
May 2005

PROLOGUE: AVOID THE TOURS!

In previous editions of this guide, I developed the habit of putting the most important message of my book in the first paragraph. Here it is this time around: *Any golfer with (1) a little time, (2) a telephone, and (3) this book can plan a good golf trip to Scotland and save hundreds or thousands of dollars by avoiding the tour operators. Now, with the internet, it's easier than ever.*

I used to be a nice guy and let the villains go unnamed. But those days are over. No more Mr. Nice Guy. If you've thought about buying a tour from PerryGolf, Value Golf Vacations, Golf International, Jerry Quinlan's Celtic Golf, Pioneer Golf, Carr Golf, or any of a dozen others just lying in wait, I have one word of advice: DON'T—unless, of course, you enjoy lighting cigars with one hundred dollar bills and tossing money down the toilet.

My interest is in Scotland, but what I am about to tell you applies to every other destination where the the romance of golf is sold: *Tour operators typically mark up their "product" by seventy-five percent to more than one hundred percent.*

Deception is the daily bread of tour operators. They practice deception in two ways: (1) they imply that their "buying power" allows them to deliver travel services to you, the customer, at wholesale prices; and (2) they imply that you will benefit immeasureably from their "local knowledge" or "expertise." Not to put too fine a point on it, on both counts, that is pure mallarky.

With few exceptions, tour operators are buying services at retail and re-selling them to travelers for *two times retail*. The truth is (1) with few exceptions, golf courses in Scotland don't give discounts to anyone; (2) rental car agencies in Scotland don't give significant discounts to anyone; (3) only a few hotels (e.g., Turnberry, Gleneagles, St. Andrews Bay) pay commissions or "kickbacks," as I prefer to call them (note the incentive to put customers in the most expensive hotels).

As for "expertise," this is either inconsequential or highly overrated. Going to Scotland is not exactly like making a trek to a third world country. The paths are well worn. Itineraries abound on the internet.

Going to Scotland is not exactly like making a trek to a third world country. The paths are well worn.

Basically, there are no wrong answers. In other words, it doesn't make much difference whether you stay at the Lorimer Guest House, the Dunvegan Hotel, or Rusacks in St. Andrews; at Thorncroft House, the South Beach Hotel, or the Marine in Troon. You're going to have a good experience at any of these places and they are all within a quarter-mile of a championship golf course. The only significant difference is price and that is easily determined with one phone call or a perusal of a website. No—what you are really buying from a tour operator is a very expensive bagtag, an even more expensive advertisement in a slick golf publication, a retired guy in a green coat to meet you at the airport, and, believe me, little else.

My mission is to help golfers traveling to Scotland get value for their hard-earned money and, more important, have a memorable, human experience. If the tour operators don't like me, that's ok. Ideally, I want golfers to return home with the feeling that they discovered Scotland, Scottish golf, and the Scottish people—not just the well-worn "rota courses," a few expensive hotels, and the concierges. Ideally, I want them to return to Scotland as soon as possible and, to achieve that, I want to show them how to make *two trips for the price most people pay for one trip.*

The purpose of this book is to give you, the golfer, all the information needed to plan a good trip at any price level. I am not opposed to someone spending a bundle of money if that's what they want to do. I do have my point of view—skewed to the middle-of-the road in terms of price and toward Scotland's by-ways and golf courses off the beaten path. But all the information is here, whether the trip orientation is budget, middle-of-the-road, or high-end; "rota" or "hidden gem."

Regardless of your budget, if I can show you that hiring a tour operator to organize a golf trip to Scotland (or Ireland) is the worst possible way to go, then you would be open to other possibilities—correct? Then let's begin.

Exhibit #1- An Overpriced Extravaganza

In the December 2004 issue of *Golf Digest*—one of the two most influential golf publications in the United States—contributing editor David Owen authored an article titled, "The Ultimate Guide to the Ultimate Buddies Trip." The article described a one-week trip he and seven friends took to play golf in Scotland.

This unfortunate article promoted a golf-'til-you-drop, chauffeur-driven, beer-swilling, card-playing, hermetically-sealed excursion focused on Scotland's most expensive courses and a couple of resort hotels. The cost?—about $6,700 per person *not* including air fare. In other words, "Scotland on $1,000 a day." Boy, do the tour operators love to see suckers like that coming down the pike!

This group used a tour operator (Jerry Quinlan's Celtic Golf) and played the following courses: Turnberry Ailsa (twice), Prestwick, Crail, Carnoustie, Gullane #1, North Berwick West Links, Kingsbarns, St. Andrews' Jubilee and St. Andrews' Old Course. They stayed at the Turnberry Hotel for two nights and at the St. Andrews Bay Resort for four nights. They used the *Old Course Experience* (see page 71) to pre-book a tee time on St. Andrews' Old Course— as Owen admits, costing them each about $1,200 for one round of golf!!

And Owen's summation of this trip? He says they really didn't need to use the Old Course Experience to play that ultimate course and, "the majority view was that it probably would have been more fun (if not also somewhat less expensive) to stay at a smaller hotel or bed and breakfast."

More fun?—yes. Less expensive? I should say so, by about $200 per-person per-night. What's worse—and this is strictly my summation of Owen's trip—he managed in a few short pages to glorify all that's wrong with Scottish golf: an overemphasis on conspicuous consumption at a few overpriced golf courses and resorts, all driven by the greed of tour operators and their compliant Scottish allies.

And what about those great tour operators? Owen says, "Using them isn't even necessarily much more expensive than doing it yourself because they usually get to pay wholesale prices for things like hotel rooms, rental cars, and tee times."

Surely no one outside of Golf Digest *believes that tour operators pass on price breaks to their customers! No—they pocket the cash and go whistling on their merry way.*

Let me make my analysis of Owen's statement perfectly clear: nonsense, poppycock, and bullroar. This is simply not true. A few hotels and golf courses in Scotland give tour operators a break. These include Turnberry, St. Andrews Bay, Gleneagles, and a handful of others. But, for the most part, in Scotland the price you see is the price you pay—whether tour operator or ordinary tourist. Besides, surely no one outside of *Golf Digest* believes that tour operators pass on price breaks to their customers! No—they pocket the cash and go whistling on their merry way.

David Owen's group could have booked this same trip themselves for about $4,000 and, if they had followed my recommendations, they could have made a better trip (in small hotels or B & Bs) for about $3,000. In other words, you can stay in the most expensive hotels and play the most expensive golf courses in Scotland for a week without paying more than about $4,000. If the tour operators ask for more than that, you can calculate their profit by subtracting the pertinent sum from their asking price.

So, what's a fair profit? I don't know, but I'm pretty sure that $1,000 to $2,000 per golfer for a one-week trip requiring about ten phone calls and a little legwork is beyond the pale. It's not criminal, but it's damned near.

Exhibit #2 - Stay-and-Play in St. Andrews

Thanks to the internet, PerryGolf helps us with an indictment of their own business practices. At *www.perrygolf.com*, anyone with a computer can enter the module "Plan Your Own Tour," submit information, and get a quote on a trip. The quote service is relatively inflexible—course choices are limited and the lodging choices are all expensive. Nevertheless, as a "high water mark," it's a useful tool.

It so happened that in January 2005 I finished a client's trip that I could replicate on the PerryGolf website. Here it is:

Trip Elements
1. Lodging: eight nights in St. Andrews at The Scores Hotel - double occupancy
2. Golf: seven rounds on the following courses: Carnoustie, Crail, Kingsbarns, Scotscraig, St. Andrews' Jubilee, St. Andrews Bay Devlin, St. Andrews Bay Torrance
3. Rental Vehicle: four golfers in an automatic minivan; self-drive

PERRYGOLF'S PRICE FOR THIS TRIP: $4,624 per golfer

REAL COST: With about ten phone calls this trip could be organized for about $2,455 per person—and that's paying "rack rate" in high season at The Scores Hotel. *Footnote:* I would recommend booking this trip for about $1,800 with B & B lodging. In my view, it's a mistake to stay at The Scores in high season. In review, then:

PERRYGOLF'S "CUSTOMIZED QUOTATION": $4,624 per golfer
REAL COST: $2,455
THE DIFFERENCE (your savings): $2,169 *(operator markup 88%)*

Here we have a typical operator profit of over $2,000 *per person.* For a group of four, we're talking about more than $8,000. The potential saving of $2,000+ per golfer can buy a plane ticket and all the trip expenses not covered in the land package (caddies, food, etc.).

Now, hang on to your wallet because here's what PerryGolf wants for the *nongolfer: $3,035.* Mind you, that's for twenty-five percent of the cost of a minivan for one week and eight nights at the Scores Hotel. Let's grant a contribution of perhaps $200 to the minivan. We're left with $2,835 for eight nights at a very average, three-star Best Western hotel. Quick math: that's $354 per person per night for a room you can book yourself with one phone call for about $163 per person per night in high season. In sum:

PERRYGOLF'S "CUSTOMIZED QUOTATION": $3,035 per nongolfer
REAL COST: $1,507
THE DIFFERENCE (your savings): $1,528 (operator markup 101%)

Exhibit #3 - What You See is NOT What You Get

"Bait-and-switch" salesmanship has been around since time immemorial. Tour operators in the golf business have refined the practice. When it comes to golf in Scotland, bait-and-switch tactics take two recurring forms:

• St. Andrews' Old Course is the "come-on" followed by an asterisk (*) indicating that golfers will not have a guaranteed tee time but will be entered into the daily ballot for a tee time.
• An attractively low price is followed by unappealing details.

Here's an example of the latter, courtesy of Value Golf Vacations (a misnomer if ever there was one). It was on their website in 2005 under the title, "Scottish Gems" (see ***www.valuegolfvacations.com***). They describe their "budget" trip as follows:

Trip Elements
1. Lodging: seven nights in B & Bs double occupancy - two nights in Inverness, two nights in Aberdeen, three nights in St. Andrews; add $432 ($61 per night!) for a single room.
2. Golf: six rounds on the following courses: Royal Dornoch, Nairn, Cruden Bay, Royal Aberdeen, St. Andrews' New or Jubilee, and Crail's Balcomie Links
3. A "manual transmission rental car"

VALUE GOLF VACATIONS' PRICE: $2,250

Apart from the fact that this is a poorly-conceived itinerary with too much traveling in too little time, a couple more problems present themselves. The golf portion of this trip costs $707. That leaves $1,543 for a manual transmission rental car and seven nights of lodging in B & Bs—well over $200 per day. What's wrong with this picture? First, 99.9 percent of Americans prefer to have a car with *automatic* transmission—add about $200 to $300 to the tab. Second, when staying in B & Bs, many Americans prefer to have their own room—add another $400+ to the tab. In short, the "budget" trip advertised at $2,250 could easily end up costing something like $3,000. More important, you could do it yourself for about $1,500.

Well, that's the way it goes with tour operators. It's *caveat emptor* ("buyer beware"). If you don't have information, you can't fight them. Some present their services accurately; most do not. *Not one of them will tell you their cost basis*; it's all obscured in a "package price." You have to dig up the details yourself. Once you've done that, you'll be in a position to bargain with the tour operators. More likely, once you've done that you'll be in a position to do it yourself and, in the process, create a trip that is *more fun, more rewarding,* and *less expensive* than anything offered by a tour operator.

More Notes and Some Personal Observations

Every day I work with highly-educated people—teachers, business executives, CPAs, attorneys, doctors, et. al. These are people who, in their professional and family lives, are knowledgeable and careful about financial matters. Thus, it never ceases to amaze me how so many of them will turn over their expensive travel decisions to a tour operator without doing the homework necessary to know whether the product they are buying is reasonably priced. Most of the time these are people who have done a considerable amount of golf travel on their own, at least in North America. And, yet, when it comes to making a golf trip to Scotland, they lose confidence and think they have to hire an "expert."

At the same time, I understand the process. I know what happens when people start considering a golf trip to Scotland. So often these are "bonding" experiences—among old friends and/or current golf partners; between father and son; between husband and wife. This is what I call the "Trip of a Lifetime" syndrome. With growing anticipation, the trip to Scotland starts to take on an aura of glamor and undue importance. You can't afford to let it fail; you can't afford to screw up the *trip of a lifetime.*

Now the search for an expert begins. You browse the internet. You go to the back of major golf magazines to find advertisements for the various companies that offer tours. Or you call your favorite travel agent who has brochures from those same companies. You send off for some brochures or use the internet to download information. Maybe you talk to a few buddies who have made a trip to Scotland.

At some point, you get around to making a decision. All the trips seem expensive. But, of course, this is your *trip of a lifetime.* It may be the one and only trip you'll ever make to the Home of Golf. So you don't want any mistakes. You've heard so many stories about how difficult it is to get on Scottish courses. You've heard the hotels and food are awful. All of sudden you feel like you need help.

I know. I've "been there, done that." The first time I went to Scotland, I used an operator. With three friends from high school days, I had a great time. The agency did a good job for us. I asked for a tour a bit off the beaten path and they gave it to us. No complaints.

But here's the problem with this scenario (and every other operator-planned trip): When you get to Scotland you will see the room rates at your hotel posted in a public place. When you go to the golf course you'll see the greens fees posted. And you know from previous experience the approximate cost of a rental vehicle. When you start adding up these numbers, you don't have to be a CPA to figure out who just made a very nice profit on your *trip of a lifetime*. You know what you paid (an "all-inclusive" package price). Now you know what you *could* have paid. Subtract the latter from the former and you have *operator profit*.

Was it worth the money? Only the buyer can answer that question. But I think most people who go through this experience end up feeling like they've been "taken to the cleaners." On that trip with my high-school friends, I fell in love with Scotland, but, as I learned more, I came to detest the game tour operators play with the golf public.

> *I fell in love with Scotland, but, as I learned more, I came to detest the game tour operators play with the golf public.*

And, what's the root of the decision-making problem? As usual, the answer is a lack of information. Even though information is available and increasingly easy to get, most people don't have the time or inclination to do the necessary research. And, even if they do, the accumulated research can be pretty confusing. Consequently, many intelligent people end up buying overpriced golf trips to Scotland. They simply give up and turn their travel decisions over to an "expert."

I want to change that situation. I want to make *you* the expert. Ideally, I want you to take the approach that you are going to make *two trips for the same price most people pay for one trip*. I guarantee, when you adopt that attitude, you'll feel the pressure coming off. You'll no longer feel like you have to "do it all" in one trip. All those rota courses may not seem quite so important. And the Old Course may even assume its proper perspective—one of many great courses to be played on more than one trip.

Getting There is Half the Fun

Apart from the dollars-and-cents side of travel, there's something more important—and that's what you gain from the process of creating a trip. When you really dig in and create a trip, or at least participate in the creation of a trip, it becomes an educational, learning experience. And, with an interesting and culturally-rich country like Scotland to study, you can only become wiser and better for having made the effort. Sure, it takes an investment of time and energy. But the result is worth it. That's why the first three items I send to my clients are (1) a detailed map of Scotland; (2) a questionnaire designed to elicit their thoughts about travel in Scotland; and (3) a copy of this book. I want my clients to be involved in their trip because I know the more deeply they are involved the more the trip will become *their* trip rather than the trip I designed for them. Anticipation of the event is just as important as the event. Or, as one of my clients reported, "Reading all this material is like foreplay. We just can't wait to go." Remember: getting there is, indeed, half the fun.

Knowledge is Power

After reading this book, even if a person chooses to engage a tour operator, I hope that he or she at least will have enough information to take a *bargaining* approach with an operator. Knowledge is power. If you know how to determine the real cost of a trip, you will have a powerful bargaining chip in your hand. You don't need to accept the "list price" of an operator's tour. Treat it just as you would treat the list price of a piece of real estate or a new car. If an operator wants your business, you'll be able to negotiate a discount from the list price.

Distinguishing Between Travel Agents and Tour Operators

Travel agents sell the products of tour operators. In other words, tour operators assemble attractive "package tours," then sell them directly to the buyer or sell them through travel agents. Travel agents get a sales commission of ten to fifteen percent.

My quarrel is not with travel agents. They are just conduits for the tour operators. They are information brokers. My quarrel is with the tour operators who sell the romance of golf in Scotland without regard for fair profit or for the democratic spirit of the game. This targeted and clever selling of Scottish golf to affluent consumers has had many unfortunate effects. Primary among them is that some of the finest golf courses in the world have been turned into ghettos for the rich—overpriced, overplayed, and now off limits to most visitors (including Scots) of average income. What's more—and I'll name names here—places like Gleneagles, Prestwick, Kingsbarns, Royal Troon, and Turnberry, with their exorbitant green fees, have ensured that most visitors, if they choose to play those courses at all, will play only once and never come back. For most golfers, these truly will be once-in-a-lifetime experiences, and that is unfortunate for the clubs, the hotels, and the golfers alike. It's a lose-lose-lose proposition.

> *Some of the finest golf courses in the world have been turned into ghettos for the rich—overpriced, overplayed, and now off limits to most visitors (including Scots) of average income.*

Where the price increases will stop no one knows. Scottish courses can only raise prices so far before they push people away to other, more affordable locations. One could argue that has already happened. Golf tourism to Scotland has declined precipitously since 2000. Evidence indicates that some have begun to "see the light." Management committees at top-drawer clubs like Cruden Bay, Nairn, North Berwick, and Royal Dornoch have held the line on prices in recent years and now are relatively good bargains compared to the courses mentioned in the preceeding paragraph.

Benchmark Costs for Your Trip

Following are benchmark costs *per-person* circa 2005 for a group of four golfers on a fairly typical, moderately-priced, seven-night/six-course itinerary. This is meant to give you a measuring stick for quickly sizing up trips offered by tour operators. For longer trips, take the daily average and multiply times the appropriate number of days.

Transportation - If you rent a vehicle from the right place (see Part II, Chapter 4), you will pay about **$200** for a fully insured VW Caravelle minibus with automatic transmission. A minivan is less, but minivans are not adequate for most groups of four golfers.

Lodging - Just about everywhere in Scotland, £35 to £45 ($65 to $85) will buy you a good night's sleep and breakfast at a three-star hotel *or* a four-star B & B. In St. Andrews you'll pay a little more for a hotel but not necessarily for a B & B. Assuming the upper end of this range, budget **$600** for lodging. It could be less.

Golf - Assume a mix of expensive and moderately-priced courses: *Prestwick* and *Western Gailes* in Ayrshire; *North Berwick West Links* and *Gullane #1* in East Lothian; and *St. Andrews' New Course* and *Kingsbarns* in Fife. Cost: **$998**. Add $225 for play on St. Andrews' Old Course.

TOTAL = $1,798 ÷ 7 days = $257 per day

If you see a trip similar to this priced between $2,500 and $3,000 (and you will), you will know that the margin built into the trip is about $700 to $1,400 *per golfer*—or a total of $2,800 to $5,600. It's no wonder there's such a glut of tour operators! That kind of profit is hard to resist.

Now that we've dealt with the tour operators, let's get on with the important business of planning a great trip and saving big bucks.

Telephone/Fax Calling Procedures

All UK telephone and fax numbers in this book are formatted like this: 01334-466-666 (main telephone number for the St. Andrews Links Trust). To call that number, do this:

From the United States: Dial 011 (international long distance), then 44 (country code), then the number in Scotland without the leading "0" (i.e., 011-44-1334-466-666).

In Scotland: Use the leading "0" and dial the rest of the number from anywhere in the country (i.e., 01334-466-666). For a local call, use only the last six digits.

Prices and Exchange Rate

All prices are current to 2005. Throughout, I have used an exchange rate of £1 = $1.90. Let us hope this leads to *overstating* prices throughout this book.

PART 1

DECISIONS, DECISIONS, DECISIONS:

AN OVERVIEW

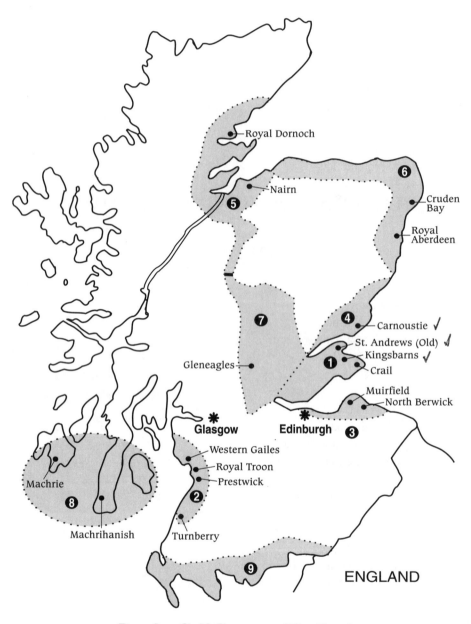

Popular Golf Courses of Scotland

CHAPTER ONE

Overview of Key Issues and Decisions

Getting Oriented - the Lay of the Land

The map on the facing page highlights the areas where most travelers go to play golf in Scotland. These areas are numbered to reflect my sense of golfer priorities—i.e., Fife (St. Andrews) first, the South Coast last, and everywhere else in between. This map is repeated in Part II, Chapter 2 ("Where to Go") and Part III, "The Directory of Courses." Those maps are accompanied by an index or indices identifying all sixty-eight courses. Here, only seventeen of the best-known courses have been labeled. In priority order, the following regions are indicated:

1 - Fife
2 - Ayrshire
3 - East Lothian
4 - Angus/East Coast
5 - Dornoch/Inverness
6 - Northeast/North Coast
7 - Perthshire/Central
8 - Arran/Kintyre/Islay
9 - South Coast

This basic orientation is important because location relates to priorities and priorities relate to itinerary planning. For example, if one wants to play St. Andrews' Old Course, Carnoustie, Royal Troon, Turnberry, Muirfield, and Royal Dornoch—and, oh yes, Cruden Bay and Royal Aberdeen—then one had better have lots of time and lots of love for the lefthand side of the road because these courses are in six different regions of Scotland!

On a typical trip of seven to ten days, a more sensible itinerary might combine several courses on the southwest coast (e.g., Turnberry, Troon, Prestwick) with several courses on the east coast (e.g., St Andrews Old Course, Kingsbarns, Carnoustie, Crail). Another approach is to do away with most of the driving and, instead, "stay and play" in a place like Carnoustie where your itinerary might include all the courses at St. Andrews and Carnoustie plus Montrose, Monifieth, and Panmure. From Carnoustie one might easily make day trips up to Cruden Bay and Royal Aberdeen. These itinerary options and more are addressed in Part II, Chapter 2.

But, here's the main point: you can't do it all in one trip. Maybe you can if you have a month to travel. But most people have seven to ten days. So, the best approach is to be keenly aware of time, distance, and golf priorities. A careful assessment of these elements will help you formulate an itinerary that makes sense.

ISSUE #1 - The "Trip of a Lifetime" or One of Several?

This is the most important issue I will raise in this chapter. Given the brief discussion above, my orientation should be clear: *I want you to go to Scotland as often as you can possibly go.*

The biggest mistake golfers make when they start thinking about a trip to Scotland is buying into the tour operators' romantic notion that this is a "once-in-a-lifetime" event. Once you accept that marketing ploy, cost consciousness goes out the window. You're ready to spend whatever it takes to have that "once-in-a-lifetime" experience.

Now, think about it. It doesn't really cost that much to get to Scotland. In September 2004 I flew Denver/Glasgow round trip for a grand total of $567. From anywhere on the east coast of the United States, air transportation to the United Kingdom is "bargain basement" most of the time.

So, what's the problem here? If at all possible, let's be rid of that once-in-a-lifetime notion. Instead, take the approach that this is going to be the first of several trips to enjoy golf as it was meant to be played in a welcoming country of unsurpassed beauty, hospitality, and character.

Let me be specific: say you've heard about and want to play the following courses—the Old Course and the New Course at St. Andrews, Kingsbarns, Muirfield, North Berwick, Royal Troon, Prestwick, Turnberry Ailsa, Western Gailes, Machrihanish, Machrie, Gleneagles, Royal Dornoch, Nairn, Cruden Bay, Royal Aberdeen, and Carnoustie.

My mission is to show you how to make two trips for the price most people pay for one trip. This is far better than buying into the "once-in-a-lifetime" trap.

That's seventeen courses—all worth playing. But how do you do that in seven to ten days? You don't.

Now, consider how much easier it becomes when you break that once-in-a-lifetime trip into two or three parts. Suddenly you feel the pressure release. You can relax. Now you can play all those courses, mix in a few "hidden gems," and get to know Scotland in a way few golf tourists do.

As I often tell my clients, "You're going to fall in love with golf in Scotland and you're going to want to go back." My mission is to show you how to make *two* trips for the price most people pay for one trip. This is far better than buying into the "once-in-a-lifetime" trap.

ISSUE #2 - How important is St. Andrews' Old Course? If it is the top priority, do you have an advance reservation?

Virtually every first-timer to Scotland wants to play the Old Course. That's understandable. If the Old Course is at the top of your priority list, it will have its effect on overall trip planning. In particular, it will affect when you can go. It may also affect how long you stay in St. Andrews and, thus, how much time you can give to other parts of the country. These issues are explored in Part II, Chapter 1 ("When to Go"), and in Part II, Chapter 3 (from page 68, "Eight Ways to Get a Tee Time on the Old Course").

Most important, this issue relates directly to Issue #1 above. If the once-in-a-lifetime syndrome is weighing on your trip and you don't have an advance reservation on the Old Course, that one course becomes a controlling factor in trip planning. Everything revolves around the Old Course.

If one takes the view that this is the first of several trips to Scotland, the Old Course takes on a different kind of importance. It may still be "first among equals," but it becomes less obsessively controlling. It becomes one of many courses to be played—if not on this first trip, then on a second, third, or fourth trip. And it *will* be played, perhaps many times. This is a much different perspective than the once-in-a-lifetime view of golf in Scotland.

DECISION #1 - When to go

The short answer: sometime between early April and mid-October. A longer answer is in Part II, Chapter 1.

Here are the basics:

- the weather can be great or miserable any time. Odds are best for warm weather from May through August, but that doesn't mean much, so go whenever you can and whenever you want to go.
- April-May and September-October flank the busiest travel months and, thus, are generally preferable in terms of lodging availability, tee times, prices, and crowds. I think the April-May period is better than September-October for four reasons: (1) those months are closer to the summer solstice so you get more hours of daylight for golf; (2) spring is beautiful and the yellow flower of the gorse is in bloom on the golf courses; (3) people in the travel industry are fresher (like spring) and tend to give better service; and because . . .
- (4) *St. Andrews is a nightmare in September.* There's an RAF base at nearby Leuchers and their annual Air Show comes early in the month. Then there's the fall meeting of the Royal and Ancient; the Queen Victoria Cup; various golf club events; the beginning of the fall term at St. Andrews University; and the Dunhill Cup, now played at the end of the month (an early-October event until 2004).

In fact, September in St. Andrews has become so busy that the Links Management no longer takes advance reservations on the golf courses during the month. Best to stay away unless you have a specific reason to attend one of the September events and book well ahead.

- June in St. Andrews is a little better than September, but not much. Consult the St. Andrews website for course closure dates (*www.standrews.org.uk*).
- July and August are the best summer months for play at St. Andrews except when the British Open is played there in July (every five years - 2005, 2010, etc.).
- Traditionally, August is the most intense vacation month of the year for Europeans. The Edinburgh International Festival draws tens of thousands of people from all over the world to Scotland. In general, plan and book well ahead and, with respect to Edinburgh, be prepared for high prices and either make the festival part of your itinerary or avoid the city.

That's the broad outline. And this does not even touch the most unpredictable, yet frequent, source of scheduling conflicts—i.e, the myriad member "medal days" and tournaments at the various golf clubs. All the more reason to make more than one trip to Scotland because the odds are good that your itinerary planning will be complicated by one or more of these conflicts.

DECISION #2 - *How to get there*

As far as I am concerned, the only civilized way to get to Scotland is by ship. Unfortunately, ships are no longer affordable or convenient. We are left with the airplane.

Air travel is the first subject treated in Part II, Chapter 4. Here's my advice boiled down: (1) from one of several North American cities, fly either directly or with one stop to Glasgow or Edinburgh; (2) if you must fly through London or choose to fly through London (particularly Heathrow Airport), leave at least *three hours* to make your connection to Scotland. I used to say leave "at least two hours," but since September 11, 2001, the only safe thing to do is make it three hours. Why?—because even if you make the connection in less than three hours, your golf clubs probably won't. With emphasis, I would add: *Do not let a travel agent tell you that two hours is enough. It is not.*

Delta, USAirways and British Midland (a subsidiary of British Airways) offer flights from several American cities to Manchester, England, and, from there, on to various Scottish cities, usually on British Midland. Those who choose Northwest/KLM or Air France usually connect in Amsterdam or Paris.

In my view, these continental connections are not much better than flying through London. They just prolong the agony of transatlantic flight.

DECISION #3 - *Where to Go*

The long answer to this one, featuring "Ten Itineraries That Work," is in Part II, Chapter 2 ("Where to Go"). If you are a first-timer, the short, realistic answer is that you will probably want to include St. Andrews on your itinerary. And why not?—it's the Mecca of international golf, and several of my suggested itineraries focus on St. Andrews.

Apart from St. Andrews, even for first-timers, I strongly encourage a look at the Highlands even if it's only a wee taste of the north with a drive up to Pitlochry, the "Gateway to the Highlands." Why? Because if the traveler never gets outside the belt of population around and between Glasgow and Edinburgh (home to about three million people), Scotland will seem much like every other urbanized, overcrowded place in the world. Only when the traveler gets north of Stirling and Perth does the countryside open up and grab at the heartstrings with eye-popping photo ops and calendar moments. To experience even a small slice of this "other Scotland" most likely will guarantee a return to this lovely land. It is for this reason that, among the ten itineraries in Part II, Chapter 2, I am partial to Itinerary #3 for the first-timer. This itinerary could well be titled, "A Taste of Scotland," for it combines a touch of the rural Highlands with the more heavily populated stretch from Carnoustie and Dundee down to St. Andrews. It does assume a tradeoff—that is, it postpones the high-priority Ayrshire coast (Troon, Prestwick, Turnberry, etc.) to another trip. Again, my antipathy to the once-in-a-lifetime syndrome comes into play.

For the second or third-timer—well, Scotland is your oyster and anything goes. Personally, I am inclined to head straight for the Highlands and Islands where I know I'll spend less money, play what I think are the most interesting golf courses, enjoy the grandest scenery, and see more sheep than people (Itinerary #s 5, 6, and 10). Not to give too short a shrift to the south of Scotland, I would add that I am rather partial also to Itinerary #4 traversing the rolling green hills of Dumfries and Galloway and tumbling along the Tweed River Valley before making a soft landing at North Berwick, east of Edinburgh. Any one of these itineraries will fill to overflowing both your photo album and your memory bank.

DECISION #4 - *Whether to use a tour operator, a travel planner, or self-plan*

This may seem like the toughest decision to make but, contrary to all conventional wisdom, it is not. You'll learn the most if you plan your own trip. If you don't have the time or patience for that, the next best choice is to hire a travel planner for a reasonable hourly rate or a flat fee (I know where you can find a good one!). The last choice should be a tour operator.

Unfortunately, the opposite order prevails. Most golfers think they need to buy the "expertise" of a tour operator who "knows the territory." Poppycock. Any intelligent person with some internet savvy, a telephone, and little time can plan and execute a good golf trip to Scotland. Many of the trips organized by tour operators are presented on their websites. Take a look at some of them. See what you like. Steal a few ideas. If you have this book, you'll have all the phone numbers you need to make bookings. As a matter of fact, if you read this book you'll know more than most of the travel operators, themselves. As for the time investment in trip planning—true, I may be able to do it all more efficiently and with more background knowledge. But planning the typical seven-to-ten-day trip is not that hard. How far wrong can you go?—especially if you are following the beaten path.

> **Any intelligent person with some internet savvy, a telephone, and little time can plan and execute a good golf trip to Scotland.**

DECISION #5 - *The size of your golf party*

Size does matter. In fact, the size of the golf party has a more profound effect on the character of a trip than any other single factor. And, on this subject, opinion and experience are all over the board.

For obvious reasons, the most common number in a golf party is four. Students of group dynamics would probably say this number not only makes sense on the golf course but everywhere else as well. Four fit nicely into a big station wagon, a minivan, or minibus. Lodging is simplified because a group of four can stay just about anywhere either in two double rooms or four singles.

Once past the most common configuration, the factors to consider get more interesting and important:

- *Two or three golfers* have more flexibility than four. Many golf clubs are partial to threes and twos and even reserve a block of time for "two-ball play" (e.g., Prestwick, Royal Dornoch, and many others). Twos or threes play faster than fours and Scots like that. Twos and threes also have a better chance of picking up a local resident or club member to fill out a tee time and, thus, meet more Scots with all that that potentially entails—i.e., a playing partner with intimate knowledge of the course being played (no need to pay a caddie) and maybe even a post-round invitation to the members' private dining room. In St. Andrews, twos and threes can more readily hook up with a local resident and enter the "local ballot" for play on the Old Course (for more detail, see Part II, Chapter 3, page 70).

- *A single golfer* can enjoy all the flexibility and opportunities enjoyed by twos and threes *except* the ability to make an advance reservation at some golf clubs, particularly at the high-profile courses that are priorities for most visiting golfers (e.g., Carnoustie and St. Andrews' Old Course). Most golf clubs will make a reservation for a singleton, but they don't do it with great enthusiasm. Often, you'll be told, "Just turn up and we'll get you a game." On the other hand, given some patience and flexibility, a single golfer doesn't really need advance reservations. Though accepting this advice may take a leap of faith, the best advice for single golfers is to simply get on a plane to Scotland, jump in a rental vehicle, and go play golf wherever and whenever the spirit moves with a phone call ahead to pave the way. For those who prefer a little more structure, see my detailed discussion of this subject in Part II, Chapter 4 from page 89.

- *For eight or more golfers* the social aspect of a trip becomes a more dominant factor. This is likely to be a group of guys, gals, or couples who play regularly together at the same club or otherwise have some social affiliation. They are much more likely than a smaller group to engage a chauffeured bus or van ("coach" is the common term). They almost certainly will be more programmed and less flexible in terms of tee times, travel, lodging, and eating arrangements than a smaller group. For example, a group of eight or more is likely to lodge in a relatively expensive full-service hotel because, by law, a B & B may not house more than six guests. Logistically, if a group of eight chooses to self-drive, two vehicles will be required unless one of the eight doesn't mind driving a wide-body coach along the narrow roads of Scotland. In sum: what I am describing here is the liklihood of a relatively expensive trip. Contrary to the laws of "volume purchasing," it's fair to postulate a new law of golf travel: *The larger the group, the more expensive the trip.* That's not to say a large group does not have budget options or even volume-purchasing privileges in some places, but, too often, when a group gets as big as eight to twelve or more, the planning is headed toward the resort track in the hands of a tour operator rather than a budget-conscious individual.

- A group of *twelve or more* probably will be traveling in something resembling a Greyhound bus, lodging in large hotels, and marching in lockstep to the dinner table. At some point, small-group dynamics become large-group dynamics and, in my experience, in any group of twelve human beings, there's always at least one horse's behind. Personally, I just wouldn't go there. But, to each his own; no wrong answers here—only different strokes for different folks.

Decision #6: "Stay and play" or move around?

In general, the appeal of stay-and-play is in getting intimately acquainted with an area while maximizing the golf and minimizing packing and unpacking. If St. Andrews' Old Course is a high priority and a group does not have an advance reservation, then a stay-and-play approach in or near St. Andrews makes a lot of sense. There could also be significant cost savings associated with "self catering" (renting) on a week-long stay. The appeal of moving around may lie in playing more "name courses" and, more important, in becoming broadly acquainted with an appealing country and its people. A sensible middle ground on a seven to ten-day trip is to limit the moving around to two or three areas of the country. See Part II, Chapter 2, for a more thorough discussion of this interesting subject.

DECISION #7 - To drive or be driven

This subject has two facets: (1) objective cost issues; and (2) subjective risk tolerance. In terms of pure cost, here are the basics:

- It's a little unusual for a group of four or fewer to hire a chauffeur, but it can be done. The cost ratio of a chauffeured versus self-drive trip will be about $3 to $1.
- Groups of eight are more likely to consider a chauffeur. Their cost ratio compared to self-drive will be about 2:1.
- Groups larger than eight are most likely to prefer a chauffeured trip. Parity is reached at about twelve golfers and from there on up a coach and chauffeur are actually less expensive than the self-drive option.

Regardless of the size of a group, in my view a chauffeured coach is the right decision in only four situations: (1) when there is a lot of ground to be covered and a lot of partying to be done; (2) when a group is comprised of golfers and nongolfers and the nongolfers want to enjoy guided sightseeing; (3) when members of a group are either too young or too old to hire a rental vehicle; (4) when all members of a group are absolutely petrified at the thought of driving on the left side of the road.

This last point, of course, leads to the subjective facet of this decision. There's no question that driving on the left side requires some adjustment and practice for North Americans. There is heightened risk involved. Personally, I have never found this to be a serious problem. I rather enjoy the change and the challenge. At the same time, I realize that some people are not comfortable with the heightened level of risk or simply do not want to experience the stress of adjusting to left-side driving. This is understandable and every traveler needs to assess the subjective part of this equation for themselves.

Finally, if a trip is organized around a stay-and-play theme with minimal transportation requirements, it rarely makes sense to hire a coach and pay a driver for sitting around twiddling his or her thumbs all day. If you don't want to self-drive, you'll save a lot of money by getting to your destination and hiring local transportation (i.e., taxi service) to get to and from the golf courses.

Decision: #8 - How much to spend

The cost of a trip is largely dependent upon two factors: (1) where you stay and (2) where you play. Though not normally included in a "land package," the next largest cost center can easily become caddies; if one is used for every round of golf, a caddy can add $50-70 per round. The rest of the cost of a trip depends upon how expensively you eat and drink and how many souvenir sweaters you buy.

The Once-in-a-Lifetime Trip: In terms of cost, working from the most expensive downward, let's take a close look at a "once-in-a-lifetime" trip that many golfers, in fact, take or would like to take.

- Eight nights lodging including one night at Turnberry Hotel.
- Ten rounds of golf: Turnberry, Prestwick, Royal Troon Old Course & Portland (a two-course policy), Carnoustie, St. Andrews' Old Course & New Course (another two-course policy), Kingsbarns, and Muirfield (two-round day ticket).
- Transportation - automatic minivan.

Where you stay: Ferguson's Golden Mean: you can lodge comfortably in Scotland for an average of £35-45 per night. To assure a tee time at Turnberry, one should stay at the hotel. Total lodging cost on this trip with one night at Turnberry: $740-875. For lodging detail, see Part II, Chapter 4, from page 93.

> *Ferguson's Golden Mean: you can lodge comfortably in Scotland for . . . £35-45 per night.*

Where you play: Regardless of where you stay, any trip featuring golf at the courses listed above will be expensive. I call this "running the table" (on the Open rota courses). The cost, high season circa 2005: $1,840 for 10 rounds of golf.

Transportation: If you get a vehicle from the right place, per-person cost for four sharing an eight-day rental of an automatic minivan: $215 (for detail, see Part II, Chapter 4, from page 80).

TOTAL Land Package: $2,795 to $2,930

Obviously, one can spend a lot more than $3,000 depending upon where you stay. But the golf and transportation parts of this equation are fixed. My point: anyone can have a "trip-of-a-lifetime" to Scotland, playing all the most expensive courses, for about $3,000 rather than the $4,000 to $5,000 or more that tour operators typically pry out of unsuspecting victims.

The implied corollary here is that, *when one starts making less expensive subsitutions for the top-drawer golf courses, trip costs can drop dramatically.* Let me, again, be specific: let's say we substitute (1) Crail for Kingsbarns; (2) North Berwick for Muirfield; and (3) Western Gailes for Royal Troon. The lodging part of the equation remains the same, but the golf cost drops to about $1,265 and the total cost to between $2,220 and $2,355. You are no longer making a trip-of-a-lifetime, but you are spending less money and, in my view, not making much of a sacifice in terms of the overall golf experience.

To re-cap, then, here are the main issues:
- Issue #1 - The "Trip of a Lifetime" or one of several?
- Issue #2 - How important is St. Andrews' Old Course to your trip and, if it is the top priority, do you have an advance reservation?

And here are the key decisions:
- Decision #1 - When to go (Part II, Chapter 1)
- Decision #2 - How to get there (Part II, Chapter 4 - Air Travel)
- Decision #3 - Where to go (Part II, Chapter 2)
- Decision #4 - Whether to use a tour operator, a travel planner, or self-plan
- Decision #5 - Size of the golf party
- Decision #6 - Stay and play or move around (Part II, Chapter 2)
- Decision #7 - To drive or be driven (Part II, Chapter 4 - Vehicle Rental)
- Decision #8 - How much to spend

Before getting to the nitty-gritty of trip planning in Part II, the next chapter describes money-saving programs that may have a bearing on when you go and where you play. Just as important, these programs may help you connect with the Scots and with golfers from other countries in ways and places that package tours do not touch.

CHAPTER TWO

Moneysaver Opportunities:
Discount Cards and Organized Competitions

Moneysaver opportunities come in four categories:
- open club competitions
- "twofer" discount cards (2-for-1 offers)
- regional packages and course promotions
- commercial competitions: the Golf Classics

Generally, if one is interested *only* in playing the best-known "rota" courses, these programs are not going to appeal (and you may want to skip this chapter). But, if you want to fill in your itinerary with a few "hidden gems," if you're a frequent golf traveler to Scotland, if you're interested in competitive golf, if the idea of getting inside Scotland's golf culture appeals, a close reading of this chapter is recommended.

While reading, keep a couple of questions in mind: Are any of these ideas especially attractive? Do any of them fit with your specific travel dates? If you can answer "yes" to either of these questions, there's little reason not to pursue a moneysaver opportunity, for they can *enrich* your travel experience—in monetary terms, in human terms, or both.

Here's an example of what I mean: In 2005, I planned a trip for three young New Yorkers. They were to be in St. Andrews on the second weekend in May when Scotscraig Golf Club holds its annual "Gents Open," a one-day handicapped stroke-play event open to all. My clients jumped at the chance to join the "locals" on a special day. Their cost?—£10 against what normally would have been a £50 green fee. Their benefits: a saving of £40 (about $75) and the satisfying experience of playing golf with Scots on their own turf. That's the kind of opportunity these moneysaver programs offer. We'll begin with more about open competitions.

Open Competitions

Open competitions at individual clubs are nearly as old as golf in Scotland and, if the moment is right, these offer the best and cheapest ways to get beneath the surface of Scottish golf and enjoy the game at the club level. Typically one-day events, open competitions take place practically every day at some club, somewhere in Scotland, from early April to October. Events are organized for all levels of ability in every imaginable format—scratch, handicapped stroke play, seniors, mixed doubles, senior mixed doubles, Stableford, four-ball, foursomes (alternate stroke), etc., etc. The best part: the entry fee at these events, even at the most expensive courses, is rarely more than £10 to £20. Moreover, visiting golfers get to meet and play with other golfers from the UK and often from other countries as well.

Example: We have four golfers over age fifty-five ("seniors") with middlin' handicaps traveling between July 18-29, 2005. These fellows have been to Scotland before and have played the "rota" courses. They've decided to spend a few days in East Lothian with golf at Dunbar, North Berwick, and Gullane before heading north to play the great courses at Royal Dornoch, Nairn, and Brora. To complete their itinerary, they do a little research and discover they can enter senior opens at the following courses *just in these two areas* between July 18 and July 29 (entry fee in parentheses):
  • Old Musselburgh Links (£8)
  • Dunbar Winterfield (£5)
  • Bruntsfield Links, Edinburgh (£13)
  • Tain GC (£8)
  • Boat of Garten (£12)

For a grand total of £46 each, these golfers can play five rounds of golf on a handful of Scotland's most interesting "hidden gems" that normally would cost about £115. Even if they chose to play in only one senior open event, their travel experience would be enhanced.

How does one uncover these open competitions? The answer: *The Wee Yellow Book (WYB)* published by Star-King Press (0131-451-5782; *www.weeyellowbook.com*). First printed in 1987, *WYB* is the brainchild of retired businessman/entrepreneur Les Starkings. Mr. Starkings' simple idea was to annually compile the tournament dates from all the clubs between the yellow covers of one wee booklet—thus, *The Wee Yellow Book*. During the last quarter of every year, as the clubs fix their dates for the ensuing year, Mr. Starkings works frantically to compile and then publish that information by the end of January.

Events are organized (1) by date from April through October; and (2) by type of event.

Mr. Starkings counsels overseas visitors to apply early; open club events tend to fill up quickly. Late January, then, is the time to look for the most current edition of *WYB*. On the other hand, most of the events occur at more or less the same time every year. To get a jump on the competition, with an old copy of WYB in hand, one can anticipate the liklihood of an event and contact a club earlier than January.

Another way to get information on open competitions is to simply visit the websites of clubs in the vicinity of your pre-booked courses. Though not all clubs list their competition dates, many do so under page headings like "open events," "calendar," or "fixtures."

A personal note: even though many open events fill up well in advance, I have stumbled into several of these while traveling about without any advance reservations. In other words, if one is looking for a game, it never hurts to make a telephone inquiry or drop in on a club. Frequently the answer will be, "Come on ahead. Weel find room fer yae."

The other three varieties of moneysaver opportunities—"twofers," regional promotions, and the Golf Classics competitions—are of more recent vintage. All stem from a perceived need to market golf more effectively in Scotland. The motivating sources of these programs are several. Scotland, in general, and Scottish golf, in particular, have experienced increasingly stiff economic competition from Ireland, the "Celtic Tiger." Until recently, the best Irish golf courses were more reasonably-priced than their Scottish counterparts. Relative bargains drew golfers to Ireland. Now, in my view, golf is equally overpriced in both places. Whether their organizers admit it or not, marketing programs have been designed, in part, to take some of the sting out of the high cost of golf. The golf clubs won't roll back prices, but they can make their product more price-attractive by participating in some of these programs.

Another part of the motivation among the golf clubs is to spread the wealth created by the boom in international golf travel. In Scotland, most of that wealth goes to about twenty courses well-known to golfers everywhere. In general, these twenty-or-so clubs are not participants in the marketing programs. They don't need to be. Admirable exceptions are Carnoustie, Kingsbarns, Turnberry, Royal Dornoch, and St. Andrews Bay. The best moneysaver programs include Scotland's "hidden gems" like Montrose, Panmure, Monifieth, Irvine Bogside, and Kilmarnock Barassie. These are all outstanding golf courses that can absorb more visitors and can truly benefit from cooperative marketing.

A related motivation at the clubs is to fill "off-peak" times, either on a daily basis or in the calendar year. Two of the 2-for-1 programs restrict golfers to off-peak tee times as defined by the clubs. Likewise, some of the Golf Classics are in early May and late September near the "shoulder" of peak tourist season.

Finally, the regional packages and Golf Classics have the effect of encouraging golfers to "stay and play" in an area longer than they might otherwise have planned. Using package enticements and price breaks, if a regional council or event organizer can get golfers to stay in a region even one day longer, this can be of worth tens of thousands of pounds to a local economy over the course of a tourist season.

Whatever the motivation at the selling end, for the visiting golfer these programs all amount to good news. It's a plus to reduce the cost of golf, to discover the lesser-known courses, to meet the "locals" on their own ground, to experience competitive golf, or to take a stay-and-play approach to Scottish golf. Whether it's a simple 2-for-1 round or a full five days of participation in one of the Golf Classics,

Whatever the motivation at the selling end, for the visiting golfer these programs all amount to good news.

it's a win-win proposition for both the golfer and the seller of these moneysaver opportunities.

"Twofers"—Green Fee Discount Programs

Green Fee Savers, 2-Fore!-1, and Open Fairways,

These discount programs have a lot in common and, for comparative value, will be treated in the same space. Green Fee Savers (GFS) was launched by *Bunkered Magazine* in 1998 with a focus on Scotland and, since then, has expanded offerings throughout the UK and Ireland. The 2-Fore!-1 program came along at the same time and has the smallest roster of participants. Open Fairways (OF) is the granddaddy of the discount schemes, having started in 1995. From the first, OF has had the most expansive vision of serving UK, Irish, and European golf.

Some three hundred of Scotland's golf clubs participate in one or more of these programs. That's roughly fifty percent (pretty good representation). Twenty-four of the sixty-eight courses described in this book participate in the GFS program including, for example, Scotscraig and the courses at St. Andrews Bay in Fife; and Boat of Garten, Tain, and Inverness up north. The 2-Fore!-1 roster includes eighteen of my sixty-eight courses with a respectable group on the northeast coast led by Montrose, Stonehaven, Murcar, Peterhead, and Duff House Royal. The OF lineup includes twenty-five of the sixty-eight courses described here. OF has a clear edge among the most prestigious courses in the UK, including Gleneagles in Scotland and The K Club in Ireland.

All these programs feature mostly 2-for-1 and 4-for-2 deals. GFS and 2-Fore!-1 are strictly half-price; some of the top courses in OF's program (e.g., Gleneagles) make a 4-for-3 offer.

The programs diverge when it comes to price and *modus operandi*. GFS and 2-Fore!-1 are most similar. GFS offers coupons, with a minimum purchase of five, at the following price points:

- 5 coupons - £23.50   • 10 coupons - £43.50
- 15 coupons - £63.50   • 20 coupons - £83.50

Average cost here is about £4.35 per coupon. Each coupon may be used by two or four golfers for a half-price round of golf or, in some cases, a day ticket. Restrictions and policies are set by the individual clubs.

The folks at 2-Fore!-1 sell coupons too, but each coupon, priced at £2.50, is specifically for *two golfers*. Coupons can be purchased in any quantity, thus giving visiting golfers a little more flexibility than the GFS approach.

OF offers a Great Britain "Passport" good for up to to two half-price rounds at all participating courses for a flat fee of £120 in 2005. *The passport can be used by up to eight golfers* (an investment of £60 each for two golfers, £30 for four golfers or £15 for eight golfers). For any group on an extended golf trip, perhaps including both Ireland and Scotland, or even playing one expensive course like Gleneagles, this can be the best buy. The more flexible GFS and 2-Fore!-1 programs *may* be better suited to the visiting group on a typical seven-to-ten-day golf tour.

So, what's not to like?—one "catch" maybe. The GFS and 2-Fore!-1 plans were designed to help courses fill tee times at "off-peak" hours, both during the week and during the calendar year. During peak tourist season, some of the courses restrict play to Monday through Thursday. The courses are free to assign whatever times they choose to these programs. This is not necessarily bad if one does not mind playing a late afternoon round (most often) or, on occasion, making a drive off the first tee into the rising sun. Ostensibly, tee times on the OF program are unrestricted.

Coupons and cards can be ordered by telephone or online. Here's where to order and/or get more information:

Green Fee Savers
www.greenfeesavers.co.uk
ph 0141-402-8090; fax 0141-954-3963

2-Fore!-1Golf
www.2-fore-1golf.com
ph 0870-124-1000

Open Fairways
www.openfairways.com.
ph 0131-664-3117; fax 0131-664-3270

Regional Packages and Promotions

There must be at least twenty regionally-based discount passes for individual play available in Scotland. Most offer a certain number of rounds on participating courses for a set fee. Some offer percentage discounts. Some require the golf to be played over consecutive days. The St. Andrews Links Management offers unlimited golf for set fees covering three, seven, and fourteen-day periods. Typically, the various discount cards are for play from April 1 through October 31, with lower rates applicable November - March.

Frankly, most of the golf passes will not be of much interest to visiting golfers, but several important exceptions, featuring the best courses, are noted below. The Golf East Lothian Passport is described in detail as an example of how these golf passes might dovetail with a hypothetical itinerary. Other programs are more concisely presented.

Golf East Lothian Passport

This well-conceived program is ideal for visiting golfers on a short stay in East Lothian. It is representative of the many available regional discount cards featuring a number of mostly secondary but interesting courses typical of those played by most Scots most of the time. The group in East Lothian includes a particularly strong collection of courses.

The Passport program is simple: £7.50 buys a fifteen percent discount for either one round or a day ticket at twelve participating golf courses over a period of five *weekdays*. Five of the ten East Lothian courses described in "The Directory of Courses" participate in the program. These are: Craigielaw, The Glen, Longniddry, Royal Musselburgh, and Whitekirk. Other participants include the excellent auxiliary courses at Gullane (#2 and #3), the dramatic Winterfield course at Dunbar, and the historic Old Links at Musselburgh, Scotland's oldest golf ground. The East Lothian Passport is sold through the North Berwick Tourist Information Office at 01620-892-197 or can be ordered online at *www.golfeastlothian.com*.

Let's take a look at how the Passport might fit into the itinerary of some gung-ho golfers playing thirty-six holes a day on a five-day stay in East Lothian. Their priorities are the championship courses at Muirfield, Gullane #1, North Berwick West Links, and Dunbar, but they want to fill in their schedule with additional rounds on lesser-known tracks (Passport courses indicated by an asterisk):

- Day 1 - Play two rounds at Muirfield
- Day 2 - Combine play at North Berwick West Links with a round at
    The Glen* (North Berwick East Links)

• Day 3 - Combine play on Gullane #1 with a round on Gullane #2*
• Day 4 - Play Whitekirk* on the way down to Dunbar
• Day 5 - Play neighboring Craigielaw* and Longniddry *
Green fees at the five Passport courses here were £171.50 in 2005. Thus, a fifteen percent discount = £25.73 minus £7.50 Passport cost = a net saving of £18.23 per golfer (about $35)—not a huge amount of money, but enough to buy dinner at one of the fine restaurants in the area.

Ayrshire Open Qualifier Card

When the British Open is held at Royal Troon's Old Course or Turnberry's Ailsa, the local courses used for Open qualifying are Glasgow Gailes, Kilmarnock Barassie, Irvine Bogside, and Turnberry's Kintyre. These are the courses involved in the Ayrshire Open Qualifier discount card, offering two options for weekday play at a significant discount (weekend rates are also available, but, because the rates and available times are not particularly attractive, I don't recommend that purchase).

The options and prices (2005) are: (1) a pass for Glasgow Gailes, Barassie, and Irvine for £125; or (2) all of the above plus the Kintyre for £195. These prices compare to undiscounted prices of £163 or £268 respectively, yielding savings of either £38 or £73 ($72 to $139). The pass may be used over a seven-day period. On a stay-and-play trip to Ayrshire, adding these three or four courses to an itinerary with play at Royal Troon, the Ailsa at Turnberry, Prestwick, and Western Gailes will result in a trip featuring the best of golf on Scotland's southwest coast. The Ayrshire Qualifier card is administered by Wilkinson Golf and Leisure and must be ordered by phone or by mail (no online ordering). For more information, see *www.wilkinsongolf.com*, *www.celticlinks.co.uk*, or call 01383-629-940. For residents of the U.S., Wilkinson Golf has a toll free number: 1-800-868-1106.

Carnoustie Country Dream Ticket

The Carnoustie Dream Ticket goes one up on the Ayrshire Open card. Not only does it include three excellent Open qualifiers (Monifieth, Montrose, and Panmure), but it features the Open venue itself—the championship course at Carnoustie. These are the best golf courses in Angus—a perfect combo on a three or four-day stay in or around Carnoustie. Cost: £195 for weekday play as compared to undiscounted green fees of £228—a saving of £33 (about $63). The program is administered by Scotia Travel, who will add a £10 fee for credit card use. The card is unrestricted with respect to tee times and time period. For more information see *www.carnoustiecountry.com* or call 0800-975-5955.

Fife Fairways

The Fife Fairways card provides a substantial discount for weekday or weekend play on the Old Course Hotel's Duke's Course, Ladybank, and the Torrance Course at St. Andrews Bay. The weekday rate is £130; the card for weekend play is £155. These rates compare to undiscounted fees of £225 and £235 respectively—a saving of nearly £100 weekday. For anyone on a stay-and-play visit to St. Andrews, this represents good value and a strong mix of courses—one seaside and two of Scotland's best inland courses. Like the Ayrshire Open Qualifier card, this program is administered by Wilkinson Golf and Leisure (see above for contact information).

St. Andrews Courses

Of special interest to the golfer on extended stay in St. Andrews, the Links Management sells three passes for *unlimited play* on all the courses except the Old Course. The periods are for three, seven, or fourteen consecutive days, and the costs are £125, £250, and £470 respectively.

The likely purchase for most visiting golfers is the three-day ticket. If this ticket were used to play two rounds on the New Course and one on the Jubilee, or vice versa, the saving would be £40 ($76) on the undiscounted cost of £165. Throw in an extra eighteen or thirty-six holes and you have an enormous bargain. These passes are not sold in advance but, rather, must be purchased at one of the clubhouses or the starter office on the first day of

> **Throw in an extra eighteen or thirty-six holes and you have an enormous bargain.**

play. A note of assurance: booking "on the spot" at St. Andrews is not normally a problem. Space is usually available on one or another course.

A variation on the theme costs a little more. A three-day *advance reservation* pass can be purchased for £140. Times must be booked at least one month in advance, play is limited to one course per day, and the New Course may only be booked once. If playing the Jubilee twice and the New Course once, the saving is £25.

For more information on discount passes at St. Andrews, see *www.standrews.org.uk* or call advance reservations at 01334-466-666. From the home page of the website, click on Golf > Book Golf > Green Fees.

Commercial Competitions: The Golf Classics

In the spirit of saving the best until last: Since 2000, a golf travel phenomenon has taken root combining play in a mildly-competitive format on some of Scotland's finest courses with, in some cases, remarkable lodging bargains offered at participating hotels. These are the four-day "Golf Classics" staged in seven different areas of the country by various organizers. All the classics have the following in common:

- tournament play on four top-notch courses on four consecutive days, Monday through Thursday
- open to all amateurs in men's and women's divisions with maximum handicaps ranging up to 18-24 (men) and 27-36 (women)
- *net* scoring (handicaps applied) in Stableford format (double-bogie = 0 pts; bogie = 1 pt; par = 2 pts; birdie = 3 pts, etc.)
- daily and overall monetary prizes, with a total pot typically £2,000 and individual prizes up to £500
- random pairing (play with different people every day; could be mixed men and women)

The individual classics may or may not offer the following:

- five nights of discounted lodging at participating hotels in a range of price categories
- a welcome drinks reception and other social events
- a closing-night awards banquet
- organized sightseeing for nongolfers

At this writing, seven Golf Classics are firmly established in the following slots on the calendar:

- Ayrshire - first week of May
- Highlands (Dornoch) - second week of May
- Carnoustie Country - third week of May
- Fife - first week of June
- Galloway (southwest) - third week in July (following British Open)
- Aberdeenshire - second week of September
- Speyside (Highlands near Inverness) - fourth week of September

Some further background: In 2000 the Ayrshire Golf Classic was launched as an entrepreneurial venture by Ian McCaig of Plan B Leisure & Tourism. Sufficient interest was generated to justify expansion of the concept to other golf destinations (i.e., Fife, Speyside, and the courses around Royal Dornoch). Without any proprietary claim to the phrase, "Golf Classic," Mr. McCaig soon discovered that imitation is, indeed, the sincerest form of flattery as golf classics in new territories were launched by others—in some cases, with financial assistance from local tourism councils. In 2003, Mr. McCaig picked up sponsorship from Drambuie to distinguish his product from others. And there we stand today. Fortunately, visitors don't have to be concerned with the politics of the Golf Classics, but can just enjoy the benefits.

I want to stress that the competitive aspect of the classics is minimized. The Rules of Golf strictly govern play, but the social aspect of the events is far more important than who wins or loses. A golfer could go through the week of play, turn in a mediocre score or no score at all, and still have a perfectly good time. As should be clear from the relatively high handicap allowances, one need not be a great golfer to partake in these events. Anyone who relishes a touch of competition will enjoy them all the more.

In chronological order, here is a summary of the highlights of each Golf Classic, along with contact information:

Drambuie Ayrshire Golf Classic
2005 dates: May 1-5
Courses: Turnberry Ailsa, Turnberry Kintyre, Kilmarnock Barassie, Irvine Bogside
Spaces: 120
Hotel packages: Five nights at Turnberry Hotel, Lochgreen House, Marine Hotel, South Beach Hotel, and others
Other features: welcome drinks reception, closing-night awards banquet
Golf-only price: £315 (regular rate - £343) including welcome and banquet
Contact: www.scottishgolfclassics.com; ph 01292-272-956
Comment: This "flagship" tournament among the Drambuie Scottish Golf Classics offers particularly dramatic examples of bargains available to visiting golfers. Paying regular green fees, these four golf courses would cost £343, assuming the non-resident rate at the Turnberry Hotel. Now get this: during Drambuie week you can do the entire package with five nights at the Turnberry Hotel for £615. During high season, the tab for the hotel, alone, would range upward from £750 per person for five nights! Boiled down, you're getting the Turnberry Hotel during Drambuie week for about £60 per person per night double occupancy. At the three-star South Beach Hotel in Troon, the cost for the week is £490 compared to a normal golf/lodging cost of £580. In addition, of course, are the reception and the awards banquet, not to mention the opportunity to win daily and overall prize money. In 2006 the event will get even better with the participation of Prestwick Golf Club.

Drambuie Highland Golf Classic
2005 dates: May 8-12
Courses: Brora, Golspie, Royal Dornoch, Tain
Spaces: 120
Hotel packages: Five nights at Royal Golf Hotel, Burghfield House, Bank House (Eagle Hotel); four nights at Dornoch Castle Hotel
Other features: welcome drinks reception, closing-night awards banquet
Golf-only price: £259 (regular rate - £163) including welcome and banquet
Contact: www.scottishgolfclassics.com; ph 01292-272-956
Comment: Perhaps because this has been the most popular Drambuie classic

since it debuted in 2003, it does not offer significant value. In fact, you could stay at the Bank House and play the same four courses at regular rates for about £100 less than the Drambuie package price. Nevertheless, all the other attractions of the event justify the small premium and, at this time of year, with spring in the air and with the gorse in glorious bloom, there is no finer place on earth. In 2005 two Americans from North Carolina combined this event with the Ayrshire Classic to achieve two weeks of competitive golf with a stop at St. Andrews in between. That's smart golf travel.

Carnoustie Country Classic
2005 dates: May 15-19
Courses: Carnoustie Championship, Monifieth, Montrose, Panmure
Spaces: 160 (sold out late January 2005)
Hotel packages: Park Hotel, George Hotel, Murray Lodge - all in Montrose
     and package priced at £380 or £205 for the nongolfer
Other features: five social events (welcome reception, quiz night, Guthrie
     Castle tour, awards banquet at Park Hotel)
Golf-only price: £175 (regular rate - £228)
*Contact: **www.carnoustiecountry.com***; ph 01674-672-932 or email to
     secretary@montroselinks.co.uk
Comment: After struggling to drum up interest for several years, organizers of this event secured promotional financing from the Angus council in 2004 and by January 2005 had sold all 160 tournament slots for the 2005 event. This is the same group of courses involved in the Carnoustie Country Dream Ticket described earlier. The locus of the event is Montrose, though many of the participants pay the golf-only price and stay in Carnoustie near three of the four courses. No doubt more Carnoustie hotels will get on board in the future with package prices. This classic is administered by Margaret Stewart, the secretary at Montrose Links Trust. It's an excellent bargain at a great spot on the calendar to combine with the Drambuie Highland Classic or with play in and around St. Andrews.

Drambuie Fife Golf Classic
2005 dates: June 5-9
Courses: St. Andrews Bay Torrance and Devlin, Ladybank, Kingsbarns
Spaces: 120
Hotel packages: Five nights at St. Andrews Bay, Rufflets, Old Manor Country
     House, Hotel, Inn at Lathones, and others
Other features: welcome drinks reception, closing-night awards banquet
Golf-only price: £312.50 (regular rate - £380) including welcome and banquet
*Contact: **www.scottishgolfclassics.com***; ph 01292-272-956

Comment: Already good, the Fife Classic got even better with the addition of Kingsbarns to the playlist in 2004. Attractive hotel packages are on offer—all the more remarkable for their high-season dates. The discount on golf, alone, makes this a bargain. In 2005 the prize-giving banquet was held at the Old Manor Country House Hotel overlooking the golf course at Lundin Links.

Galloway Golf Classic
2005 dates: July 18-22
Courses: Stranraer, Portpatrick, Newton Stewart, Wigtownshire
Spaces: 120
Hotel packages: none
Other features: "corporate event" and complementary polo shirt
Golf-only price: £105 (regular rate - £99)
Contact: **www.gallowaygolfclassic.co.uk**; ph 0778-715-0177 (Linsey Cox)
Comment: Galloway is strategically located on the border between England and Scotland. For this reason, the organizers of the newest classic event wisely chose to position their tournament in the week following the British Open— the better to capture traffic traveling from the rota sites on either side of the border. Stranraer is also a port for ferry traffic to and from Scotland and Ireland, so the Galloway classic is picking up a fair share of Irish entrants. Started in 2004, the event has not yet gained American participation, but these are good courses in an attractive part of Scotland and perhaps that will change. There's not much money to be saved here, but these courses are already in the bargain category.

Aberdeenshire Golf Classic
2005 dates: September 11-15
Courses: Newburgh-on-Ythan, Newmachar, East Aberdeenshire, Murcar
Spaces: 120
Hotel packages: Express by Holiday Inn, Ardoe House, Skene House, Udny
    Arms, and others
Other features: welcoming event
Golf-only price: £95 (regular rate - £140) including welcome reception
Contact: **www.aberdeenshiregolfclassic.com**; ph 0845-450-8330
Comment: For two years, from 2003, Cruden Bay served as the main attraction here. Cruden Bay pulled out in 2005, perhaps spelling the death knell for the tournament. Nevertheless, as with all the classic courses, these are good ones, and Aberdeenshire is a beautiful place to be in the fall. If in the neighborhood in September, I would take advantage of this value.

Drambuie Speyside Golf Classic

2005 dates: September 25-29

Courses: Grantown-on-Spey, Kingussie, Newtonmore, Boat of Garten

Spaces: 120

Hotel packages: Five nights at Macdonald Four Seasons or Highlands,
      Aviemore Inn, Cairngorm Hotel, and others

Other features: welcome drinks reception aboard Strathspey steam railway,
      closing-night awards banquet

Golf-only price: £198 (regular rate - £97) including welcome and banquet

*Contact: **www.scottishgolfclassics.com***; ph 01292-272-956

Comment: This is the most tenuous of the Drambuie events because the featured courses are the wee "holiday" tracks of the Highlands rather than well-known Open qualifiers or a compelling attraction like Royal Dornoch or Turnberry. Purely in terms of golf fees, neither does this qualify as a bargain. Nevertheless, let it be said these are easily the most scenic inland courses in Scotland. They are plenty challenging, and the classic clubhouses are delightful. At bottom, what you are really buying here is the whole Drambuie package—in this case, bargain hotel rates, the steam railway reception, bagpipes and haggis on closing night, and perfect camaradrie in the crisp autumn air of the Spey Valley.

Most likely, these discount cards or competitions would constitute only one component of a larger, longer trip. The open club events and the Golf Classics, in particular, offer effective ways to meet the Scots on their own turf. And, if one is staying in an area long enough to play three or four courses, there is every reason to take advantage of programs like the Ayrshire Open Qualifier Card. With this information now "on the table," and having reviewed major issues and decisions in Chapter 1, we now turn to the detail of trip planning, beginning with "Where to Go."

 Telephone/Fax Calling Procedures

From the United States:
Dial 011 (international long distance), then 44
(country code), then the number in Scotland
without the leading "0" (i.e., 011-44-1334-466-666).

PART II

HOW TO PLAN A GOLF TRIP TO SCOTLAND:

DETAILED INSTRUCTIONS

CHAPTER ONE

When To Go

The most frequently-asked question I get is, "What's the best time to go to Scotland?" One answer is, "Whenever you can." Scotland can accommodate any time of year. You might be surprised to learn that most golf courses in the various coastal "micro-climates" are open throughout the winter. What that means, of course, is that while it may be cold there's not much snow.

As a practical matter, most people want to be as warm as possible and enjoy the longest days of the year. This means going sometime during the five months from May through September. Family, school, and job considerations often limit travel options to the summer months of June, July, and August. Now we move toward a definition of high season for Scottish golf tourism. To be most precise, the busiest months of the year are: (1) August, particularly the first half; (2) June and July; (3) September; (4) May; (5) April and October about equal. Most innkeepers consider May through September the high season. Thus, good lodging bargains abound during the "shoulder months" of April and October. Many B & Bs and guest houses close their doors for five months from November 1 to March 31.

Generalizations About the Weather

Implicit in the question, "What's the best time to go to Scotland?" is another question: "What can I expect from the weather?". The only remotely intelligent answer to that question is, "You can expect the weather to be *unpredictable*." I've been so cold in Scotland in June that I had to go shopping for a wool sweater. On the other hand, I've played golf in seventy-degree weather in May and October. In the early 1990s Scotland suffered a severe summer drought that turned the golf courses to hardened, brown runways;

> *"What can I expect from the weather?". The only remotely intelligent answer to that question is, "You can expect the weather to be unpredictable."*

the winter of 2000-01 brought heavy rains and flooding to many parts of the UK; recent years have seen unusually blustery and wet weather.

So, if unpredictability is the key word, what generalizations can one make? For golfers, three generalizations are important:

✓ *The west coast is wetter than the east coast.* For example, though no more than sixty miles apart, Glasgow gets almost twice as much rain as Edinburgh during September and October. The ratio narrows during other months.

✓ *The west coast is warmer than the east coast.* All along Scotland's west coast, from south to north, you'll find semi-tropical plants growing in open air gardens during the summer. To my knowledge, nothing like that exists on Scotland's east coast. Why? Because the gulf stream waters wash the west coast. On the east coast, despite justifiable pride in their "micro-climates," they can get brutally cold winds off the North Sea at any time of year—and no one, not even the Scottish tourist board, can deny it.

✓ A typical Scottish day may bring sunshine, clouds, mist, rain, wind, and calm. This is the reason you are advised by all who have been there to *dress in layers.* Don't be surprised if, during a round of golf, you go from short-sleeved golf shirt to sweater to rain jacket to full rain suit before returning to sweater and golf shirt.

Temperature

The chart on the next page shows average high and low Fahrenheit temperatures in Edinburgh for twelve months. As a measure, Edinburgh is as good as any. Temperatures don't vary much from north to south. For example, the average high temperature during January is precisely the same in the Orkney Islands and Inverness

Extremes are rare—it doesn't get very cold and it doesn't get very hot.

as it is in Edinburgh. East (Edinburgh) to west (Glasgow), on average, the west coast might be a degree or two colder in winter and a degree or two warmer in summer.

This chart illustrates a fundamental point: *extremes are rare*—it doesn't get very cold and it doesn't get very hot. During the peak tourist season, May through September, daily high temperatures typically range between 55° and 75° Fahrenheit. For golfers, this is wonderful weather—soft, cool air and no oppressive, humid heat to beat you down and sap your strength (as in many parts of the United States and, for that matter, the rest of the world). The United Kingdom, indeed, is blessed with a climate congenial to golf.

Here are the details:

Edinburgh - High and Low Temperatures - Monthly Averages

Jan	43	May	58	Sept	61
	34		43		49
Feb	43	June	63	Oct	54
	34		49		45
Mar	47	July	65	Nov	49
	36		52		40
Apr	52	Aug	65	Dec	45
	40		52		36

A further note on temperature: The UK, like most countries in the world, uses the Celsius (metric) temperature scale. Math majors may love the complicated formula for converting Celsius to Fahrenheit, but it's not necessary. Keep it simple. Most May-September temperatures will be between 10° and 20° C. Just remember:

10° C = 50° F   15° C = 60° F   20° C = 70° F

Before I get caught up short by the math majors, I know these are not precise numbers. They are close. With the weather, close is good enough.

Rainfall

You must bring good rain gear to Scotland. On the west coast from Oban on up, from August through April, it's wet a lot of the time—from six to ten inches a month. Fortunately, there aren't many golf courses in that part of the country.

For golfers, the driest part of Scotland is around Edinburgh (Fife and the Lothians). What does that mean? It means, on average, about two to three inches of rain during each of the summer months. That's not bad, especially when it comes in the form of a soft Scottish mist that hangs about all day and doesn't really get in the way of play. On the other hand, it can come in sheets and buckets and stay all day. Fortunately, those days are relatively rare and there's always a castle or museum or pub nearby where one can seek shelter. Most often, the sky will be intermittently cloudy and, out of the clouds, might come a quick burst of showers followed by warm sunshine. Who knows? Take everything said here (and everywhere else) with a grain of salt and remember this little Scots limerick:

> Whether it rains or whether it shines,
> Whether it's chilly or hot,
> You must weather the weather,
> Whatever the weather,
> Whether you like it or not.

The point is, there's *no* point in being concerned about the weather. No one needs another chart on rainfall. Just go on your trip and take what comes. And be prepared!

While all commentary about weather in Scotland may begin and end with the word, "unpredictable," the basic truth is that you should expect rain. That's what makes Scotland blossom into a breathtaking land of green and yellow and lavender. That's what creates her mountain rivulets and trickling burns and flowing rivers. Warm rains are the stuff of elephantine leaves and semi-tropical plants on the west coast, of heather on the hills in the Highlands, and of springy turf and silky-smooth greens in all parts of the country. Whatever the weather, you'll enjoy Scotland for her beauty in sunshine or in shadow, in mist or pouring rain.

Daylight Hours

Related to weather, remember that Scotland is one of the northernmost countries in the world. Scotland is on latitude with Hudson Bay in Canada, Norway, and the southern reaches of Siberia. Consequently, in the months around the summer solstice (mid-June) the nights are short and the days are long. In May, June, and July you can play golf until 9 or 10 p.m. Twilight is long and lovely. This subject arises when my clients say, "I want to play early in the morning," and I say, "You can't get on that golf course early in the morning. The only available time is after lunch—and, by the way, you can play until ten o'clock at night." And they say, "Oh, yeah, I hadn't thought about that."

The tradeoff for the long days of May, June, and July are the short days of early spring and fall. Earth's time machine moves more rapidly in these northern climes. Starting September 1, daylight hours shrink at a rate of about forty-five minutes every two weeks. Thus, sunset in Glasgow on September 1 is at 7:11 p.m.; by October 15 it's at 5:17 p.m.; by the end of October sunset is at 4:40 p.m. At the winter solstice you had better be done with your round of golf by about 3:15 p.m. (For detail, see *Appendix D*.)

The Case for April and October

If your heart's desire is to play the Old Course and you want to get the best rates at hotels, the best months to be in Scotland are April and October. One case in point: the four-star Old Manor Country House Hotel overlooking the golf course at Lundin Links routinely cuts its prices in half after the first week in October. That is typical of hotels throughout Scotland—many starting in late September. In St. Andrews, most of the major hotels offer attractive package deals after play for the Dunhill Cup concludes in late September-early October. And the golf courses can be surprisingly free of traffic. Personal testimony: On a Wednesday in late April 2002, I was one of *three* singles playing on world-famous Cruden Bay. The same story at Brora—just me, the sheep, and few other lone wolves.

A special attraction of spring and fall travel is the beauty of the countryside. In spring, daffodils line many of the highways and byways offering up a dazzling yellow display of welcome to Earth's new year. In the fall, an equally-appealing palette of autumnal browns and golds spreads over fields of newly-mown and gathered hay.

But tradeoffs are part of the bargain. In the spring, putting greens are not likely to be in "top nick." Course maintenance is conducted at that time, just as it is at most golf courses. In the fall, the heather is past its prime, gardens have lost their luster, and most nongolf attractions have either closed or adopted drastically shortened hours. In both spring and fall, daylight hours are shorter and one must risk the possibility of enduringly cold, nasty weather. For all the benefits, I think it's a good gamble and, if pressed on the point, I would choose April over October.

Calendar Highlights

By month, following are additional factors that might influence your decision on when to go.

May-June

✓ Late May and June are visually stunning. Spring has sprung and bright yellow flowers on the gorse are in full bloom. The gorse will cost you strokes on the golf course, but at least you'll enjoy the view. In May you'll be a bit ahead of the summer tourist curve.

July

✓ Late in the month, if the British Open is in Scotland, you'll have to plan well ahead—that is, plan ahead to make your reservations near the Open venue or plan on being somewhere else. Here are the announced future venues for the Open: 2006 - Royal Liverpool, England; 2007 - Carnoustie, Scotland; 2008 - Royal Birkdale, England. Turnberry stands a good chance of hosting the Open in 2009 and, presumably, 2010 will see the event back in St. Andrews.

August

✓ Like May, August is a visual stunner with heather in bloom, casting its lavender glow over the countryside. The Highlands are especially beautiful.

✓ August is the busiest month because (a) that's when UK families take their traditional summer holiday; and (b) the Edinburgh International Festival draws thousands of tourists from around the world. In other words, you are fighting for space not only with tourists from North America but with the Brits and every other nationality within striking distance of Scotland. Reservations must be made well in advance to lodge in Edinburgh and are recommended for most parts of the Highlands. Multi-night stays may be required, especially at weekends.

✓ Plan to arrive around the third week of the month when UK schools resume. You'll see a discernible drop in the level of tourist activity, particularly in the Highlands.

September
    ✓ Don't assume this is a relatively quieter month. It's the most popular month for "empty nesters." In St. Andrews, in addition to all the golf events (see below), September also sees the Leuchers Air Show and matriculation at St. Andrews University. It's a zoo. The only time to be in St. Andrews for play on the Old Course is early in the month.

The Old Course and Your Travel Plans
    For many golfers, playing the Old Course at St. Andrews is the "bottom line," the *sine quo non*, of a trip to Scotland. Whether applying for an advance reservation or angling for your best shot in the daily ballot, *you can't play the Old Course if it's not open to the public.* Therefore, travel dates must be picked carefully. You will want to avoid or anticipate:

> **You can't play the Old Course if it's not open to the public.**

    ✓ *May - first or second full week:* Spring meeting of the Royal and Ancient Golf Club; other events during the month (Links Trophy, St. Rule Trophy) impinge on Fridays and Saturdays.

    ✓ *June - second and third week:* Rotary International; graduation at St. Andrews University. Book early (e.g., six months ahead) or plan on staying somewhere outside the town.

    ✓ *First three weeks of July every fifth year* (2005, 2010, etc.) when the British Open is played at the Old Course. In 2005 the course closed in late June and re-opened on the first Tuesday (July 19) after the Open.

    ✓ *September - second, third, and fourth weeks:* Queen Victoria Jubilee Vase Tournament; Bing Crosby Tournament; Royal and Ancient autumn meeting; Dunhill Cup.

✓ *Mid-November through March:* you will be issued a piece of astroturf for playing shots from the fairways. Fairway mats are also issued at Carnoustie. This is to preserve the turf at those hallowed links during the harsh winter months. Check with the courses for the exact dates. Most visiting golfers are not interested in playing Carnoustie and St. Andrews from mats, in effect eliminating four months from consideration.

The above notes on Old Course closings are for general guidance only. Normally the calendar is fixed by late November for the ensuing year. *For a complete calendar of events, check with the St. Andrews Management or visit their website **www.standrews.org.uk**.* From the home page, click on Events > Local Clubs. For a wider discussion of the Old Course in your travel plans, see Chapter 3 in this section.

Now that you have some ideas about when to go, let's turn to the next important issue: *where* to go.

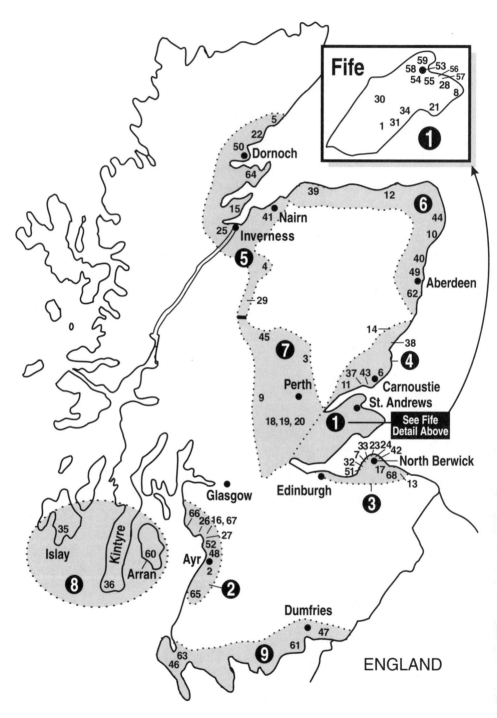

Sixty-Eight Golf Courses in Nine Regions of Scotland

CHAPTER TWO

Where to Go—Ten Itineraries That Work

The map on the facing page reflects my sense of the relative popularity of regions where tourists go to play golf in Scotland. All but one of these are coastal regions that feature "links" golf, though all the courses in a coastal region are not necessarily links courses. The *numbers in dark circles* (e.g., ❷) indicate the relative popularity of each region, from #1 (Fife - St. Andrews) to #9 (the South Coast). The smaller numbers from 1 to 68 correspond to courses described and arranged alphabetically in Part III, "The Directory of Courses."

A large percentage of Scotland's eighteen-hole golf courses are located within these nine regions. *Virtually all the courses most visitors want to play are within these nine regions.* I have not included golf courses in Glasgow and Edinburgh. Does that mean no courses there are worthy of play? Of course not. It's just that most visitors don't want to play golf when they're in those cities. They want to see the cities.

Think of these regions as building blocks for itineraries. In describing itineraries, I use the term "base" interchangeably with "region" and "area." With these bases clearly defined, we can create trips featuring various combinations of bases.

If you want to focus on the high-end "rota" courses and their neighbors, go to region #s 1, 2, and/or 3. To head for the Highlands, combining great golf and scenery, choose region #s 5 & 6 or 6 & 7. Want to get off the most beaten paths?—try region #s 8 and 9. Maybe you'd like a combination of classic courses and less-traveled byways—then pair a low number with a high number (e.g., 1 and 7, 2 and 8, 2 and 9). Still another option is to "stay and play" in any one region. As I often say to clients, "There are no wrong answers, only choices to make. They're all good."

Geographic Arrangement of Sixty-Eight Courses
(located by number on map)
+ = British Open Qualifying Course
* = Current or historic venue for British Open

Region #1 - Fife (from Tayport, south along coast and back)
Scotscraig+ (59)
The Duke's Course (58)
St. Andrews Old*/New/Jubilee (53, 54, 55)
St. Andrews Bay Devlin/Torrance (56, 57)
Kingsbarns (28)
Crail (8)
Golf House Club - Elie (21)
Lundin Links+ (34)
Leven Links+ (31)
Balbirnie Park (1)
Ladybank+ (30)

Region #2 - Ayrshire (north to south)
West Kilbride (66)
Irvine - Bogside+ (26)
Glasgow Gailes+ (16)
Western Gailes+ (67)
Kilmarnock - Barassie+ (27)
Royal Troon* (52)
Prestwick* (48)
Belleisle (2)
Turnberry - Ailsa* (65)

Region #3 - East Lothian (west to east)
Royal Musselburgh (51)
Longniddry+ (32)
Craigielaw (7)
Luffness New+ (33)
Gullane #1+ (23)
Honourable Company of Edinburgh Golfers - Muirfield* (24)
North Berwick - West Links+ (42)
The Glen - North Berwick (17)
Whitekirk (68)
Dunbar+ (13)

Region #4 - Angus/East Coast (from Dundee north to Edzell)
Downfield+ (11)
Monifieth+ (37)
Panmure+ (43)
Carnoustie* (6)
Montrose+ (38)
Edzell (14)

Region #5 - Inverness/Dornoch (south to north)
Kingussie (29)
Boat of Garten (4)
Nairn (41)
Inverness (25)
Fortrose & Rosemarkie (15)
Tain (64)
Royal Dornoch (50)
Golspie (22)
Brora (5)

Region #6 - Northeast/North Coast (south to north to west)
Stonehaven (62)
Royal Aberdeen (49)
Murcar (40)
Cruden Bay (10)
Peterhead (44)
Duff House Royal (12)
Old Moray (39)

Region #7 - Perthshire/Central (south to north)
Gleneagles - King's/Queen's/PGA Centenary (18, 19, 20)
Crieff (9)
Blairgowrie Rosemount (3)
Pitlochry (45)

Region #8 - Arran/Kintyre/Islay
Shiskine (60)
Machrihanish (36)
Machrie (35)

Region #9 - South Coast (west to east)
Powfoot (46)
Southerness (61)
Stranraer (63)
Portpatrick (47)

Constructing Itineraries

Where you go depends upon three main factors—your personal preferences, the length of your trip, and, most likely, how many times you've been to Scotland. If you're a first-timer, you're probably not going to choose the Kintyre Peninsula over St. Andrews. On the other hand, if you've visited St. Andrews and played the Old Course, you may be quite keen to make the pilgrimage to Machrihanish on remote Kintyre.

For the typical seven to ten-day trip I recommend limiting yourself to two or, at most, three bases. Beyond ten days, the number of bases can increase as the length of a trip increases. If you are among the lucky ones who can spend three or more weeks, then you can cover more ground and your options increase dramatically.

On a two or three-base trip, this means three or four nights in each locale. With that much time, you'll feel more like you're "at home." You can get unpacked and stay unpacked for awhile. You can get to know your lodging hosts. You can get to know the streets and shops, the restaurants and the corner bartender. You can make day-trip forays out to the countryside or into the nearest city. Most important, you can spend your time playing golf instead of packing up, driving for several hours, then finding your next place to bunk down. The last thing you want to do on a golf trip is get into the tourist trap: "If this is Tuesday, it must be Carnoustie."

Some tour operators sell a seven-day package touting the world-famous courses at Troon, Dornoch, Cruden Bay, Carnoustie, and St. Andrews. That kind of routing is absurd—five bases in seven days, covering about 800 miles, requiring you to spend most of your free time in a car or bus and leaving no time to "savor the clubhouse" (not to mention the countryside). This is not the right way to tour Scotland.

Likewise, some golfers will fly into and out of the airport at Machrihanish in one day just to say they've played that great course. But, in doing that, they miss the best part of the Machrihanish experience—the process of *getting there* by sea or land and, once there, exploring the wild and remote reaches of the Kintyre Peninsula. The golfer who flies in and out of Kintyre in one day will never know the thrill of driving down a one-lane road to Southend where, on a clear day, you can see all the way to Ireland; or of stopping at the Dunaverty Golf Club for a quick round on a course that will take you back to the nineteenth century as a reminder of the way golf used to be played. At unattended Dunaverty you'll drop your fee in an "honesty box" before leaving the first tee. You'll probably "play through" several bovine hazards as well. That's the kind of experience a traveler can savor long after the buzz of a championship course is forgotten. But it's not an experience a *hurried* traveler will ever have. No matter where you go, this is the single most important piece of advice I can give: *Don't hurry. Slow down and savor the clubhouse* (the golf equivalent of "smelling the roses").

The next important piece of advice I can give is to *book the golf before dealing with the lodging.* The pieces of the golf puzzle must fit. You can always find a place to stay. For example, in Ayrshire, Royal Troon takes visitors only on Monday, Tuesday, and Thursday. Western Gailes takes visitors on Monday, Wednesday, Friday, and a small window of time on Sunday. Prestwick will take visitors about any time during the week except Thursday afternoon. If you've been planning on playing Troon on a Wednesday and doubling up Western

> **No matter where you go, this is the single most important piece of advice I can give: Don't hurry. Slow down and savor the clubhouse (the golf equivalent of "smelling the roses").**

Gailes and Prestwick on a Thursday, all of a sudden it's "back to the drawing board." In Part III, "The Directory of Courses," these policy details are noted in the course entries in the data area under the heading *Visitor Policies.* For information on the booking process, see Part II, Chapter 4, from page 87.

A Few Notes on the Most Popular Combinations of Bases

Without question, and understandably, the most popular combinations of bases come from Regions 1 (Fife), 2 (Ayrshire), and 3 (East Lothian) with a sidetrip up to Carnoustie in Region 4. Fully seventy-five percent of the trips I organize cover two or more of these areas with St. Andrews, Troon, and Gullane/North Berwick the focal points. It's a lot of ground to cover, but all four of these bases can be visited in a twelve-day trip. With all the planets aligned, a "dream trip" for many golfers might end up looking a lot like this:

Saturday - depart
Sunday - arrive; play Turnberry
Monday - play Prestwick and/or Western Gailes
Tuesday - play Royal Troon's Old Course and Portland; transfer to Gullane/
  North Berwick
Wednesday - play North Berwick
Thursday - play Muirfield; transfer to St. Andrews
Friday - play St. Andrews' Old Course
Saturday - play St. Andrews' New Course
Sunday - play Kingsbarns or another course in Fife
Monday - play Carnoustie; return to airport area for overnight
Tuesday - return home

That's at least ten rounds of golf and nine nights of lodging in four locations. For this, a tour operator will charge $5,000 and up, circa 2005. It can be done for a lot less but, even if camped out in a pup tent, the golfer is going to spend about $2,000 on golf alone because these are Scotland's most expensive courses. My point and attempt here is to give you a sense of how much time and money might be required to execute such a "dream trip." Obviously, if one has less than twelve days to travel or is not inclined to spend so much money, then you cut and trim to suit the circumstances—i.e., most likely leaving out Region #2 or #3.

Particularly with respect to Muirfield, if a golfer has the luxury of planning *fifteen months ahead*, I encourage application for an advance booking simply because this is such a difficult ticket to get between April and September. A new online booking system was installed at Muirfield in early 2005. It operates on a lead time of up to fifteen months (February 2006 for April 2007, March 2006 for May 2007, etc.). The times sell fast. With lead time shorter than fifteen months, a golf party is not likely to have Muirfield on its itinerary and this could affect decisions on where to go. For more information on booking at Muirfield, see "Honourable Company of Edinburgh Golfers" in Part III, "The Directory of Courses."

In the case of St. Andrews, booking policies put in place in 2005 by the Links Management suggest an optimum planning window of eight to twelve months for securing an advance reservation on the Old Course. Reservation requests are now being accepted beginning the first Wednesday in September for the ensuing year (September 2005 for 2006, etc.). Unlike at Muirfield, however, if a golfer is not prepared to submit a request for an advance reservation at the best time, there are lots of other ways to "skin the cat" and these are explored in Part II, Chapter 3, under the heading "Eight Ways to Get a Tee Time on the Old Course." As I've said elsewhere, the importance and place of St. Andrews in a trip—whether the Old Course is pre-booked or a group is in a balloting situation—will affect the shape of every itinerary.

With the exception of these two special cases at Muirfield and St. Andrews, I want to stress (and will do so more than once) that *golf tourists to Scotland do not need to book tee times eight to fifteen months ahead of their travel dates.* That is a myth promulgated by tour operators. In fact, at most courses, it is not possible to book any earlier than the last quarter of the year before intended date of play because the "diaries" are not open. The only thing the clubs will do is accept a letter of request and put it in a file for future action. In other words, don't worry, be happy. Your golf party can go pretty much anywhere, anytime

> *Golf tourists to Scotland do not need to book tee times eight to fifteen months ahead of their travel dates. That is a myth promulgated by tour operators.*

it wants and, in most cases, could be booking tee times a few months, a few weeks, or a few days ahead of play. The only other exception I would make to this rule is to suggest an early booking (six to nine months out) at Royal Troon. For more on booking tee times, see Part II, Chapter 4.

Stay and Play

One-base, one-week golf trips are becoming increasingly common in Scotland. Regional tourism councils, independent promotional groups, and some enterprising hotels are making the pitch to "stay and play," often accompanied by package deals that reduce costs at participating venues. Many of the "Moneysaver Opportunities" described in Part I, Chapter 2, are designed to extend the golfer's stay in an area. If a program among these appeals (particularly one of the various "Golf Classics"), it will provide at least a partial answer to the question of where to go.

As one can see on the map and in the Geographic Index at the beginning of this chapter, each area offers a wealth of courses when a decision is made to stay and play. Even in Regions 8 and 9 where I have included only a few courses, rest assured, there are many more. On the Isle of Arran, for example, no less than seven golf courses await the visitor—four 18-holers, two 9-holers, and the 12-hole Shiskine club featured in this book. Admittedly, these are not "championship" courses, but they are interesting "holiday" courses and are fun to play.

Two further benefits of the stay-and-play approach: First, you can almost always negotiate a multi-night discount at a B & B or hotel. The magic number on this matter is usually three or more nights, but most places don't have a specific policy or, if they do, they don't announce it, so it's best to be direct and ask for the discount. Second, a stay-and-play approach sets up the possibility of even greater savings and convenience through "self-catering." This is the British term for what Americans call "rentals." Generally, self-catering units are priced by the week and assume a Saturday-through-Saturday stay. Rentals can save a group a lot of money but, more important, they offer the comforts of home, including fully-equipped kitchens. For some, that is appealing. For others, that's what they are trying to escape. The point is, this approach to golf travel is far different than the whirlwind approach offered by tour operators. For more detail on self-catering, see Part II, Chapter 4, from page 94.

With that much introduction, let's take a quick look at several of the most popular stay-and-play choices.

St. Andrews and Fife—The Obvious First Choice

If St. Andrews' Old Course is the absolute first priority of a trip, and if a group is without an advance reservation, the most sensible thing to do is simply go to St. Andrews and stay for the duration. Quite apart from that particular situation, St. Andrews is a pleasant and interesting place to be for a week. With or without an Old Course reservation, on a seven-night stay with five days dedicated to golf, you could play *two* great courses a day in Fife and still leave others unplayed. Start with five courses in St. Andrews (Old, New, Jubilee, Eden, The Duke's); add Kingsbarns, Crail, Elie, Lundin Links, and Leven Links. That leaves Scotscraig, Balbirnie Park, Ladybank, and the courses at St. Andrews Bay to play on another trip. This is a "no-brainer" for anyone who wants to stay put for a week.

The Case for Carnoustie

As an alternative to St. Andrews, after considerable thought and experience, I've come to the conclusion that Carnoustie is the best base for a week of stay-and-play up and down the east coast. Elsewhere I've said that Carnoustie is not the most scintillating of towns. But, really, who cares? From a practical point of view, consider the following: (1) Carnoustie's championship golf course is superb and relatively easy to book; (2) all the courses at St Andrews can be easily reached from Carnoustie (ballot the Old Course while based at Carnoustie); (3) the great golf courses at Monifieth, Panmure, Downfield, and Montrose are nearby; (4) Carnoustie Championship participates in both the Carnoustie Country Dream

> *Carnoustie is the best base for a week of stay-and-play up and down the east coast.*

Ticket and the Carnoustie Country Classic; (5) it's easy to travel up the coast on day trips to Stonehaven, Cruden Bay, and Royal Aberdeen; (6) Carnoustie offers good lodging options at about half the price of lodging in St. Andrews; (7) Carnoustie has several excellent restaurants; (8) nongolf attractions in and around Dundee and Perth are easy to reach (e.g., Discovery Point, Glamis Castle and Scone Palace). This is a powerful set of pluses for Carnoustie. This stay-and-play itinerary can be visualized in truncated form as Itinerary #9 (see page 54), extending from St. Andrews to about thirty miles north of Aberdeen. For more detail on Carnoustie, see my description in "The Directory of Courses."

A Week in Ayrshire

In 2004 I worked with a group of guys who had been to Scotland the previous year, following the traditional "rota" loop from Ayrshire to East Lothian to Fife (see Itinerary #1, page 46). This time they decided to cut out the travel, stay put, and just play golf. They didn't even rent a vehicle. Instead, they checked into *single rooms* at the South Beach Hotel in Troon for six nights and hired local tranportation (i.e., taxis) to get to the golf courses. They bought an Ayrshire Open Qualifier Card providing discounted golf at Kilmarnock Barassie, Irvine Bogside, Glasgow Gailes, and Turnberry's Kintyre. To these they added play at Prestwick, Western Gailes, Belleisle, Royal Troon's Old Course and Portland, and Turnberry's Ailsa—an impressive dance card. Their per-person cost for (a) a week of golf on ten superb courses; (b) private rooms at a full-service hotel; and (c) local transportation: about $2,350. This is smart golf travel.

Let me re-emphasize that any one of my nine golf regions can support a stay-and-play trip. Incidentally, the lesser-known areas are the ones that draw the Brits and Europeans. Avoiding the most expensive regions (1, 2, and 3), they'll more often be found in the southern hills of Galloway, on the Isle of Arran, at Pitlochry (the geographic center of Scotland), in the Spey Valley, up around Dornoch and Bora, or in the countryside surrounding Aberdeen. More often than not, their preference is for self-catering on stays of a week or more. Americans could learn a lot from this mode of travel.

————

Ten Itineraries That Work

Following are ten itineraries best suited to trips of at least ten to fourteen days. Most of these trips could start in either Glasgow or Edinburgh. Though surprisingly few travelers fly into Inverness or Aberdeen, those cities also can be used as the beginning and/or end point of an itinerary. Itinerary #8 is an example of a trip starting and ending in Aberdeen or Inverness. Itinerary #s 9 and 10 traverse the length of Scotland, either beginning or ending in Inverness—ideal for someone traveling to or from England.

While browsing through these itineraries, bear in mind they are only suggestions designed to stimulate your thinking. If you have fewer than ten days to travel, maybe some *portion* of one of these itineraries will appeal. With more than two weeks for travel and golf, some combination of itineraries might appeal. My purpose here is to include all the regions where you'll find the golf courses described in Part III, "The Directory of Courses."

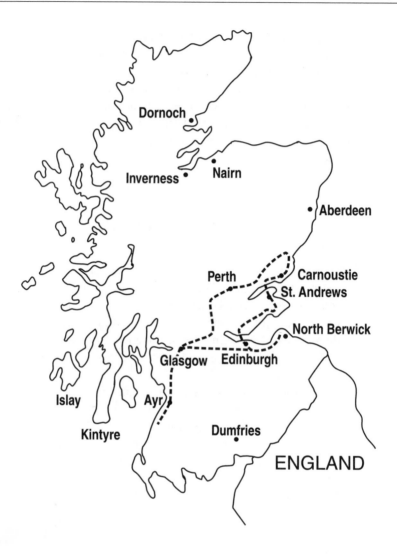

Itinerary # 1 - The Open "Rota" Courses: *Combining Ayrshire (Region #2), Angus/East Coast (Region #4), Fife (Region #1), and East Lothian (Region #3).* The focus here is golf on seven past and current venues of the British Open. With St. Andrews' Old Course and Muirfield in the picture, depending upon the time of year, *considerable advance planning (twelve to fifteen months) might be required to actually accomplish this trip.* Variations on the theme can be accomplished with less lead time (i.e., without advance booking at St. Andrews or Muirfield). This trip could include the following courses: *Ayrshire:* Prestwick, Royal Troon, Turnberry; *Angus:* Montrose, Carnoustie; *Fife:* St. Andrews Old, Crail; *East Lothian:* Muirfield, North Berwick, Old Musselburgh.

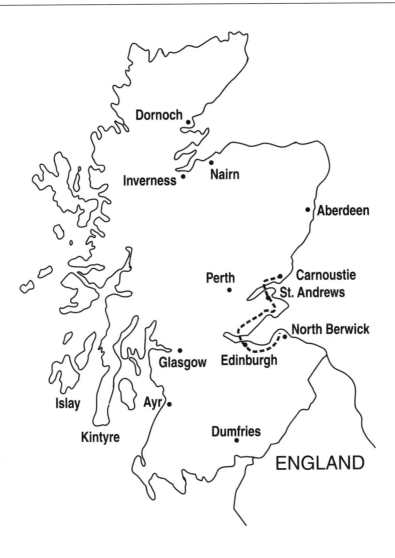

Itinerary #2 - The Historic Homes of Golf - Edinburgh and the East Coast: *Combining East Lothian (#3); Fife (#1); and Angus/East Coast (#4).* This is a shortened version of Itinerary #1. It's a focused trip requiring relatively little driving to and from Scotland's oldest golf grounds at Musselburgh, North Berwick, St. Andrews, and Carnoustie. Locations provide easy access to Edinburgh for sightseeing and shopping (a good itinerary for non-golfers). Any one of these areas could serve as home base for a stay-and-play trip.

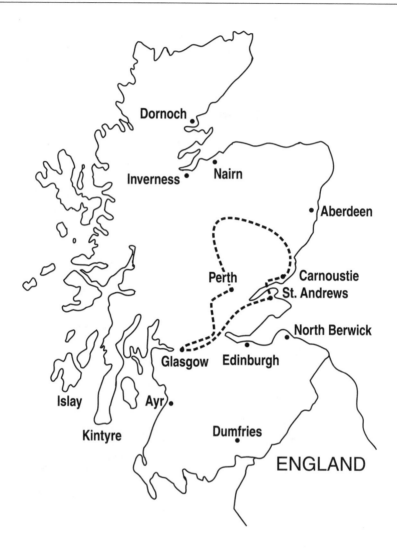

Itinerary #3 - Parkland to Seaside: *Combining Perthshire (#7), Angus/East Coast (#4), and Fife (#1).* This itinerary suggests the courses at Gleneagles, Blairgowrie, and Pitlochry; then on to Montrose and Carnoustie with a finish in and around St. Andrews. In Part I, Chapter 1 ("Overview"), I indicated a liking of this itinerary for first-timers. The reason: it combines a slice of the Highlands and inland golf with historic links courses at Montrose, Carnoustie, and St. Andrews. The loop above Perth indicates travel on the scenic A93 traversing the Dee Valley and skirting Balmoral Castle. This is a seductive itinerary designed to give travelers "a taste of Scotland," enticing them to return as soon as possible.

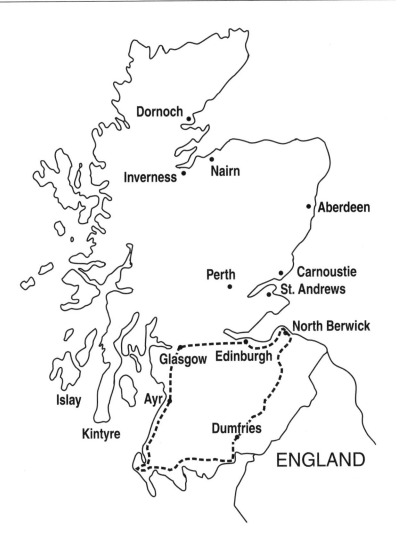

Itinerary #4 - The Southern Loop: *Combining Ayrshire (#2), South Coast (#9), and East Lothian (#3).* This big loop (easily shortened) combines the great courses of Ayrshire with scenic driving and golf in the less-traveled south of Scotland. The superb courses of the South Coast are bargain-priced. The courses of East Lothian are both historic and relatively good bargains. For those of literary bent, this trip traverses the haunts of Robert Burns and Sir Walter Scott. Glorious gardens and castles abound. Easy access to Edinburgh also figures into the equation. Either the Drambuie Ayrshire Golf Classic or the Galloway Golf Classic could provide a five-day focus to this itinerary (see Part I, Chapter 2 for details).

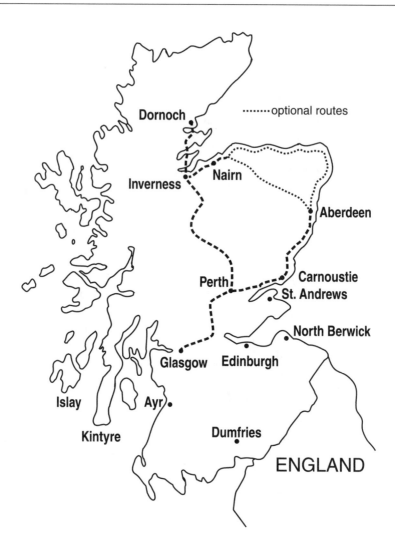

Itinerary #5 - Highlands Loop to the East: *Combining Perthshire (#7), Inverness/Dornoch (#5), Northeast/North Coast (#6), and Angus (#4).* This trip leaves behind the heavily-populated lowlands to increase the drama of both the golf experience and the travel experience. Starting in the lush Perthshire countryside, we push on to the Highlands at least as far north as Dornoch, fifty miles above Inverness. Then down to Cruden Bay/Aberdeen (Scotland's most dramatic dune-filled linksland) either through the Cairngorm Mountains or along the north coast, then southward to visit the courses of Angus, especially Carnoustie, before returning to Glasgow or Edinburgh.

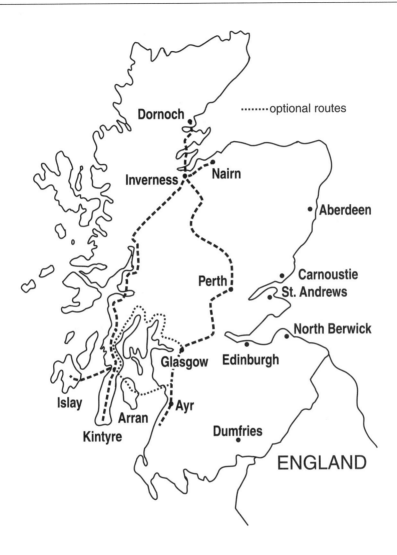

Itinerary #6 - Highlands Loop to the West: *Combining Perthshire (#7), Inverness/Dornoch (#5), Arran/Kintyre/Islay (#8), and Ayrshire (#2).* A variant on Itinerary #5, this features the dramatic scenery of the west coast and islands with golf on Arran, Kintyre, and Islay. Two weeks or more are needed to do justice to this full itinerary. The reason: Shiskine, Machrihanish, and Machrie all should be played at least twice to gain familiarity with a host of blind shots. Optional routes by ferry or land to the Kintyre Peninsula are indicated. Ferries to Islay leave from Kennacraig. Additional western islands to explore: Iona, Mull, and Skye.

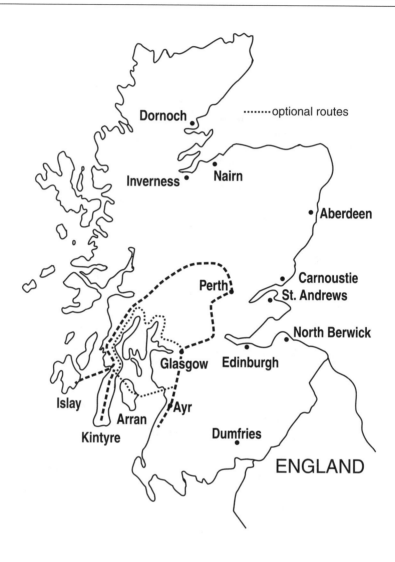

Itinerary #7 - Ayrshire and Scenic Scotland: *Combining Ayrshire (#2), Arran/ Kintyre/Islay (#8), and Perthshire (#7).* A variant on Itinerary #6—for those on a shorter trip—this trip features the great courses of Ayrshire before setting out for the Kintyre Peninsula (either driving or by ferry via the Isle of Arran). Alternative to the Ardrossan-Brodick ferry to Arran, one can get to Arran from Claonig on the Kintyre peninsula. Islay is reached by ferry from Kennacraig. From Islay, return to the mainland for sightseeing and golf in Perthshire before returning from Glasgow or Edinburgh.

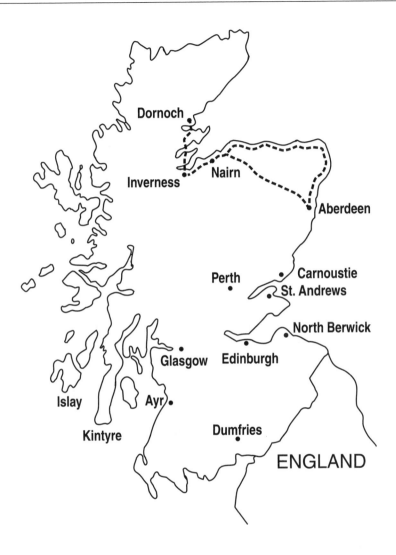

Itinerary #8 - The Highlands and the Northeast/North Coast: *Combining Northeast/North Coast (#6) and Inverness/Dornoch (#5).* A focused trip encompassing all the best Scotland has to offer: great golf, the "Castle Trail," the "Whisky Trail," the "Coastal Trail," plus the dramatic scenery and friendly people of the Highlands. This trip could start at either Inverness or Aberdeen, Scotland's third largest city. Consider some of the course options: Royal Aberdeen, Cruden Bay, Moray Old, Nairn, Royal Dornoch, Brora, and Tain. This is a good itinerary for a week of self-catering in two locations. The best part: a leisurely pace on "roads less traveled."

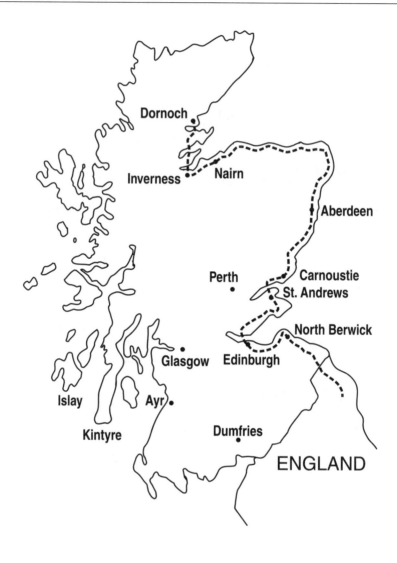

Itinerary #9 - East Side: A One-Way Trip to From the Highlands.
Combining East Lothian (#4), Fife (#1), Angus/East Coast (#3), North/Northeast (#6), and Inverness/Dornoch (#5). Traveling to or from England? Here's a way to do it playing links golf all the way. Just imagine: Dunbar, North Berwick, Old Musselburgh, Crail, St. Andrews, Carnoustie, Montrose, Cruden Bay, Moray Old, Royal Dornoch, and many more. You may think you've died and gone to golfer's heaven. Elsewhere I've suggested a truncated version of this route, stretching from St. Andrews to Cruden Bay about 30 miles north of Aberdeen, as a stay-and-play itinerary based in Carnoustie (see page 44).

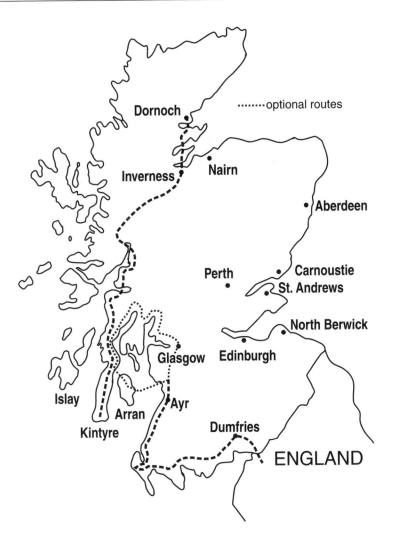

Itinerary #10 - West Side: A One-Way Trip to or From the Highlands.
Combining the South Coast (#9), Ayrshire (#2), Arran/Kintyre/Islay (#8), and Inverness/Dornoch (#5). A variant on #9, but this time up (or down) the craggy and wild west coast. Links golf is featured at Southerness, Portpatrick, Turnberry, Prestwick, and Troon, with Royal Dornoch and other northern courses the icing on the cake. With history and scenery and gardens galore, this is a strong itinerary for the non-golfing fellow traveler.

In Anticipation of Chapter Three

St. Andrews is included in four of the ten itineraries outlined here. As a practical matter, St. Andrews is included in the itineraries of most first-time golf travelers to Scotland, Rarely do I encounter a first-timer who doesn't want to visit the Auld Grey Toon and have a look at the Old Course, take a shot at the daily ballot, and at least play next door to it on the New Course or the Jubilee. And that's fine. As we shall see, "Everyone Wants to Go—and Why Not!".

Fortunately, even in the dead of summer it's not as hard to get a tee time at the Old Course as it is at several of the other well-known Scottish courses. I'll have more to say about that in the ensuing pages. In the context of this chapter, it is more important to answer the common question, *"Among the historic and current 'rota' courses, which are the hardest courses to get on?"*. In my experience, in order of degree of difficulty in high season, they are: (1) Muirfield; (2) Royal Troon; (3) St. Andrews' Old Course; (4) Turnberry; (5) Prestwick; and (6) Carnoustie.

Due to limited availability, Muirfield leads the pack any time of year. Royal Troon is more difficult than St. Andrews because it is a private club where visitor play is limited to three days a week. St. Andrews is third due to sheer demand; if all things were equal (i.e., access policy), it would rank fifth or sixth. The Ailsa at Turnberry is tied to the resort hotel and, as long as there's room in the hotel and you're willing to pay up, a tee time is assured. Prestwick and Carnoustie are a tossup. Demand at Carnoustie is greater, but Prestwick's somewhat more restrictive visitor policies sometimes make it a bit more difficult to manage.

More course-specific information is presented in Part III, "The Directory of Courses." But before we get to the details of trip planning, it's time to take a closer look at the place everyone wants go—St. Andrews.

CHAPTER THREE

St. Andrews Up Close:
Everyone Wants to Go—and Why Not!

Traveling to St. Andrews carries with it an undeniable sense of drama. I think of it as a modern-day pilgrimage to Shangri-La or Oz. You know there's a shining city upon a hill awaiting, and you're pretty sure there's a pot of gold at the end of this rainbow. And, you know, you're right. St. Andrews does not disappoint. It's everything one hopes for and maybe a little more.

From Edinburgh, you cross the Forth Bridge (nine miles from the Edinburgh airport) on the M90, leaving airports and cities and crowds far behind. Only a few minutes along, the A92 branches eastward off the M90 and then sharply northward into the Kingdom of Fife. Now, shedding another layer of modernity, the dual carriageway disappears near Glenrothes as you press on through rolling farmland past Freuchie and Ladybank to join the A91 just fifteen miles outside St. Andrews. Time elapsed: only about forty minutes to this point but so different as to be in some other time and place.

Getting to this point from Glasgow takes a little longer—about ninety minutes, first northward on the M80, then eastward along the length of the A91, skirting Stirling and the golden bluffs of the Ochil Hills, slowing at tiny farm villages, driving ever more deeply into the peaceful countryside of Fife. The tensions of travel ease and the drive begins to feel like a pilgrimage. You're on your way to the place where the game of golf was conceived, nurtured, and codified. You're ever so close to St. Andrews.

Now the A91 takes you straight through the bustling market center of Cupar, ten miles west of your destination. After clearing Cupar, a few miles along, you cross a flowing stream marked, "Eden." Could this place name be entirely coincidental?

Now, as the A91 slides gracefully to the southeast, you round a bend and there St. Andrews appears on high ground above the Fife countryside. You wind your way into town past university playing fields, take a left on Golf Place just past the second roundabout, and . . . there you are. In an instant all you've seen in books and on television is before your eyes. In one grand sweep you take it in: the vast, flat field encompassing the first and eighteenth fairways of the Old Course; the golden beach curving off into the distance; the intimidating first tee exposed for all to see; the mammoth eighteenth green ringed around by white fence and idling observers; the imposing Royal and Ancient clubhouse, looking as though it has stood since time immemorial.

The imposing Royal & Ancient clubhouse overlooking the first tee at St. Andrews' Old Course.

Now more details catch your eye: the British Golf Museum across the street behind the R & A; the starter house, the caddie pavilion and putting green bounded by more white fence; the Victorian stone buildings alongside the eighteenth fairway; Tom Morris's golf shop; Rusacks Hotel; the Old Course Hotel off in the distance near the seventeenth hole. There's "Grannie Clark's Wynd" where people are walking and cars are driving right across the middle of the first and eighteenth fairways! And, beyond it, the Golfers' Bridge across Swilken Burn.

Eventually you make your way down the West Sands Road to the car park and the Links Clubhouse where you find all the golfer's amenities for a stay in St. Andrews—information desk, changing rooms, pro shop, and the starter's office for the New Course and Jubilee. Maybe it's time for some refreshment in the handsome lounge, or a jaunt up to the rooftop observatory for a bird's-eye view over the linksland.

Finally, you've arrived at St. Andrews! Now it's time to find your accommodations, get settled, and explore the Auld Grey Toon.

The Lay of the Land

St. Andrews, with a permanent population of about 20,000 including university students, is compactly laid out and entirely walkable. Six golf courses spread out in the shape of a giant fan on the flat, low ground to the west/northwest of town. Town buildings occupy high ground above the linksland and rocky cliffs that separate the West Sands (golf courses) from the East Sands about a mile away around a bend in the coastline.

Looking at a town plan of St. Andrews, the medieval character of the place is plain to see. Once the ecclesiastical center of Scotland, the heart of the old city was at the east end of town where the dramatic cathedral and cemetery grounds meet the coastline.

TRAVEL TIP

To get a bird's eye view of St. Andrews, climb the 138 steps up St. Rule's Tower on the cathedral/cemetery grounds. Nearby, back down on the ground, are the gravesites of Alan Robertson and Willie Auchterlonie.

Here, along Abbey Walk, Castle Street, and the Pends, one can trace the remains of old city walls that lead to the ruins of a 13th-century castle—first the bishop's home—perched on a promontory above the rocky shore.

Just as the town's golf courses fan out from the first tee of the Old Course, four streets fan out from the cathedral grounds to define the commercial and spiritual core of modern St. Andrews. Three of these streets—North Street, Market Street, and South Street—offer up a lot of traffic and most of St. Andrews' shops and restaurants, pubs and other public places. None is longer than about three-eighths of a mile. A fourth street, between North Street and the coast, is called "The Scores." This street leads directly and symbolically from the bishop's

St. Andrews' busy Market Street—a graceful warren of shops and services.

castle to the first tee of the Old Course and is remarkable for its peaceful contrast to the trio of commercial streets just mentioned. To the east of Murray Park, The Scores is a leafy one-lane track lined by ivy-covered walls and university buildings. Between Murray Park and the R & A clubhouse, The Scores and its university roots give way to a long block of offices and expensive ocean-front hotels.

Marked on the map on the following page, on Market Street and South Street, are several places of special interest to golfers and non-golfers alike. At 70 Market St., you'll find the Tourist Information Office ❶. Start here for information about "What's On" in Fife and St. Andrews during your stay. It's a well-stocked TI with excellent staff. Next, on the north side of South St. between Church St. and Bell St. is the main Post Office ❷ where you can go to send postcards to all your golf buddies back home (and, incidentally, pick up a phone card). Other nearby practical destinations are the public library ❸ and the Tesco food store ❹ near the corner of Market and Bell.

Looking for entertainment in St. Andrews? There's golf history at the British Golf Museum ❺ near the R & A clubhouse. Try a feature film at the local cinema ❻ or performing arts at the Byre Theatre ❼. But the best entertainment in St. Andrews is all around you—that is, in pounding the paved streets of this enchanting town. It's a place with ancient roots and, as author Michael Tobert advises, "Look up when you walk the streets of St. Andrews. That's where the history is. It's in the details of the buildings." And, finally, my favorites: for peaceful relief from the streets, there are the beaches and the shady walk along Lades Brae ❽ through quiet neighborhoods where the land falls off precipitously to the south behind Queen's Terrace.

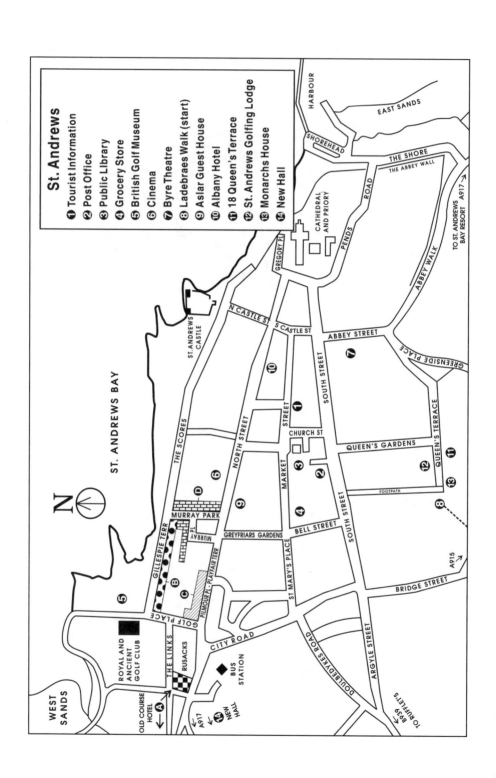

St. Andrews

- ❶ Tourist Information
- ❷ Post Office
- ❸ Public Library
- ❹ Grocery Store
- ❺ British Golf Museum
- ❻ Cinema
- ❼ Byre Theatre
- ❽ Ladebraes Walk (start)
- ❾ Aslar Guest House
- ❿ Albany Hotel
- ⓫ 18 Queen's Terrace
- ⓬ St. Andrews Golfing Lodge
- ⓭ Monarchs House
- ⓮ New Hall

ST. ANDREWS BAY

WEST SANDS

EAST SANDS

HARBOUR

SHOREHEAD

THE SHORE

THE ABBEY WALL

TO ST ANDREWS BAY RESORT A917

CATHEDRAL AND PRIORY

PENDS

ROAD

GREGORY PL

ABBEY WALL

GREENSIDE PLACE

ABBEY STREET

QUEEN'S TERRACE

QUEEN'S GARDENS

FOOTPATH

N CASTLE ST

S CASTLE ST

SOUTH STREET

ST. ANDREWS CASTLE

THE SCORES

NORTH STREET

STREET

CHURCH ST

MARKET STREET

GREYFRIARS GARDENS

BELL STREET

MURRAY PARK

GILLESPIE TERR

MURRAY PL

PILMOUR PL

PLAYFAIR TERR

GOLF PLACE

ST MARY'S PLACE

SOUTH STREET

BRIDGE STREET

A915

TO RUFFLETS B939

ARGYLE STREET

DOUBLEDYKES ROAD

CITY ROAD

ROYAL AND ANCIENT GOLF CLUB

OLD COURSE HOTEL

THE LINKS

RUSACKS

A917

NEW HALL

BUS STATION

Lodging In and Around St. Andrews

A prospective client once called me in considerable confusion. He didn't have a lot of money to spend and said a travel agent had told him, "The only hotels in St. Andrews are the Old Course Hotel, Rusacks Hotel, and Rufflets." Of course, nothing could be farther from the truth. As one of Scotland's major tourist destinations, St. Andrews is blessed with a wealth of lodging options in every price category. St. Andrews is not just for the well-heeled.

This section presents an overview of choices and directions to internet sites where you can get more information. To that end, I've organized my comments on St. Andrews lodging generally by proximity to the golf courses and, among the first four groups, generally by price. Proximity and price tend to coincide around the links so, rather than locate all the individual hotels on the map, I've indicated four main areas (A, B, C, D) of lodging choices near the links. All price estimates are quoted *per person per night (pppn) double occupancy* high season 2005 (exchange rate £1 = $1.90).

The Crème de la Crème (Area A)

In town that would be *The Old Course Hotel* (01334-474-371; *www.oldcoursehotel.co.uk*) and *Rusacks Hotel* (0870-400-8128; *www.macdonaldhotels.co.uk*). *Rufflet's Country House Hotel* (01334-472-594; *www.rufflets.co.uk*) is about a mile and one-half west on Strathkiness Road. A newcomer to this group in 2002, the monumental *St. Andrews Bay Resort Hotel*, rises on high ground three miles south of town (01334-837-000; *www.standrewsbay.com*). The least expensive room in these places costs about £95 pppn ($180). Want to face the Old Course from suites at Rusacks or The Old Course Hotel?—that will be about £150 to £210 pppn ($285 to $400). Of course, if you want to use the helipad, that's a whole 'nother ball game.

The Scores (Gillespie Terrace) (Area B)

Eastward from the corner of Golf Place and The Scores, four hotels offer million-dollar views from oceanfront windows at rates a cut or two below the *crème de la crème*. In order, from the corner to Murray Park, these are: The Scores Hotel, the St. Andrews Golf Hotel, the Hazelbank Hotel, and the Russell Hotel.

The Scores Hotel (01334-472-451; *www.bestwestern.com*) has thirty rooms and a classy pub called the "The Chariot Bar"—so named to honor the feature film, "Chariots of Fire," filmed primarily on the West Sands of St. Andrews. On the cherry-wood walls of the Chariot Bar are hung photographs, sketches, and oil portraits of 127 famous Scots from several centuries and all walks of life.

High-season rates at The Scores: £85 to £100 pppn ($160 to $190). This is not a good deal for a three-star Best Western hotel.

The *St. Andrews Golf Hotel* (01334-472-611; *www.standrews-golf.co.uk*), a bit farther along, is a family-run, four-star hotel with twenty-two comfortable rooms, a first-class restaurant, and strikingly handsome public rooms. Prices here are comparable to those at The Scores Hotel.

Near the corner of The Scores and Murray Park, are the *Hazelbank Hotel* (01334-472-466; *www.hazelbank.com*) and the *Russell Hotel* (01334-473-447; *www.russellhotelstandrews.co.uk*). Each is family run and has ten rather average rooms costing about £55 to £65 pppn ($105 to $125). The Russell has an attractive dining room popular with locals.

In every case here, we're talking location, location, location. I've quoted a range of prices because an ocean-view room costs more than an "inside" room. The best idea: save these hotels for the shoulder season or off-season when special offers are available at significantly reduced rates.

Pilmour Place/Playfair Terrace (Area C)

Eastward from the other corner of Golf Place are three more small hotels—the Dunvegan Hotel on the corner of Golf Place and Pilmour Place; the Ardgowan Hotel a little farther along on Playfair Terrace; and The Inn on North Street up by Murray Park. These are small hotels run in the best Scottish tradition—popular gathering places with full bar and restaurant facilities. They frequently show up on mid-price tour packages and, given their popularity and small size, one should book well in advance. Prices are similar to those at the Hazelbank and Russell, though in a wider range. Expect to pay from £48 to £65 pppn ($90 to $125) with the Ardgowan at the lower end of that range and the Dunvegan at the upper.

The Dunvegan Hotel on Golf Place—St. Andrews' most popular small hotel.

The *Dunvegan Hotel* (01334-473-105; *www.dunvegan-hotel.com*) is St. Andrews' most famous small hotel. In 2002 it got bigger fast with the acquisition of the three "Auchterlonie Suites" in the historic corner building across the street from the main hotel. Layered onto the hotel's popular golfers' lounge and Claret Jug Restaurant, these spacious rooms increase still further the Dunvegan's appeal to small groups of golfers. The owners here are Jack and Sheena Willoughby. Jack is a transplanted Texan (A & M) who first lived in Aberdeen where he was involved with North Sea oil exploration and drilling. When the opportunity came to buy the Dunvegan in 1994, he settled in St. Andrews and has since become a local institution and minor celebrity in international golf with hundreds of guests returning annually to enjoy his and Sheena's welcoming little inn.

In late 2003 the *Ardgowan Hotel* (01334-472-970; *www.ardgowanhotel.co.uk*) at #2 Playfair Terrace was acquired by Dr. Roy McGlauchlin who promptly embarked upon major refurbishment of a comfortable but dated structure. With prices starting at £48 pppn ($90) in high season, this one is popular on many "budget" golf tours and is perhaps the best full-service hotel bargain near the golf courses. The hotel has a good restaurant and attractive lounge, "Playfair's Restaurant/Bar," at street level.

At the corner of Murray Park and Pilmour, the thirteen-room *Inn on North Street* (01334-473-387; *www.theinnonnorthstreet.com*) has a subterranean pub popular with locals. The menu in the small "Cidsin" dining room is among the most extensive in town and of consistently good quality.

Murray Park and Murray Place (Area D)

Remarkably affordable lodging near the golf courses can be found on Murray Park and Murray Place. These two Murrays are lined entirely with B & Bs ranging in quality from two-star to four-star. We're not talking fancy here, but clean, well-lighted places near town center, within easy walking distance to the golf courses, priced

Both sides of Murray Park are lined with reasonably-priced B & Bs near the golf courses.

from about £32 to £45 pppn ($60 to $85)—in other words, about half the price of most of the hotels in this area. Every bit the bargain for a town as pricey as St. Andrews. Most of these establishments have their own website, but they also can be found on one or more of the promotional associations (e.g., *www.smoothhound.co.uk*). There are too many to mention, but among them are the *Annandale Guest House, Arran House, Burness House, Cameron House, Craigmore Guest House, Duone House, Lorimer House,* and *Glenderran Guest House*—all good choices for the savvy traveler. When

TRAVEL TIP
Attention singletons! Several guest houses on the Murrays have small rooms typically priced around £35 designed specifically for singles. These include Cameron House, Glenderran Guest House, and Duone House.

considering these, keep in mind that address numbers ascend from North Street to The Scores—so, while Burness House at #1 is up by busy North Street, the Annandale at #23 is on the corner at the relatively quieter Scores across from the Russell Hotel.

Just outside this area, but close enough to include here, is the *Aslar Guest House* ❾ (01334-473-460; *www.aslar.com*) across from the cinema near the corner of Murray Park and North Street. Efficiently managed and impeccably furnished by Jean Pardoe, the six-room Aslar is St. Andrews' best four-star guest house (and value) in the center of town. Prices start at £39 pppn ($74) but are reduced for stays of three or more nights. Incidentally, the Aslar website includes an extensive set of links to local and national sources of information.

Parking in the Golf Quadrangle

With the exception of the luxury hotels, what I've described to this point is lodging in the quadrangle of blocks directly east of the R & A clubhouse and the first tee of the Old Course. A major problem for all these establishments— thus, for *you* and, indeed, for all of St. Andrews—is parking. The medieval streets in the central part of this fair city are simply not designed to accommodate the modern automobile in anything like the numbers vying for space every day. What to do? First, take whatever advice and help your lodging host can provide. Second, take whatever space you can find and be damned glad you got it. Third, before getting into your car, think about the possibility of walking.

Alternatively, consider other accommodations where the parking challenge is not so severe. To that end, following are suggestions in two more lodging groups—the first, in St. Andrews but outside the Golf Quadrangle; the second, literally outside of St. Andrews.

Other Options in St. Andrews

In a category of its own, housing is available in the summer through the University of St. Andrews ⓮ (01334-462-000; *www.st-andrews.ac.uk*). New Hall, not far from the Old Course and three-star rated by VisitScotland, offers perfectly acceptable lodging for the budget traveler. For that same budget traveler, excellent B & Bs in private homes scattered throughout the greater St. Andrews area are available for the lowest rates in town (typically £20 to £25 pppn for singles and £30 to £40 pppn doubles). Most belong to the St. Andrews Private B & B Association (*www.standrewsbandbs.com*).

In the small-hotel category is the *Albany Hotel* ❿ on the cathedral end of North St. (ph 01334-477-737; *www.standrewsalbany.co.uk*). The Albany is comparable to the hotels in Group C above. It's a restored Georgian with twenty-one rooms—popular on mid-price golf tours and, though on busy North St., just far enough away from town center to improve the parking odds. Cost: about £60 pppn ($115). With six rooms specifically for singles priced at £75 pppn ($142), this is the best hotel choice in St. Andrews for single occupancy.

Three properties on Queen's Terrace, one block off South Street, deserve special mention. *Eighteen Queen's Terrace* ❶ (01334-478-849; *www.aboutscotland.com/fife/queensterrace.html*) is a four-room Victorian row house where the weary traveler is surrounded by good taste and personal attention from an excellent hostess, Jill Hardie. All the rooms feature antiques, fine art, and top-of-the-line fixtures. And, yet, the atmosphere is relaxed and homey. At £50 single ($95) and £40 pppn double ($152), this is the kind of special place available in St. Andrews at about one-third the cost of the five-star hotels and, for that matter, considerably less than the three-star hotels.

Across the street at *The St. Andrews Golfing Lodge* ❷ (01334-477-676; *www.st-andrews-golf-lodge.com*), Chris Toll and Claire Cook preside over the newest concept in St. Andrews lodging—it's a private home, five-star rated by VisitScotland, renovated in sleek Scandinavian modern and available to groups for a per-diem fixed price (£700 B & B in 2005). Like "self catering," but with the option of breakfast service and rental by the night (rather than a mandatory full week), this is a perfect arrangement for eight golfers who want their own place with a kitchen, lounge, billiard table, private parking, patio, and other amenities. Split the cost and it's comparable to one of the expensive hotels in the Golf Quadrangle (e.g., £700 ÷ 8 = £87.50 or $166 pppn).

An even better bargain at the deluxe level is available at *Monarchs House* (01334-477-218; *www.monarchshouse.com*) ❸ at #26 Queen's Terrace. Under American ownership, this is a baronial property with seven bedrooms and eight bathrooms for up to eight people. From the formal Tom Morris dining room, through the comfortable library, to the spacious bedrooms, Monarchs House exudes class from top to bottom. Available only from Saturday through Saturday, Monarchs' weekly rental in 2005 is $8,500, payable in U.S. dollars (thus non-fluxuating), and includes the usual B & B plus three four-course dinners and an initial bar setup comprising a case each of wine and beer, and a bottle each of vodka and single-malt whisky. A special feature of Monarchs House is the presence of General Manager Angus Mitchell, longtime St. Andrews resident who serves as a sort of personal assistant to house guests. Angus is a member of the Royal & Ancient and is on the Links Trust Management Committee. In short, he knows where all the bodies are buried and he helps make Monarchs House so much more than a self-catering property. This is quite simply the best choice in town for up to eight golfers looking for luxury and personal attention on a week-long stay-and-play trip to St. Andrews. Think about it: split eight ways, the cost is about $150 pppn for quality, comfort, and ambience far exceeding the offerings of an impersonal resort hotel. Incidentally, an advantage of all the properties on Queen's Terrace: this is a dead-end street, so there is no through-traffic—a true luxury in St. Andrews.

Outside St. Andrews

In "The Directory of Courses" I have cited lodging choices at Glenrothes (see *Balbirnie Park Golf Club*); Lundin Links (see *Lundin Golf Club*); and Crail (see *Crail Golfing Society*). To these I would add:

• *Eden House Hotel* (01334-652-510; *www.edenhousehotel.com*) in Cupar, on the A91 ten miles east of St. Andrews. A good "golfers' hotel" on the train line to and from Edinburgh.

• *Inn at Lathones* (01334-840-494; *www.theinn.co.uk*). Great location five miles southwest of St. Andrews on the A915. A 400-year-old coaching inn with a popular restaurant; pricey but special.

• *The Old Station* (01334-880-505; *www.theoldstation.co.uk*). Classy modern property in a quiet countryside location two miles south of St. Andrews off the A917 near St. Andrews Bay Resort.

So, you see, there's a lot more to lodging in and around St. Andrews than the Old Course Hotel, Rusacks, and Rufflets. You can pay a lot or a little. Demand is high, but competition is keen, and that works to the benefit of the tourist. Consider your preferences, then start digging. There's something for everyone in St. Andrews.

The Golf Courses at St. Andrews

The St. Andrews Links Trust and Links Management Committee

In 1974 the St. Andrews Links Trust was established by an Act of Parliament to deal with the increasing numbers of visitors descending upon St. Andrews to play golf on the ancient links. The Trust was charged with maintaining the courses as *public* courses with assured access to all and with particular regard for the citizens of St. Andrews.

In carrying out its charge, the Links Management Committee has taken a variety of actions—some popular, some controversial. Surely the most popular was wholesale redesign of The Jubilee Course by Donald Steel in 1988-9, thus giving St. Andrews three championship-level courses side by side. Next, to accommodate beginning and high-handicap golfers, a new 18-hole course (The Strathtyrum) and a nine-holer (The Balcove) were opened in 1993. Additionally, a Golf Practice Center was carved out of The Eden Course (some say to the everlasting ruin of the little track adjacent to the Old Course). A large clubhouse to accommodate visiting golfers was built in 1995 ("unnecessary," grumbled the old-timers). A smaller clubhouse at The Eden was finished in 2000. In 2000-01 an extensive, expensive, and controversial irrigation system was installed on the Old Course. In 2003 the committee announced plans for a seventh public course on ground situated one mile south off the A917 between the St. Andrews Bay Resort Hotel and town center. This one will be constructed to championship standards by Scotsman David MacLay Kidd of Bandon Dunes fame.

To pay for all these changes, the Links Management Committee revised fee structures (constantly upward, of course), with special attention to visitors' wallets. In the mid-1970s a visitor could play the Old Course for about £5; by the mid-1980s the cost was £15; by the late 1990s, the fee reached £60. In 2001 the rate was pegged at £85. In 2003 it jumped to £105. Now, in 2005, the tariff is £115. Has inflation increased 2,300 percent in thirty years?—no. Is the Old Course twenty-three times better than it was thirty years ago?—of course not. Is demand twenty-three times greater?—yes, probably so, and then some.

Devising a system responsive to visitor demand, while continuing to guarantee democratic, affordable access to the Old Course *and* some preference for local residents, required the wisdom of Solomon. The Management Committee's multipart answer was an advance reservation system, the now-famous daily ballot for visitors, and the local ballot for residents. Unfortunately, the committee created serious controversy in 1995 when, to maximize revenue and simplify administration, it entered into a ten-year contract with a London-based travel agency to manage and sell about 1,000 tee times annually to the public and to "the trade" (i.e., tour operators and travel agencies) *without* retaining control over the agency's pricing policies (see my discussion of *The Old Course Experience* below). This action introduced elitism and obscurity to the previously democratic, straightforward booking process at St. Andrews. With expiration of the Prowse contract in 2005, controversy has continued to brew. Current speculation has the contract on annual renewal with a two-year cancellation provision. Even though the Links Trust operates as a publicly-funded charitable trust established by an Act of Parliament, management has been less than forthcoming about its arrangement with the Prowse agency.

The net result of links management history since 1974: lots of money for the Trust; a booking system that manages demand reasonably well, though not so democratically or cleanly as one would hope; a basketload of controversy over the years; and, at bottom, Europe's largest golf complex with ninety-nine holes on six courses. Thanks to the Links Management Committee, comprised over the years of individuals dedicated to golf at St. Andrews, there's something for everyone at The Home of Golf. That much is not debated. Detailed information about the courses at St. Andrews, links news, and management policies can be found at the Links Trust's excellent website, *www.standrews.org.uk*.

Eight Ways to Get a Tee Time on the Old Course

When I begin to explore itinerary options with a potential client, early in the conversation I ask one key question: *How important is the Old Course to your trip?* The answer to that question influences all aspects of trip planning. Before addressing that question here, I want to provide some context for the discussion—namely, an explanation of how to get a tee time on the Old Course. You have *eight options:*

✓ *Make an advance reservation.* In 2005 the Links Trust announced an important new advance-reservation policy. Golfers seeking an advance reservation are asked to submit an application *on or after the first Wednesday in September* for play during the ensuing year. Applicants contacting the management before that date will be asked to reapply at the designated time. Application may be made by email at reservations@standrews.org.uk; by fax to 011-44-1334-477-036; or by mail to Reservations, Pilmour House, St. Andrews Links Trust, St. Andrews KY16 9SF. Obviously, those in queue on or soon after that first Wednesday in September will have the best shot at the best times, but that should not deter anyone from applying at a later date. Management promises to respond to requests *by mail* within four weeks. If you've secured a time, you can proceed with planning the rest of your trip. If your bid has failed, you can weigh your other options.

This is a process more easily described than accomplished. Making an advance reservation at St. Andrews requires considerable forethought, as well as the freedom to make a date-specific commitment as much as twelve months prior to play. The Links Management requests information that may be a challenge to present. They want: (1) a "lead golfer" to receive all correspondence and make payment; (2) the names of all golfers; (3) their handicaps; (4) their home courses; (5) a specific date of requested play (Monday through Friday; all play on Saturdays is by ballot); and (6) choice of a second course to play (an advance date on the Old Course requires play on another of the St. Andrews courses). This level of detail is required to help prevent speculative booking by tour operators. A minor modification might be made along the way (e.g., substitution of one player for another), but wholesale variations from the original request are not tolerated. A single golfer may apply for an advance reservation. Depending upon the month, from May to September ten to fifteen slots per month are allocated to singles. For more information on the advance-reservation process, see *www.standrews.org.uk*. From the home page ("Welcome"), click on Golf > Book Golf > Advanced Tee Time Requests.

In Part II, Chapter 1, I stressed the importance of checking the Old Course calendar for conflicts and closure dates, with the admonition that, "You can't play the Old Course if it's not open." I reiterate that admonition. Check the Links Trust website and/or call the reservations office if you have any doubt about the availability of a date. On the website, from the home page, click on Events > Local Clubs. If you request a date when the Old Course is not available by advance reservation, you will be notified and asked to re-submit for another date. In 2003 the Links Management announced a policy of no advance reservations during June and September due to conflicts with annually-scheduled tournaments and other special events. The Old Course is not open on Sundays.

✓ *Apply for canceled dates.* Naturally, when reservations are made, cancellations follow. After that initial wave of advance-reservation responses, cancellations or unpaid reservations inevitably occur. Some people ask for dates they can't keep. Some people have business or family emergencies that force them to cancel travel plans. Some people get sick. Some people die. With any of these eventualities, openings occur and the Links Management periodically posts notification of openings on its website. In recent years, cancellation openings have been posted first in late January and then sporadically after that. The protocol: announcement by the Links Trust typically a week or two ahead of a specific date when they will accept application for open tee times *by phone* on a first-come, first-served basis. This means getting up early in North America to dial (and probably re-dial) with hope of getting through to the reservations office. Interestingly enough, over the past two years I have had at least a dozen groups secure Old Course tee times with this method. Bottom line: it pays to keep an eye on the St. Andrews website, particularly during the first quarter of the year. The number to call: 011-44-1334-466-666.

✓ *Enter the daily visitor ballot.* On this subject I quote directly from the Links Management website:

> Around 50% of all starting times over the year are put into the daily ballot (lottery) which is drawn every day for next day's play except Sunday—the Saturday draw is for Monday play. Success in the ballot is not guaranteed and chances vary according to the time of year, how busy the course is, and the weather. A minimum two golfers can enter. Either telephone or apply in person before 2 p.m. on the day before play. The results are shown by 4 p.m. on the web, at the clubhouses, the starters' boxes, the caddie pavilion, and local golf clubs.

This is the way most visitors to St. Andrews get a tee time on the Old Course. Odds are about even in April and October; perhaps more like one in three chances during peak months May to September. Let me stress that, among all my clients without an advance reservation (most of them), rarely have I had anyone come back from St. Andrews without having played the Old Course. How rarely?—roughly one in twenty-five. Those are pretty good odds. Again, the caveat: without a reservation you just have to give St. Andrews about three days to achieve that kind of success ratio through the ballot. To see results of the daily ballot, from the home page of the St. Andrews website, click on Golf > Today's Ballot.

✓ *Enter the daily local ballot.* Each day, tee times from 8-9 a.m. and 5-6 p.m. are reserved for residents of St. Andrews. The pool of applicants in the local ballot is much smaller than in the visitor ballot. Thus, if you can get into the local pool, your odds of getting onto the Old Course improve. To enter the local ballot, you need to pair up with a resident of St. Andrews who will play a round of golf with you and who will enter your name or names in the ballot. How do you that? Maybe you already know someone who lives in St. Andrews or belongs to one of the golf clubs there. If not, when you get into town, start talking to people. Chat up the bartender, the shopkeeper, the waiter, or a university student. Most important, talk to your lodging host. He or she most assuredly will know a local resident who might be looking for a game. This method of getting on the Old Course is not "by the book" (except when you buy this book), but it's entirely legitimate. It's a great way for a single golfer to avoid the walk-on queue.

✓ *Walk on.* Though a few advance reservation slots are allotted to singles, joining the walk-on queue is the most common way single golfers get on the Old Course. Obviously, this is another option for groups of golfers willing to split up. Since many advance reservations and ballot applications are made for two or three golfers, each day the starter has a varying number of open slots. And, because many Scots play in twos and threes, this is also your best shot at playing with locals who know the course. With a first tee time of 7 a.m. in the summer, single golfers, often with coffee and continental breakfast in hand, start queuing up at the Old Course Starter House at about 5:30 a.m. (or earlier). Alternative to the morning queue, one might check with the starter mid-to-late afternoon to inquire about the possibility of evening play. Inclement weather can bring the best opportunity for walking on any time of day. While a little rain won't stop visitors who have traveled thousands of miles to play the Old Course, locals, who can play any time, may prefer to sit out a rainy day.

> The cost of these first five methods of getting on the Old Course is the current green fee plus, in the case of advance reservation, another green fee on the New Course, Jubilee, Eden, or Strathtyrum. From here on, the options get considerably more expensive.

✓ *Buy a St. Andrews hotel or guest house package that includes an Old Course tee time.* Each year members of the St. Andrews Hotel and Guest House Association are allocated about one hundred tee times (total). Most of the times go to the largest, most prestigious hotels—the Old Course Hotel, Rusacks, Rufflets, The Scores Hotel, and the St. Andrews Golf Hotel. Small hotels like the Dunvegan or The Russell get only a handful (four or five) to sell. The allocation is made in the fall when the Links Management allocates other advance **This is the least likely way** reservations. You can request a reservation at a **to get on the Old Course.** hotel contingent upon receiving one of their allocated tee times. Should they agree to sell to you, for a package price putting a premium on the Old Course round, they will require play on two courses, a minimum three-night stay, and dinners at the hotel. They'll also be looking for a full contingent—that is, four golfers with four non-golfing spouses—to maximize their revenue from these little nuggets of golfing gold. In practice, most of the hotel tee times go to longtime patrons—people who come back year after year to vacation in St. Andrews—or to favored tour operators who bring trade to the hotels. This is the *least* likely way to get on the Old Course.

✓ *Buy a tour package.* The Links Management has created a class of "protected operators" who get a small allocation of tee times. These are Scottish operators or the UK offices of American companies like PerryGolf and InterGolf. Of course they only sell the tee times as part of a larger tour package. Generally, the Scottish operators run more reasonably-priced tours than their American counterparts. To get a list of these protected operators, inquire at the Links Management office.

Other tour operators buy Old Course tee times at "trade" prices from the Keith Prowse Agency (see *The Old Course Experience* below). They then wrap the tee times into package tours and re-sell them to the public. As indicated in the Prologue to this book, the problem with these tours is their cost. You can get a tee time on the Old Course this way, but, to get it, you will probably have to stay at the Old Course Hotel, not to mention Gleneagles, the Marine Hotel in Troon, and the Turnberry Hotel. In other words, you can play the Old Course, but only by paying top dollar all the way through your tour of Scotland's luxury resorts.

✓ *Buy "The Old Course Experience."* Tour operators can be removed from the picture by dealing directly with the Keith Prowse Agency. You can read in detail about The Old Course Experience at *www.oldcourse-experience.com*. The Old Course Experience offers two, three, and four-night packages depending upon the time of year. From June through September the minimum purchase is a three-night package. Hotel participants in the program are The Old Course Hotel (most expensive), St. Andrews Bay, Rusacks, the Carnoustie Golf Course Hotel, and St. Andrews Golf Hotel (least expensive). Assuming high season and the least expensive hotel option, here's a summary of the product and price circa 2005, June to September. You get: (1) tee times on the Old Course; either the New or Jubilee; and either Kingsbarns or Carnoustie; (2) three nights of bed and breakfast at the St. Andrews Golf Hotel; and (3) two dinners. Oh, yes, I almost forgot: the lucky customer also gets "full use of the links clubhouse" (open to the public at no charge) and "souvenir video and merchandise." The price for this "experience"?—a mere £1,665

The Old Course Experience—even the bus is expensive.

($3,164). If you want to stay at the Old Course Hotel, the cost will be £1850 ($3,515). And, by the way, that's *per golfer* double occupancy.

If a person could get a tee time on the Old Course in a reasonable way (e.g., by advance reservation or in the daily ballot), and assuming the choice of Carnoustie rather than Kingsbarns, the actual cost of the package described above would be about £623 ($1,184). In other words, the Keith Prowse Agency is selling that high-season tee time on the Old Course for about $1,980. Is any golf course worth $1,980? I don't think so.

In my view, there are only two remotely reasonable occasions to buy into the Old Course Experience: (1) in April, May, or October when the two-night program is available; and (2) when a golfer has a terminal disease and *must* play the Old Course before he or she dies. In the latter case, I would try to arrange my death in April, May, or October immediately after playing the Old Course. Otherwise, the world would be better off if all the money that goes to the Old Course Experience went instead to charity.

How Important is the Old Course to Your Trip?

With some context in place, let's take another look at this question. For many people, playing the Old Course is the "bottom line" of a trip to Scotland. The guarantee has to be in place. Without it, they'd rather stay home. If you fall into that category, you have four options: (1) secure an advance reservation by application; (2) persuade one of the hotels or B & Bs to sell a package to you; (3) sign up for a tour package; or (4) buy the Old Course Experience. None of the other methods of getting on the Old Course carries a guarantee of success.

If you can plan far enough ahead to apply for an advance reservation and succeed, you are miles ahead of everyone else. In my view, it's the only reasonable way to buy a "guaranteed" tee time.

But most people either don't know they need to apply eight to twelve months ahead of anticipated play or they just start planning too late. Every spring I get calls from people who say they want to go to Scotland in the summer and, of course, they *must* play the Old Course. Usually I'm successful in convincing them to stay-and-play in St. Andrews and put their trust in the daily ballot, but, in recalcitrant cases, these are times when I suggest consideration of The Old Course Experience rather than a package tour. With this approach, one can pay the Keith Prowse piper, while retaining the flexibility to plan the rest of a trip for a reasonable price—in effect, creating a "tour within a tour." But—Old Course Experience or a tour—it doesn't make much difference. Either way, it's expensive. When it comes to the Old Course, guarantees cost a lot of money—except by advance reservation.

Most often, golfers simply cannot or will not buy into the outrageously priced Old Course Experience. Yet the Old Course remains their primary objective. In this case, if the idea of a package tour also has been rejected, the options become: (1) the daily visitor ballot; (2) the daily local ballot; or (3) walking on as a single. In the first two cases, I recommend an itinerary that keeps you within striking distance of St. Andrews so that the Old Course bell can be answered when it rings. This means a stay-and-play itinerary in Fife or a circumscribed itinerary combining, for example, Fife with East Lothian or Angus. Your objective is to ballot the Old Course for a full week, if necessary. Given that much time, your success in getting on the Old Course is virtually assured. Here's what I recommend to make this approach work most effectively and efficiently:

• Arrive in Scotland on Saturday; ballot the Old Course by 2 p.m. for Monday play (or have your hotel do it for you). Check the ballot results after 4 p.m. If you have been chosen for play on Monday, call your pre-booked Monday course to cancel or re-schedule the tee time.
• On Sunday, since the Old Course is closed, play an expensive priority course like Kingsbarns or Carnoustie.
• If not chosen in the ballot on Saturday, ballot again on Monday for Tuesday play and continue that process throughout the week if necessary.
• For Monday through Friday play, book yourself at courses that require only a modest deposit. In Fife, these might include Crail, Lundin Links, Leven Links, Ladybank, and Scotscraig (see "The Directory of Courses" for details and more ideas). If cancellation becomes necessary, the monetary damage is mitigated.
• Toward the end of the week, leave some unbooked time for the possibility of play on St. Andrews' New Course or Jubilee. Though

pre-booking these courses is an option, I don't usually recommend it because (a) 100 percent pre-payment is required and (b) due to frequent cancellations, it's normally easy to walk-on at one or the other course during the week. I'd rather have the flexibility than the pre-booked time. It also helps to have an open day to leave space for re-scheduling one or more of the pre-booked courses to accommodate play on the Old Course.

• One further note: during the week, if you choose to book an expensive course like Kingsbarns or one of the courses at St. Andrews Bay, rest assured these courses will work with you to re-schedule a tee time to accommodate play on the Old Course.

This approach to the Old Course, almost assuredly, will get you a tee time and, more important, an affordable trip focused on a small area of Scotland. Believe me, even if you don't get on the Old Course, you'll have a great trip and play a lot of good golf.

Closing Words on the Old Course

This is my basic advice regarding the Old Course and Scottish golf: *To the extent that you can disenthrall yourself of the Old Course, you will have a greater range of itinerary options.* In other words, fixation on the Old Course limits your ability to discover the rest of Scotland.

Fixation on the Old Course limits your ability to discover the rest of Scotland.

To be more specific: *without an advance reservation* on the Old Course, it is not logically consistent to say that, in seven days, your main priority is to play the Old Course, but you also want to play Royal Troon, Prestwick, Turnberry, Carnoustie, and Royal Dornoch. If your main priority is to play the Old Course, then you must plan accordingly. That means staying in or within striking distance of St. Andrews and minimizing schedule conflicts with other high-priority courses. But, with the Old Course in proper perspective, championship courses in various parts of the country can be scheduled.

So, what is "proper perspective"? Ideally, the Old Course should be treated as icing on the cake. If you get on, fine. If you don't, fine—maybe next time. I can understand those situations that truly are once-in-a-lifetime trips—a father and son's last opportunity to play golf together; an 80-year-old's birthday trip to the Old Country; a dying golfer's last wish. Those are special occasions that deserve extraordinary measures to get on the Old Course.

Otherwise, why take a once-in-a-lifetime approach to Scottish golf? If you like Scottish golf—and most likely you will—then you can go back time

Golfers' Bridge across Swilken Burn at the home hole on St. Andrews' Old Course—ideally, ONE of many great Scottish courses to play on more than one trip.

and time again. And, if you can afford to go once, surely you can afford to go twice—particularly if you've read this book and have avoided the tours. At bottom, the entire case I've made to this point is that you can make two trips for the price most people pay for one trip. In that context, the Old Course takes on "proper perspective"— ONE of many great Scottish courses to be played on more than one trip.

 Telephone/Fax Calling Procedures

From the United States:
Dial 011 (international long distance), then 44 (country code), then the number in Scotland without the leading "0" (i.e., 011-44-1334-466-666).

CHAPTER FOUR

The Four Elements of a Golf Trip:
Air Travel, Vehicle Rental, Tee Times, Lodging

Air Travel

These days everyone has their own approach to purchasing airline tickets. Some people use their trusty travel agent. Others prefer to call an airline straight away. An increasing number of people are booking via the internet. Some people use frequent-flyer miles. Others use miles accumulated through credit-card purchases.

Given all these options—and the ever-changing dynamics of the airline industry—it would be foolish to print specific information on prices and routes in a book like this. What I *can* do is give you some advice, partly specific to current conditions, but generally based on the bigger picture that comes from years of experience.

Frankly, it bothers me a bit when clients plan a trip to Scotland only to delay buying their airline tickets until they can get "the best deal." To put this phenomenon in perspective: some people will blithely spend something like $500 for one night at the Turnberry Hotel but put off buying an airline ticket with the hope of saving $100! I guess it's the fun of playing Russian Roulette with the airlines. But I digress.

Following are two pieces of advice to guide your air arrangements. Both these items are based on an important principle: *it's no fun for a golfer to be in Scotland without golf clubs.* Barring a traffic accident, the worst thing that can happen on your trip is for you to arrive at your destination while your clubs are in London, Paris, Frankfurt, or Amsterdam—not just for a few hours but for a few days. If you are on a five or six-day trip and you don't get your clubs until the third or fourth day, you are going to be a decidedly "unhappy camper." Unfortunately, it happens. Why? The main reason is spelled H-e-a-t-h-r-o-w. This is another subject on which I've become an expert through personal experience.

The largest percentage of visitors to the United Kingdom arrive via London's Heathrow Airport—mainly because most major cities in the U.S. are served by routes to London and the cheapest flights are to that city. At London

Heathrow one can connect via British Midland to airports at Glasgow, Edinburgh, Aberdeen, and Inverness in Scotland. Now, here's my first piece of advice:

✓ *If you fly through London's Heathrow International Airport, leave at least **three hours** between arrival time and your connecting flight to Scotland.*

I used to say two hours, but since September 11, 2001, the only safe allowance is three hours. London is the world's second largest city. The airport at Heathrow is huge. Literally thousands of people are "processed" through Heathrow every hour. Given the size of the airport and the crush of humanity there, it seems logistically impossible to get oversize luggage (i.e., golf clubs) from Point A (International Arrivals) to Point C (Domestic Departures) in less than two hours.

Actually, it's nearly impossible to get *yourself* from Point A to Point C in less than two hours. I say, "Point C," advisedly because in between Point A and Point C you have to clear Customs (Point B). Along the way you'll endure two bus rides through a labyrinth of Heathrow's back streets. What a welcome to the UK!

In short, if your travel agent says, "I have your ticket to Glasgow and you only have to wait *one hour and thirty minutes* to connect in London," your reply should be, "Go back to the drawing board and give me three hours to make that connecting flight." To be safe, I would offer the same advice regarding all the major connecting points. The most frequently used are Amsterdam (KLM), Paris (Air France), and Frankfurt (Lufthansa).

Having allowed enough time for you and your luggage to make a connection, if your bags still do not arrive in Scotland when you do, you will need to go the "Baggage Claims" office where, bleary-eyed from lack of sleep, you will fill out claim forms and your patience will be taxed to the limit. Most often your luggage will arrive on the next flight and will be forwarded at the airline's expense to your first lodging address. Ironically, *if you choose an international flight with a connection, there is clear advantage to connecting through London rather than through a city outside the UK.* The reason: through most of the business day, British Midland (your most likely connecting carrier) runs flights every two hours from London to Glasgow and Edinburgh. Thus, your luggage most often will be delayed for only two hours. From cities outside the UK, with fewer flights each day, the wait most assuredly will be several hours at best.

All this rather depressing discussion of connecting points and delayed or lost luggage leads to my second piece of related advice:

✓ *Fly nonstop to Glasgow or Edinburgh if you can.*

When you fly directly into Glasgow or Edinburgh you'll arrive at a relatively peaceful, pleasant place, without the "cattle car" environment of major airports. More important, you'll have an umbilical link with your golf clubs and clothes that were put on the plane at your point of departure. At this writing (April 2005), nonstop flights to Glasgow and/or Edinburgh originate from the U.S. at Chicago (American Airlines), Newark (Continental Airlines), and Philadelphia (USAirways). Air Canada flies to Glasgow from Toronto. Due to the popularity of the Continental #16 flight from Newark to Glasgow, in 2005 the airline added a flight (#106) to further serve summer travelers. Likewise, the Continental flight (#36) to Edinburgh from Newark operates only during the summer months. The USAirways flight from Philadelphia to Glasgow commences early May. *Check with the airlines for the most current information.* All these options have in common the least amount of time in the air and at the airports and the best assurance that the golfer will not be separated from his or her clubs.

One-Stop Options

Another way to get to Glasgow or Edinburgh without going through London is on Aer Lingus from Boston, Chicago, Los Angeles, or New York (JFK) via Dublin, Ireland. From Dublin, Aer Lingus has daily flights to Glasgow and Edinburgh. Unfortunately, the layovers on most of these connections are not completely satisfactory unless you'd really like to hang out in the Dublin airport for about four hours. Although Aer Lingus also has flights from several U.S. cities to Shannon Airport at Limerick, Ireland, they can only get you from Shannon to Glasgow or Edinburgh by first stopping in Dublin. Ryanair runs a nonstop from Shannon to Prestwick (near Glasgow), but Ryanair's severe baggage restrictions and high fees for excess baggage and sporting equipment make that impractical for incoming golfers. Nevertheless, golfers on a trip combining Scotland and Ireland should be aware of these options on Aer Lingus.

A better choice is on either Delta Airlines (from Atlanta) or British Midland (from Chicago or Washington - Dulles) to Manchester, England, with connecting flights on British Midland to Glasgow, Edinburgh, Inverness, or Aberdeen. I do not have any personal experience with the Manchester airport, but it has to be more palatable than Heathrow. In any case, when making a connecting stop in the UK, one must leave sufficient time between flights to clear customs.

The best choice among the one-stops is on Icelandair to Glasgow through Reykjavik from Boston, Baltimore-Washington (BWI), Orlando, Minneapolis-St. Paul, or New York (JFK). The layover at Reykjavik is only about one hour, so it's nearly as good as a direct flight and it's fun to see the moonscape terrain of Iceland from the air. Icelandair does not fly to Edinburgh.

Following is telephone and website information for the airlines mentioned above. The country code for Ireland (Ryanair) is 353. easyJet is in England (44). For international calls, dial 011, then the country code, then the rest of the number.

Aer Lingus	800-474-7424	*aerlingus.com*
Air Canada	888-247-2262	*aircanada.com*
American Airlines	800-443-7300	*aa.com*
British Midland	800-788-0555	*flybmi.com*
Continental Airlines	800-525-0280	*flycontinental.com*
Delta Airlines	800-241-4141	*delta.com*
easyJet	870-600-0000	*easyjet.com*
Icelandair	800-223-5500	*icelandair.com*
Ryanair	871-246-0000	*ryanair.com*
USAirways	800-221-1212	*usair.com*

For toll-free numbers to other airlines, see *www.inter800.com*.

Vehicle Rental

Self-drive Versus Chauffeur-Driven Trips

This is an important issue probably influenced most by group size. The larger the group (8-12+ golfers/nongolfers), the more likely you are to use a coach (bus) and chauffeur. The accent is upon togetherness, socializing, and getting a big group safely through a trip. Cost is not much of a factor because per-person cost diminishes as the number of travelers increases. Per-person cost in a group of twelve will not be much different than per-person cost for four on a self-drive trip.

For groups of four to eight, the issue is a tougher call. For eight, the cost differential is about 2:1. Assuming you rent your vehicle from the right place (see below), a group of eight on a self-drive trip will spend about $30 per person per day on two minibuses. The same individuals on a chauffeur-driven trip will spend about $50-60+. The ratio for a group of four will be more like 3:1. Clearly, self-driving is the most economical way to travel.

Chauffeured transportation has lots of appeal, but for a group of eight golfers it's about twice as expensive as a self-drive trip.

The rest of the decision is qualitative. Your choice will affect the kind of trip you have. Personally, I like to drive; I want to see Scotland "where the rubber meets the road." I like the flexibility and freedom to come and go when and where I want. A group of eight, requiring two vehicles, also gains the flexibility to go more than one direction for either golf or nongolf activities. In sum, this approach provides more individual freedom and less "group think." On the other hand, group think is fun too and chauffeuring takes the adventure out of driving on the left side of the road, negotiating roundabouts, and interpreting foreign traffic signs. And, if you get a personable and compatible driver, you can make a friend for life and receive the undoubted benefit of the driver's local knowledge.

If you choose the chauffeuring option, avoid the big tour companies that herd tourists around the UK every summer. You can tell who they are by the content of their websites. With these companies you are more likely to get a comatose driver and, contrary to theories of "economy of scale," they are invariably more expensive than small companies.

Make sure your coach company is bonded, insured, and has a PCV license (passenger carry vehicle). Look for company-owned Mercedes and Volkswagen coaches as signs of customized quality. Unless your trip is circumscribed and driving distances are minimal, you do *not* want to hire a freelance driver who is going to get a contract and then go out and rent a van from a car rental agency. But, with these caveats in mind, there is every reason to choose a small, family-run business where you will receive personal attention and the best price. Scotland is loaded with them and, over the past couple of years, I've made a point of uncovering some in various parts of the country. Here are a few:

• *J.K.R. Luxury Coaches,* Strathhaven (nr Glasgow), contact Joe Russell, (01357-521-553)

• *RowanTravel*, Dundee, contact Steve Mackie (01382-320-376; *www.rowantravel.co.uk*)

• *Tim Dearman Coaches*, Ardross (nr Inverness), contact Tim Dearman (01349-883-585; *www.timdearmancoaches.co.uk*)

Self-Drive Rental

If the choice is a self-drive trip, reserve your vehicle as early as possible. There's no reason to wait. If cancellation is necessary, any deposits or prepayments made are normally fully refundable with sufficient notice. Penalties are not assessed for changes in pickup/dropoff plans.

This is a major expense that can cause way too much brain damage and cost way too much money. Call any of the name brands in the business. After you tell them you want to rent a vehicle in, say, Glasgow, the first question they ask is, "For what dates?". Then the fun begins: "Automatic or manual?" "Do you want loss damage waiver insurance?" "Zero liability insurance?" "Will that be one way or return?" "You want to add another driver?—that will be another $7.20 per day." "Oh, by the way, our price doesn't include a local airport surcharge of £17 and a daily road tax. Those are locally collected."

TRAVEL TIP

Groups with two vehicles can stay in touch on the road with two-way "walkie-talkies" that range up to several miles.

Go through this song and dance with three different companies and you could be pulling your hair out. It makes dealing with the airlines seem simple. By the time you get to the bottom line—with all the "add-ons" and surcharges not included in the base price—you can end up with an expensive rental and a giant headache.

My mission in this book is to make travel planning easy. Therefore I want to pass along two words designed to bypass all the rigmarole of shopping for a rental car in Scotland. Those words are: ARNOLD CLARK. Arnold Clark is the largest automobile dealership in Scotland. They are also in the rental car business. They have the biggest and best fleet of vehicles *with automatic transmission* for visiting golfers. My advice on this subject: Forget about the "brand name" companies and go straight to Arnold Clark for your rental. Here is their main reservations number:

Arnold Clark Central Reservations   0845-602-1895

Arnold Clark initiated online booking in early 2005 at *www.arnoldclarkrental.co.uk.* Unfortunately, because UK drivers typically prefer vehicles with manual transmission, the website fails to make clear that the automatic-transmission minvans and minibuses preferred by golf groups from North America are available at the same price. After a shake-down cruise, the website will improve.

In the spirit of full disclosure, let it be known that because of the volume of business Ferguson Golf does with Arnold Clark we have preferred rates and we book vehicles for golfers during normal business hours at 800-835-6692. Even if I had no business relationship with Arnold Clark, I would recommend them as the leader in their field. The plain truth is that Arnold Clark is so much better than the rest of the car rental agencies in the market, there really is no other choice and will not be until other companies follow their example. Why?— let me count the ways:

✓ First, Arnold Clark prices typically beat the brand names by twenty to thirty percent (see example below).

✓ Second, *all charges* are included in an Arnold Clark quote. As their brochure says, "The price you see is the price you pay." Prices include the value-added tax (17.5%), road tax, full insurance coverage (incuding CDW), and unlimited mileage. No surprises. Everything's on the table.

✓ Third, Arnold Clark has plenty of vehicles with automatic transmission in every class above the compacts, particularly among the minivans and minibuses that most golf parties need. Among the larger vehicles, there is no "upcharge" for automatic transmission.

✓ Fourth, you won't pay an airport surcharge (£17) when you rent from Arnold Clark because they are an off-site agency with branches conveniently located near Scotland's major airports.

✓ Fifth, Arnold Clark has the lowest additional-driver charge in the industry. It's a flat fee of £10 (compared to the *daily* rate of £4 or more charged by the brand names).

✓ Sixth, Arnold Clark has the lowest "excess" (deductible) levels in the industry. That's the maximum amount you're liable for in case of damage to your rental vehicle. Arnold Clark's £100 deductible for compact and mid-size vehicles compares to £250 or more in the rest of the industry. Their £250 maximum for minivans and minibuses compares to £500 or more at other companies.

✓ Seventh, with thirty-four locations around the country, an Arnold Clark branch is never far away.

✓ Eighth, while other travelers are standing in line waiting to be served by one clerk at the brand-name agencies, you'll be out the airport door, into a shuttle bus, and off to a nearby site where you will receive prompt and undivided attention.

If this sounds too good to be true, all I can say is that when you find a company like Arnold Clark—straight-shooting, no bait-and-switch, no phony advertising—you had best count your lucky stars and take your business straight to their door. You won't be sorry.

Here's an example of how Arnold Clark pricing compared to AutoEurope (a broker for Avis, Budget, Hertz, National, and EuropCar) on a given day in April 2005:

The Request: an automatic minivan for 7 days in early July 2005 with one additional driver.
   Arnold Clark's all-inclusive price from website: £450
      1. one additional driver £10
      TOTAL £460 ($874)

AutoEurope's response (quoted in U.S. dollars). Lowest price on automatic minvan through Europcar:

1. $1,140 - "Inclusive" base rate (incl VAT and full insurance)
2. Less $57 discount - *100% prepayment* before end of month
3. Less $57 discount - AAA membership
4. Plus $36 location (airport) tax (£17)
5. Plus $19.60 road tax ($2.80 per day)
6. Plus $51.10 additional driver ($7.10 per day)
   TOTAL $1,094

"Apples to apples," the saving with Arnold Clark in this case is $220—enough to pay for a round of golf at The Old Course! Even without buying EuropCar's insurance, the price differential still would be over $125. Just as important, Arnold Clark's prices are predictable, straightforward, and easy to understand. In today's marketplace, that's worth a lot.

One weakness of Arnold Clark: the company has only nine branches outside Scotland and none at London airports. Another homegrown company with branches at most UK airports is Woods Car Rental (01293-820-8888; *www.woods.co.uk*). Woods is price competitive with Arnold Clark but does not have so large a fleet as the Clark agency. Woods has automatic vehicles in mid-size categories and a small fleet of automatic minivans at Glasgow and Edinburgh airport locations. They do not have VW Caravelle minibuses.

The Brand Names

If you want to test my advice on this subject, if you are a loyal Hertz or Avis customer, or you really *want* to shop the brand names, following are suggestions on how to proceed:

✓ *Check the internet first, but call to followup with the question, "Is this the best you can do?"*.

✓ *Always check more than one source.* Why? Your first pass establishes a price benchmark. From there you can do some bargaining. If you ask them, rental car companies will usually match the price of a competitor. Most of them have a "beat-rate" supervisor—someone with authority to make a deal. Your goal is to ratchet the price downward as far as it will go—or at least to get add-ons subtracted or reduced. Remember, it never hurts to ask. Ask for a lower price. Ask for a free upgrade. Ask for a specific car. Ask them to eliminate the fee for an additional driver. If you don't ask, you won't get.

✓ *Invoke your affiliations.* Be sure to ask about any discounts you might secure by virtue of associations, memberships, employment, etc. These might include AARP, AAA, frequent flyer memberships, government or corporate affiliation. But don't ask for the discounted rate until *after* you've received a quote for a basic rate. Most often the reply will be, "That is our lowest rate," but the response might be, "I can reduce that rate by five percent." If you ask for the discounted rate first, you'll never know whether you were just quoted a basic rate that got called a "discounted rate."

Who to call? At Scottish airports you'll find the usual cast of characters— Alamo, Budget, National, Avis, Hertz, plus a European agency, EuropCar. Often, best rates are available on the internet. Here are toll-free telephone numbers for the major car rental companies:

Alamo	800-522-9696
AutoEurope	800-223-5555
Avis	800-331-1212
Budget	800-472-3325
Dollar	800-800-4000
EuropCar	877-940-6900
Hertz	800-654-3131
National	888-868-6204
Thrifty	800-847-4389

On the following page is a worksheet to help you track car agency data with the objective of comparing "apples to apples."

 Telephone/Fax Calling Procedures

From the United States:
Dial 011 (international long distance), then 44 (country code), then the number in Scotland without the leading "0" (i.e., 011-44-1334-466-666).

RENTAL VEHICLE WORKSHEET

Company _____

Phone Number _____

Airport: On-site _____   Off-site _____

Confirmation # _____

Date of Inquiry _____   Clerk ID _____

Vehicle Size: subcompact, compact, mid-size sedan, large sedan, station wagon, minivan, minibus

Pickup Date: _____   Approx Time _____

Return Date: _____   Approx Time _____

Days _____

Automatic Transmission _____   Manual Transmission _____

_____ Basic Rate (typically includes 17.5% VAT, unlimited mileage, fire/third party insurance)

_____ Discounted Basic Rate - Notes _____

_____ ADD Location (airport) Surcharge

_____ ADD Road Tax _____ per day x _____ days

_____ ADD Additional Driver(s) _____ per driver per day x _____ driver(s) x _____ days OR flat fee _____

_____ ADD Collision Damage Waiver (CDW) _____ per day x _____ days

_____ ADD One-way Dropoff

_____ ADD other insurance (e.g., theft, zero liability)

_____ **TOTAL** x $1.90 if quoted in pounds sterling = **$**_____

NOTES:

Common Questions

Do I need an international driver's license to rent a car in Scotland? No. You need a valid driver's license and your passport.

What is the age limit for drivers? Depending upon car size and individual company policy, minimum ages vary from 21 to 25. At the upper end, the age limits vary from 71 to 75.

What should I do if I have an accident? Your rental car company will provide full instructions and contact numbers.

Is a minivan big enough for four golfers? Generally, no. I recommend a VW Caravelle minibus for four golfers. A minivan usually will suffice for two golfers and two nongolfers.

Ideal for four golfers—a VW Caravelle minibus with automatic transmission.

Tee Times

Contacting the Clubs

Before cheap long-distance phone service, fax machines, and email, the common way to make a reservation at a Scottish course was by written request accompanied by a formal "letter of introduction" from your club professional. That is emphatically *not* the case today. The Scots are polite and somewhat more formal than Americans, but they are modern people, quite good at extracting money from tourists as efficiently as possible rather than by "snail mail."

Thus, the quickest, most effective way to reserve a tee time at most courses is to make a telephone call. If you do that from the west coast of North America, it means getting up pretty early. The time differential is 8 hours, so you'll need to make calls before 8 a.m. and not later than 9 a.m. Most offices at the well-traveled courses are open until at least 4 p.m. or 5 p.m. At the lesser-known clubs you may find the secretary's hours sporadic or confined to the morning hours. If that's the case, then you'll probably be communicating by fax or email. Here are the time differentials in the United States:

- Pacific Time - 8 hrs. - call before 8 a.m.
- Mountain Time - 7 hrs. - call before 9 a.m.
- Central Time - 6 hrs. - call before 10 a.m.
- Eastern Time - 5 hrs. - call before 11 a.m.

When making a tee time you'll most often talk, not with a club secretary, but with a booking secretary—like one of the friendly and efficient ladies at Crail Golfing Society.

I recommend a phone call because you can get answers most quickly that way and a phone call gives you maximum flexibility to confirm details regarding alternative available times, visitor restrictions, deposits, club rental, caddie hire, directions, etc. Sometimes you can get a feel for the ambience of a club just by talking with people on the phone. This is also a good time to request lodging recommendations. If you have trouble reaching someone with authority to book a time, then send an email or a fax and wait for a reply.

Most often you will *not* talk with the secretary of a club. You'll probably talk with an office assistant or maybe even a bartender. Usually at least two communications will be necessary—the first to formally request a time, then a second to confirm group composition and payment details by fax or email. If it can all be done with one phone call, so much the better.

The Efficiency of Fax Machines and Email

Admittedly, fax machines and email cost less than phone calls, and there's a certain satisfaction gained from firing off a half-dozen communiqués to Scotland at 10 p.m., then waking up the next morning to find that most of your trip was booked overnight while you were sleeping! It's an efficient way to start the process even if some follow-up work is necessary. If you like this approach, on the next page is a sample letter for you to adapt in making a booking inquiry. All detail necessary to customize this letter for individual courses is in "Part III, The Directory of Courses."

Online Booking Services

Fee-based online booking services have begun to develop. None is satisfactory. The most visible has been ***www.teetimescotland.com***. The problem is, "Garbage in, garbage out." The clubs are mostly interested in selling their "off-peak" times and at a high-profile golf club like Royal Troon, for example, there is no way an online system can substitute for a telephone call and a personal conversation with a booking assistant. Apart from all that, the booking services charge a premium for making a tee time. So, what's the point?—why use an online booking service when you could be on the phone talking to the someone at the club where you want to play? The value of personal contact cannot be overestimated.

SAMPLE - ADVANCE RESERVATION REQUEST LETTER

Date

ATT: Alistair MacDonald, Secretary, Lundin Golf Club
RE: Visitor inquiry - advance reservation

Dear Mr. MacDonald:

This is to inquire whether Lundin Golf Club can accommodate four visiting golfers, preferably with a morning tee time, on 13 September (Wednesday) 2006. If so, following is information for confirming an advance reservation and making the required deposit.

LEAD GOLFER: A Ferguson, hdp 9, Wellshire GC, Denver CO
CREDIT CARD: MC 0000-0000-0000-0000   Exp 09/07
OTHER GOLFERS: Donald Rex, hdp 13, City Park GC, Denver CO; Robert Thompson, hdp 12, Overland Park GC, Denver CO; Donald Bruning, hdp 17, Deer Creek GC, Denver CO.

THANK YOU in advance for your assistance with this request.

Allan Ferguson
1743 S. Marion St.
Denver CO 80210
ph/fax: 303-722-3441
aferguson@fergusongolf.com

Important Information for Single Golfers

Often a client will say to me, "I've heard that a single golfer can't make a tee time in Scotland." This is a myth. On the contrary, the single golfer has distinct advantages in making tee times.

The only important exceptions to this generalization are at Muirfield, St. Andrews, and Carnoustie. Muirfield books only twos and fours; advance reservations for singles at St. Andrews are severely limited; Carnoustie limits single advance booking to three days before play. Otherwise, a single can make an advance booking at virtually all other courses, including Royal Troon, Prestwick, Royal Dornoch, Western Gailes, North Berwick, Gullane #1, and Kingsbarns. Understanding this subject is both interesting and instructive because it relates to the Scottish attitude toward golf and course management.

The Scots will *not* routinely "fill a foursome" the way course managers do in the United States. There are two reasons for this: first, they are more interested in the pace of play than they are in filling a course to capacity. They favor two-ball and three-ball groups to fours, and many courses reserve early and late hours for the two-ball matches often preferred by club members. The Scots would rather get a dozen two-ball matches around in three hours than six or seven four-ball groups in four-plus hours. A five-hour round is out of the question.

Second, if two or three golfers have made a tee time during visitor hours, the Scots won't automatically put other golfers with that group until they ask permission of the booked golfers. In other words, you don't have to play golf with someone you don't know unless you agree to do so. What a novel idea!— enough to make an American club pro cringe. This is a broad generalization. The most heavily-played courses *will* pair singles and twos with other golfers before date of play.

In the pairing procedure, a single golfer looking for a game may be asked for his or her handicap. Why? Because, for the enjoyment of all, the Scots won't put a total duffer out with a single-digit handicapper. Another novel idea American course managers could well emulate.

So, what does all this mean for the single golfer? Well, it's good news. First, it means that at most courses you'll find lots of "holes" in the schedule of tee times—lots of places for a single golfer to slide into a game with two or three other players. Second, it means most often you'll be playing with golfers of comparable ability. The process can lead to hooking up with compatible singletons during your stay in Scotland.

Since my wife is a nongolfer, I have considerable experience as a single golfer in Scotland. Here's my approach:

✓ If a course is on my "must-play" list, I'll pre-book it.

✓ I'll leave most days unbooked—thus avoiding prepayments and deposits and, at the same time, creating maximum flexibility for golf or nongolf activities depending upon weather, mood, etc. Then I'll have a list of "optional" courses for play and start phoning through the list in priority order until I find a tee time that works best for our schedule.

✓ Normally, I'll call a course the day before I want to play and ask to speak to the secretary, the booking assistant, or, most likely, the professional. I'll explain that I'm there as a single golfer and would be interested in a game with a club member if that can be arranged. Sometimes I'm successful with that approach to play with an "insider," sometimes I'm not—but rarely do I encounter a course that is fully booked.

One further note on the opportunities of a single golfer: The greatest plus for a single golfer in Scotland is the opportunity to meet other travelers, locals, and club members for a round of golf. From these encounters a great range of positive, serendipitous consequences can follow. To facilitate those opportunities, especially at the courses lightly traveled by visitors, the golfer must be proactive. Apart from the opportunities involved, there is a simple matter of sociability. Without taking some initiative, a single golfer could end up playing a lot of rounds alone. For some, this is not a concern. Others really don't enjoy the game without company on the course. If you are among the latter, I strongly advise a call to the professional shop a day or two in advance of play to make it clear that you would like to "join or be joined" with other golfers. To be even more proactive about it, another idea is to contact the *club secretary* a few weeks in advance of play and ask him or her to post a message on the members' bulletin board. To make it easy and ready to post, send the note by fax on a half-sheet of paper. The note might read something like this:

Single Visiting Golfer Seeks Playing Partner

I'm a single golfer from the USA who would enjoy meeting one or more club members for a round of golf.

My tee time - **Wednesday, August 17, 10:30 a.m.**

If you would like to join in a round of friendly international competition, please contact me. I'll be pleased to hear from you.

Allan Ferguson
1743 S. Marion St.
Denver CO 80210
aferguson@fergusongolf.com
303-722-3441 (ph/fax)
handicap - 10

Step-by-Step Booking Advice

Using Part II, Chapter 2 ("Where to Go"), and Part III, "The Directory of Courses," pick the courses you want to play and determine their visitor policies. Then take the following three-step approach:

✓ *Arrange your courses in priority order. Start provisional booking from the top down—from "must-play" to "optional."* Certain courses on your ideal itinerary are likely to be "linchpin" courses—ones that either allow the rest of the schedule to work logistically or are at or near the top of a must-play list. For example, if Royal Troon is on your must-play list, it's usually a good idea to schedule the Ayrshire coast early in the week because Troon accepts visitors only on Mondays, Tuesdays, and Thursdays. Your odds of booking are best if you have the flexibility to play either Monday or Tuesday rather than only on Thursday.

✓ *Schedule "daily fee," public, and resort courses on the weekends.* At most private clubs (i.e., most golf courses in Scotland), visitor access on weekends is restricted. Maximum flexibility to play when you want to play on Saturdays and Sundays can be achieved by booking the daily fee, public, and resort courses on those days. Examples of these are: Kingsbarns, The Duke's Course, and the courses at St. Andrews Bay in Fife (Region #1); the courses at Gleneagles in Perthshire (Region #7); Turnberry and Belleisle in Ayrshire (Region #2); and Whitekirk in East Lothian (Region #3). In St. Andrews, the Old Course is closed on Sunday; the other courses are open.

✓ *Secure all your tee times before you make arrangements for lodging.* As Robert Burns wrote, "The best-laid plans of mice and men gang aft agley" (often go awry). All the pieces of the tee-time puzzle must fit before you start booking accommodations. You could have a well-laid plan only to find out that two of the courses on your must-play list are closed to visitor play on the days you want to be there. What to do? Well, at that point, you either change your priorities or start rearranging the itinerary to accommodate your must-play courses.

Common Questions

Do I have to prepay green fees? That depends upon the course. Some require full prepayment; most require a deposit ranging from a token (e.g., five or ten percent) to a substantial amount (fifty percent); some require no advance payment at all. See the deposit entries in "The Directory of Courses" for details.

Can I use my credit card to book a tee time? With few exceptions, yes. Just make sure it's MasterCard or VISA; American Express won't get you far in Scotland. This is not a commercial; it's the truth.

Can I use a different credit card from each member of my group for deposits? The clubs prefer to deal with a "lead golfer." It would then be up to the lead golfer to get reimbursed by the other golfers. Once there, individual cards may be used for paying balances due.

What information do I need to provide? A lead golfer's name, number of golfers, contact information, and credit card details. The St. Andrews Links Management will ask for all golfers names, handicaps, and home clubs (where handicaps are kept). In general, female golfers are more likely to be asked about handicaps than male golfers. Singles and twos of either gender may be asked for handicap information in the interest of pairing players of comparable ability.

Lodging

Scotland probably has a greater range and quantity of accommodations per capita than any place in the world. The country is dotted with literally thousands of modest bed-and-breakfast operations while boasting palatial international resorts among the finest in the world. In between are some of the finest small hotels and country houses you will ever hope to find, as well as larger, "purpose-built" hotels and an increasing number of standardized, American-style hotel chains. Tourism is big business in Scotland.

Most of these accommodations are graded and cataloged annually by VisitScotland (formerly the Scottish Tourist Board) in two publications available in any good bookstore or Tourist Information Office in Scotland. These are: *Where to Stay: Bed and Breakfast (year)* and *Where to Stay: Hotels and Guest Houses (year)*. See *Appendix E* for complete citations. VisitScotland also publishes volumes on camping and "self-catering" (rental) accommodations. These publications are hard to obtain in North America but, fortunately, all the information is available online at *www.visitscotland.com*. For general travel information, citizens of the U.S. and Canada can contact VisitBritain, 551 Fifth Avenue, Suite 701, New York NY 10176 (ph 1-800-462-2748).

The VisitScotland publications are not guidebooks. They are inclusive listings of all member establishments. Guidebooks, by definition, are selective, though I find the most popular of the general guidebooks (Fodor's, Frommer's, Lonely Planet) unsatisfactory when it comes to accommodations. Specialized publications are better. But here's another idea: when you call your courses to make tee times, ask the secretary or booking assistant about accommodations in your price range. Usually they'll give you good recommendations and you'll be getting those recommendations from a local source.

Internet Searching

Many hotels, guest houses, and B & Bs have their own websites. Certainly that is the trend. But the vast majority—particularly among guest houses and B & Bs—do not have their own sites. Rather, they gain access to the web via one or another promotional group. Primary among these is the tourist board's *www.visitscotland.com*. Less comprehensive but well organized is *www.smoothhound.co.uk*. Others are the Automobile Association's site, *www.theaa.com*, and *www.aboutscotland.com*, the most selective of the services. Together, these provide a thorough overview of lodging options in all price categories. See Appendix B for more listings of promotional services.

B & Bs, Guest Houses, and Hotels

The distinction between B & Bs and guest houses in Scotland is blurry but, essentially, the difference is that a B & B is smaller than a guest house. By law, a B & B may accommodate no more than six lodgers. A guest house will have at least four rooms (usually more than four). In times past, there was a further distinction: many guest houses offered an evening meal. Today, some still do— but not many. With few exceptions, an evening meal is not an option at a B & B. Virtually all hotels—even small hotels (up to twenty rooms)— have a liquor license and a dining room/bar for lunches and evening meals. Hotel bars and dining rooms often are gathering places for locals. Most hotels have a sitting room or lounge— usually a feature also of guest houses and B & Bs. All establishments serve a traditional "Scottish Breakfast." These days you'll also have healthier fruit and cereal options (see the next chapter for a sample breakfast menu).

Self-Catering

This is the British term for what Americans call "rentals." Just as with conventional lodging choices, comfort levels and vintages run the gamut from basic to luxurious and from contemporary to refurbished rustic. Many self-catering units are transformed farm cottages and croft houses in rural locations. Others are modern apartment units in towns and cities or are "purpose-built" specifically as income-producing properties on private land. *Most self-catering units assume a full week stay from arrival on Saturday through departure on the following Saturday morning.* Prices vary by season, but one can generally be assured of getting a lot more value for a lot less money compared to conventional accommodations.

To give you a clearer idea of what a self-catering unit offers, on a trip a few years ago I made the following partial inventory of kitchen and living room amenities at a self-catering farmhouse in Aberdeenshire:

Self-Catering Inventory

Kitchen: stove, toaster, microwave, cutlery, two sets of dishes, refrigerator, paper towels, pitchers, coffee maker, cutting boards, bread bin, sugar, cooking oil, vinegar, salt, pepper, spices, flour, thermos, coffee pot, drinking glasses, wine glasses, highball glasses, apron, pots, pans, hotpads. *Living room:* fireplace, kindling, wood, easy chairs, sofa, sound system, television, stacks of tourism brochures and information, wallmaps of Scotland and the local area. *Other*: vacuum, grocery bags, broom, dust pan, iron, detergent, cleansers, washing machine.

Any golf party on a stay-and-play trip of at least a week, should consider self-catering. Self-catering opens up the option of eating in or eating out. Food and drink become less expensive because you're buying food in a grocery store and buying that expensive single malt at a liquor store instead of a pub. If the big Scottish breakfast does not appeal, a self-caterer has more control over breakfast options. In short, a rental unit offers the comforts of home, including a fully-equipped kitchen. For some, that is appealing. For others, that's what they are trying to escape.

Early booking (several months ahead) is advisable with self-catering properties for two reasons: first, they are fewer in number than conventional choices and, second, this is the preferred method of lodging for many Europeans. The good properties tend to get grabbed up early, particularly for dates in August and September. Many rental properties are listed with the tourist board and can be found on the self-catering module at ***www.visitscotland.com***. Self caterers also have their own association and a website at ***www.aasc.co.uk***. Together, these provide comprehensive coverage of the category.

The Star System and Pricing

VisitScotland grades all establishments on a five-star scale. Among hotels, five stars are reserved for "world-class" establishments—the Turnberrys and Gleneagles of the world. Four stars mean "excellent;" three stars are "very good;" two stars indicate "good;" and one star—well, you don't want to go there.

Four stars are often found on country-house manors and mansions adapted to the hotel trade—in fact, you can look for those magic words, "Country House Hotel" and be pretty sure you're going to have an extraordinary lodging experience.

Three-star hotels are consistently good, frequently full of character, and most price-attractive to the majority of tourists. I've cited a dozen or so of this class in Part III, "The Directory of Courses" and in Appendix B as favorites of golfers. *Typically, a three-star hotel will be priced in a range of £35 to £45 ($55-70) per person per night.* From this benchmark, price extrapolations can be made downward and upward (i.e., two-star £20-30; four-star £50-£60+ per person per night).

Prices in each category vary—not surprisingly, dependent upon location. For example, Edinburgh is significantly more expensive than Inverness and the three-star hotels in St. Andrews are £10-20 more than the three-star norm. The best bargains will often be found at the two-star hotels, but you need to be careful

Four-star B & Bs offer best value and a host who "knows the territory." Here, golfers are greeted at The Glebe House in North Berwick.

in that group. These tend to be the smallest of hostelries and they can be either very good or just not big enough to maintain a high standard.

Interestingly enough, while four and five-star hotels are pricey and few in number, you'll find lots of guest houses and B & Bs with these rankings. Typically, they are priced in the same range as the three-star hotels and, for my money, they offer the best value and best personal experiences for golfers and nongolfers alike. Compared to most hotels, these B & Bs offer more spacious lodging and the personal touch of hosts who "know the territory."

Making Reservations

After consulting guide-books, browsing the internet, and talking to folks at the clubs, you should be ready to contact your chosen hostelry. Again, I prefer the rapid response, flexibility, and personal contact afforded by a telephone call. Here's what to consider and ask about when you call:

✓ *Priced per person or per room?* The aggravating European tradition of pricing per person per night (pppn), hangs on in Scotland and is worth special comment. Single travelers or unrelated travelers sharing space will find lodging in Scotland a good bargain—remember, those £35 (more or less) are buying you a breakfast so big that you can easily skip lunch. On the other hand, even ordinary lodging quickly gets expensive for a family pairing in a room, because that money is all coming out of one bank account! This pricing tradition is slowly changing due to pressure from chains like Holiday Inn, Travel Inn, and TraveLodge—all of whom offer space on a per-room basis. Be sure to ask whether quoted prices are *per person* or *per room.*

✓ *Single room or single supplemented room?* Even when traveling in a group, many people prefer to have their own single room. Some lodgings—including B & Bs and guest houses—have rooms specifically designed for singles. Always ask. A single room will cost less than a "single supplemented" room where a single lodger is taking space designed for double occupancy. Typically this surcharge might increase the cost of a room from, say, £35 to £50, whereas the room would cost £70 double occupancy. In this hypothetical example, the "supplement" is £15.

✓ *Multinight stay discount.* Many lodgings will grant a modest discount on stays of three nights or more. Some will offer that verbally or in writing but more often you have to ask.

✓ *Bed sizes; double or twin-bedded rooms.* Scots distinguish between double rooms and *twin-bedded* doubles. In their lexicon, a "double room" typically has one double bed. A "twin-bedded" room has two single beds or a single and a double—ideal for same-sex golf parties. Some beds can be converted from one configuration to another ("zip-and-link" twins convert to a king-size double). Apart from the zip-and-links, you won't find many queen or king-size beds typical of American lodging. Among couples, if one person is a picky sleeper, the twin-bedded room may be preferable. In a similar vein, if you're accustomed to space afforded by a king-size bed, a standard European double (4'6") probably won't do. Whatever the case, this is something to ask about.

✓ *Bath/shower facility.* Most Americans are partial to showers. Be sure to ask about this if it is important to you. Most hotel rooms have showers, though they may be jerryrigged over a bathtub rather than built-in. Some B & Bs and guest houses may not have a shower in all rooms.

An alternative to booking accommodations yourself is to use the services of VisitScotland's *Tourist Information Offices* (TIs). For a small fee, these offices will make bookings for you at member hotels, guest houses, and B & Bs. This is a particularly useful service for those traveling without advance reservations, but it is a service available to anyone at any time (see Appendix C for a list of TI offices in the golf areas).

One final note: I firmly believe *the more money you spend on lodging the more you separate yourself from the ordinary people, the customs, the heart and soul of Scotland* (or, for that matter, any other place). Taken to extreme, this philosophy might point you towards flea-bag hotels and youth hostels. Of course, that's not what I mean. I mean simply that many accommodations are available in the mid-price range of £35 to £45 ($65 to $85 per person per night). That's why I don't recommend places like the Old Course Hotel or Rusacks in St. Andrews; the Carnoustie Golf Course Hotel; the Marine Hotel in Troon; or the Newton Hotel in Nairn. These places are popular with tour operators. But they are places where you're just another number—one of thousands of tourists (usually Americans) to pass through their relatively impersonal doors every year.

> **The more money you spend on lodging the more you separate yourself from the ordinary people, the customs, the heart and soul of Scotland.**

Scotland is one of the special places in the Anglo-American world where a traveler can still experience a tradition of B & Bs, guest houses, and small hotels of distinction, with unique character and highly personal service—a tradition all but extinct in the United States. That's the kind of tradition a savvy traveler will seek out rather than choose a hotel one might as easily find at Myrtle Beach, Palm Springs, or Dallas.

Common Questions

Do I need to make reservations? Most golfers want to have everything pinned down so, sure, get the reservations made. My basic advice here is to confirm the tee times first and then address the lodging. Certainly, it is feasible for a single golfer or a couple to freelance and take what comes. Even then, decisions may be dictated by time and place. If you want to stay on the Isle of Skye in August, for example, it would be foolish not to make a lodging reservation. Edinburgh in August is another time to make a reservation; that's when the International Festival draws huge crowds from around the world. On the other hand, most of the time, in a large town or city like Inverness, Aberdeen, Glasgow, or Edinburgh, a stop at the local Tourist Information Office will get you a room straightaway.

Do I have to stay at the Turnberry Hotel to play the Ailsa course? Technically, no. But it's a very busy hotel and residents have priority at the course. For non-residents, the drill involves calling for a tee time within two weeks of desired date of play. Personal testimony: I have never failed to get non-resident golfers onto the Ailsa, even in high season. No guarantees, but, to my mind, this approach sure beats paying for the hotel. For more information, see "The Directory of Courses - Turnberry Hotel."

Do I have to stay at the Carnoustie Golf Course Hotel to play the championship course at Carnoustie? No. For more information, see "The Directory of Courses - Carnoustie Golf Links."

What does "en suite" mean? It's a silly, highfalutin' term picked up from the French and it means a bath/shower and toilet are in the room. Even though virtually all hotel rooms in Scotland include toilet and bath/shower these days, the term hangs on from an earlier age when the "WC" was down the hall or around the corner. If a room is described "with private bath," it means the bathroom is not in the sleeping room but is nearby and is reserved for sole use by the occupant. Usually these bedrooms have a wash basin in the room.

Should I take a hairdryer? You'll find them in most rooms, though they may be hidden in a dresser drawer. If there is none, ask at the desk. Nine out of ten times they'll have one for you. Bottom line: don't bother to pack one.

Will I have a shower in my room? And what about water pressure? I've heard it's awful. If having a shower is important to you, ask before you book. Most hotels now have showers, but some B & Bs do not. Most of the time you're probably going to be disappointed in the Scottish idea of water pressure. As the kids say these days, "live with it"—that's just the way it is. Look at it this way: you'll probably have a heated towel rack in your room and, unlike in America, each room will be unique.

Notes

CHAPTER FIVE

A Potpourri of Useful Information

General

✓ *Passport.* Don't forget it. You'll need it to get in and out of the UK. Also good to have with you when shopping.

✓ *Traveler's Insurance.* Some people buy it; some don't. Prepaid golf and hotel deposits often will be refunded if adequate cancellation notice is provided. The big factor here is air fare. Check with your travel agent or search the internet.

✓ *Luggage.* Read your carrier's guidelines. Current international rules for most airlines: (1) checked luggage - 70 lb. limit; (2) golf bag - 33 lbs; use it to pack shoes, sweaters, and other bulky items; (3) a carry-on no larger than 9" x 14" x 22" (45"). Extra weight is allowed, but you will be charged for it.

✓ *Lightweight and Drip-Dry.* This is old-hat advice, but, it's true, you'll have a better trip when you focus on what *not* to pack and then think about how to minimize the weight and maximize the efficiency of what you do pack. The best line of lightweight travel gear is at ***www.packinglight.net***.

✓ *Carry-on Luggage.* Unfortunately, luggage and golf clubs don't always arrive when you do. Just in case, pack a change of clothes in your carry-on luggage. You can rent or borrow clubs, but it's no fun to go shopping for clothes on your first day in Scotland.

✓ *Protecting Your Golf Clubs.* If using a soft-side carry bag, tie the heads of the irons together and turn the woods upside down in your golf bag. Stuff the rain cover with towels and clothes to pad the exposed end of the golf bag.

✓ *"Left Luggage."* This is a British term for short-term storage of luggage. This is something to consider if you carry golf clubs in a hard-shell case. I'll avoid the hard-shell versus soft-side carrier debate, but what do you do with all those hard-shell cases when you get to your destination? One solution is to leave them behind

The Left Luggage office at Glasgow Airport.

at Left Luggage for about £3.50 per piece per day. You'll find Left Luggage at all the major airports and train stations.

✓ *Flight Survival Kit.* Earplugs, blindfold, water, thermos, breath mints, eyedrops, aspirin or equivalent, towelettes. Pack your toiletries kit in your carry-on; that toothbrushing can sure feel good midway over the Atlantic.

✓ *Jet Lag.* Lots of advice out there about how to deal with jet lag. You'll probably arrive at your Scottish destination sometime late morning. Once you get to your hotel, here's what I recommend: get unpacked; lay down; take a nap, but set an alarm and *don't allow yourself to sleep for more than about 1-2 hours*; get up; exercise; have dinner; go to bed at a normal time. You should sleep well and be ready to play golf the next day. Some folks prefer to play golf on day of arrival—doesn't appeal to me, but I'm no spring chicken.

✓ *Money Management for Threesomes, Foursomes or More.* Designate a "treasurer" to manage a fund for cash payment of incidentals like lunch, a round of drinks at the 19th hole, etc. This eliminates check-splitting and hassling over minor expenses. When the "kitty" is empty, ante up a set amount per person and start over.

✓ *Water.* Carry it wherever you go. The Brits just don't believe in public water fountains. You won't find any on most of the golf courses either. Ask for water in restaurants. Keep hydrated.

✓ *Directions.* Take a compass with you. It can come in handy when hiking in the countryside, walking in a town or city with winding streets, or regaining your bearings while driving.

✓ *Additional Expenses.* How much will you spend above and beyond air fare and "land package" (lodging, golf, rental car)? Here's a rule of thumb: add 1/3 to your air + land package. Example: $900 air + $2100 land package = $3,000; add $1,000 more or less for food, petrol, additional golf expenses (trolleys, yardage books, caddies), and miscellaneous spending. How much "more or less"?—that depends on how much you drive, how expensively you eat, how many sweaters you buy, and, most important, how many caddies you hire.

✓ *Prepaid telephone calling cards* for domestic and international use are available at phone stores, stationery stores, grocery stores, and post offices. Cell phones can be purchased at grocery superstores and phone stores starting at about £60.

✓ *Provisions.* My first stop after leaving the rental-car agency is a Tesco or Safeway superstore to buy fuel, get cash, and stock up on fruit, vegetables, bottled water, and other liquid refreshments.

Driving in Scotland

✓ Before driving off from the rental-car agency, *check your fuel level.* Renters are not required to return a car with a full tank but only with approximately the same amount of fuel that was in the car when they rented it. That means the tank could be empty.

✓ When your tank is low, *fill up* when you can. Scotland does not have a gas station on every other corner.

✓ Somewhere on the dash or visor, your rental car may have a reminder, "drive left" or "stay left." Use a sticky note or its equivalent and put another sign on the dash: "**look right**." Americans are so used to looking left before turning at intersections, it's a difficult habit to reverse. One lapse could be your last lapse. Obviously, it's best to look both ways, but *always* look right.

✓ The *light change sequence* from red to yellow to green at traffic lights is short. Do not try to scoot through an intersection on yellow.

✓ On multi-lane and major two-lane "A" highways, *parking areas* appear about every five miles and are marked by a square sign with a white "P" on a blue field. An advance-warning sign is normally positioned about one-quarter of a mile before the pulloff. These are one-lane sidings without services other than perhaps a trash bin. It's a good place to pull over and read a map rather than trying to drive and read a map at the same time.

Parking areas or "lay-bys" appear every five miles on major highways

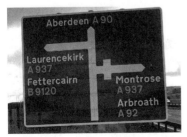

Highway signs are big and bold and quite tourist-friendly.

✓*Directional signs* are big and bold. Just as on the interstate system in the U.S., directional signs on the major highways feature white lettering on a green field. Signs with white lettering on a brown field announce major tourist attractions. Secondary roads tend to retain old markers with black letters on a white field.

✓ To really enjoy driving in Scotland, get onto the "B" roads and the "single tracks." On the single tracks, the going is slow but, after you've adjusted to the pullover protocol for oncoming traffic, you'll enjoy the pace and see parts of the countryside that most tourists never see. The protocol? If you're closest to a pullover, then pull over; flash your lights to signal the oncoming driver to proceed.

✓ *Drive times* are more important than drive distances. Here are the basics on popular point-to-point routes:

Edinburgh - North Berwick: 45"	St. Andrews - Carnoustie: 45"
Edinburgh - St. Andrews: 1 hr	St. Andrews - North Berwick: 2 hrs
	St. Andrews - Gleneagles: 1 hr, 15"
Glasgow - Edinburgh: 1 hr	St. Andrews - Troon: 2 hrs, 45"
Glasgow - Troon: 45"	
Glasgow - Turnberry: 1 hr, 15"	Carnoustie - Aberdeen: 1 hr, 30"
Glasgow - St. Andrews: 2 hrs	Aberdeen - Cruden Bay: 35"
Glasgow - Inverness: 3 hrs, 30"	Cruden Bay - Inverness: 3 hrs"
Glasgow - Aberdeen: 3 hrs	Aberdeen - St. Andrews: 2 hrs, 15"
Inverness - Dornoch: 55"	Dornoch - Tain: 10"
Inverness - Aberdeen: 3+ hrs	Dornoch - Golspie: 15"
Inverness - Machrihanish: 6+ hrs	Dornoch - Brora: 25"

✓*Roundabouts* are designed to keep traffic moving. Those who live in the New England states know they work pretty well most of the time. You'll see few intersections controlled by traffic lights in Scotland. All traffic moves clockwise. Yield to to traffic on the right (remember, "Right is Might"). In two lanes leading to a roundabout, stay left if turning left. Use the right lane if turning right (you will circle three-quarters of the roundabout and exit rightward). Either lane may exit straight ahead. How ingenious!

✓ *Prevent theft.* Always lock your vehicle. It's the only way to guarantee insurance coverage. More important, take your golf clubs out of the vehicle and store them in your lodging when not at a golf course. This is particularly important if you are driving a minibus or minivan bearing a rental-car agency sticker. These are great vehicles, but they are rolling advertisements announcing, "Affluent golfers with expensive golf clubs within."

Food

✓ For *best values,* look for "Bar Meal" signs. Protocol: go to the bar to read the menu and place your order; pay at the bar; your food will be brought to you or your name will be called for pickup at the bar. Tipping? Ten percent is plenty.

✓ *Portions* are large and the Scots don't mind your sharing. No extra plate charge. Money-saving advice: order two soups and one entree; share the entree and you'll have lunch or dinner for two for about $30.

✓ Virtually every golf course has an informal lounge with a respectable menu of soup, sandwiches and other fare. The Scots have a way with soup. The soup's always on and almost always good and hot (*very* hot - watch out).

✓ *Breakfast.* Tour operators like to plug a "full Scottish breakfast" as a benefit of their tours. The fact is, breakfast is served almost everywhere for everyone and is included in the price of lodging. Some of the chain hotels offer breakfast at additional cost. What is included in a full Scottish breakfast and what other options are presented? Here's a sample menu from a B & B:

BREAKFAST MENU

Fruit Juices: orange, grapefruit, tomato, pineapple

Cereals: Cornflakes, Rice Krispies, Weetabix, Crunchy Nut Cornflakes, museli, porridge

Full Cooked Breakfast: bacon, sausage, black pudding, lorne sausage, tomato, mushroom, scones, and fried egg OR choose from the following to create your own breakfast: bacon, sausage, lorne sausage, black pudding, tomato, mushroom, fried bread, fried potato, fried egg, scrambled egg, poached egg, boiled egg, grilled boneless kippers

Toast and Bread: white or wholemeal, croissants

Condiments: marmalade, jam, butter, Flora (margarine brand)

Beverages: tea, coffee, drinking chocolate

BREAKFAST IS SERVED 7 - 9:30 A.M. DAILY

Black pudding is "blood sausage"—a gift of dubious distinction from Germany. "Scones" are a uniquely Scottish treat made from potato and normally grilled or fried. At most establishments, the breakfast buffet table includes yogurt, fresh fruits, and a fruit compote, most often of grapefruit sections and/or prunes. No reason to start the day hungry in Scotland. Jokes can be made about rolling out the door to the golf course, but, truly, breakfast in the UK is a satisfying, civilized way to start the day.

Clothing and Dress—for Golf and Otherwise

✓ *Dress in layers.* The least useful article of apparel: a short-sleeve golf shirt, but take a couple anyway for a bottom layer. Most often you'll be most comfortable in a long-sleeve, lightweight jersey of some kind. Then layer with variously-weighted sweaters, windbreakers, etc.

✓ *Men - pack a tie and a sport jacket and take them with you to the course.* The idea here is to be prepared for that moment when you meet a local club member and get invited into what is usually called the "members' dining room" or "members' lounge" where jacket and tie are mandatory. All courses have a less formal lounge/dining area for visitors and members. At most hotels you'll find the atmosphere quite relaxed. Just as at home, "dressy casual" is the watchword.

✓ *Shorts.* Leave them at home. They're not often seen on the street, on the course, or in the clubhouse. Given the vagaries of weather, they're just not practical. Apart from that, "short pants" are generally associated with school-boy attire. It's a cultural thing.

✓ *Shoes.* My greatest space saver—black leather athletic shoes suitable for any occasion, including golf. I don't even pack golf shoes—just a pair of ribbed overshoes for waterproof covering (see Isotoner's Tote brand "Rubber Rain Boot Loafer" at *www.totes.com*). My shoes stay dry *and* clean. Actually, this is a fairly serious issue. It can take a couple of days for a pair of soaked golf shoes to dry out. In other words, if you take golf shoes, take two pair. Incidentally, steel spikes are still ok at most clubs.

✓ *Hats off!* Remember to take your hat off upon entering the clubhouse. Failure to do so is a "pet peeve" of the Scots.

✓ *Laundry.* It always pays to travel light. The best way to do that is to leave all the extra clothes at home. Take enough for one week. Then, on longer trips, have your laundry done for you weekly at a *laundry service.* These are not self-serve laundromats common to North America. Drop your clothes off and pick them up later that day or the next day—cleaned and folded. I've never paid more than £10 pounds for a load of wash. CAUTION: Do *not* have your laundry done by a hotel. You will pay an arm, a leg, and several other appendages. Following are laundry services in some of Scotland's golf centers:

Carnoustie - Kleenomat
#2 Dundee St., 01241-853-676

Inverness - New City Laundrette
17 Young St., 01463-242-507

North Berwick - Kleaning Ark
27 Quality St., 01620-894-790

Pitlochry - Laundrette & Dry Cleaners
3 W. Moulin Rd., 01796-474-044

St. Andrews - SA Laundry Service
14B Woodburn Terrace, 01334-475-150

Johnson's Dry Cleaning
153 South St., 01334-474-524

Tain (nr Dornoch) - Tain Dry Cleaners
13 King St., 01862-894-443

Troon - Darly Laundrette
149 Dundonald Rd., 01292-314-997

The laundry on Woodburn Terrace in St. Andrews. Drop off your clothes and pick them up later that day or the next day—cleaned and folded.

For the best in local information, make a Tourist Information (TI) Office one of your first stops.

Nongolf Activities/Shopping and Money

✓ *Make a Tourist Information Office (TI) and/or bookstore one of your first stops.* Good information is the key to a good trip. Maps, history books, golf guides, tourist site brochures, and specialized publications—all can enhance your travel experience.

✓ Good *hikes* can be found close by, no matter where you are. Look for "Forest Enterprise" signs; ask your lodging hosts or the nearest Tourist Information Office.

✓ *Shop Hours/VAT.* Most shops open at 9 a.m. and close by 6 p.m. You can reclaim the Value Added Tax (VAT) of 17.5% on goods carried out of the country (not on hotel or green fees). When you make relatively expensive purchases (e.g., £20 or more), ask for a Tax-Free Shopping Form. Shopkeepers administer this program. VAT reimbursement forms issued by shopkeepers at their discretion *must* be processed at your point of international departure. For more detail, ask for Customs and Excise Notice 704, *Traveller's Guide to the Retail Export Scheme*. Is it worth the hassle? If you spend a lot of money, it is. Otherwise, I'm not sure.

✓*Credit cards* are accepted at most stores and restaurants. American Express is the *least* widely accepted. Purchasing on credit is the best way to track major expenses. With widespread availability of ATMs, travelers' checks are practically a thing of the past.

Moats and Malts—Castles and Whisky

Castles and whisky distilleries—not necessarily in that order—are the attractions cited most frequently on the golfer's list of nongolf interests. One or two of each can add a nice finishing touch to any golf trip. In the case of castles, that's easily accomplished. Figuratively speaking, in Scotland there's a castle or ruined abbey around every other bend in the road. Whisky distilleries are fewer and farther between and, for that reason, I've included a map locating some distilleries on page 111.

Royal Dundonald castle was the Ayrshire home of the powerful Stewart (Stuart) dynasty. Now a ruined pile, it sits on a high hill a few miles northeast of Troon.

Many of Scotland's most important, heavily-traveled, and oft-photographed castles lie outside my nine major golf areas. In the lowlands, these are the great castle at Edinburgh; Stirling Castle at Stirling (think William Wallace, Mel Gibson and *Brave Heart*); and Duone Castle (think *Monty Python*) at Duone village a few miles north of Stirling. For anyone heading northward on the A9, these latter two are easily accessible. The west coast and islands of Scotland are dotted with romantic ruins including Eilean Donan, seat of power of the Macraes and Mackenzies; and the famous Urquhart Castle on Loch Ness. Balmoral Castle, the Highland home of Britain's royal family since Victoria's day, is just off the A93 in the Dee River valley near Braemar.

Within my designated golf areas, following are one or more of the most compelling castle attractions in each area. More information can be sought from local Tourist Information offices. The best web page I have found on the subject is at ***www.electricscotland.com/history/castles/index.html***.

Region #1 (Fife) - Falkland Palace at Falkland; St. Andrews Castle.

Region #2 (Ayrshire) - Culzean Castle (18th century) a few miles north of Turnberry on the A719; Royal Dundonald a few miles northeast of Troon on the road to Kilmarnock (A759).

Region #3 (E Lothian) - Dirleton Castle at Dirleton village near Gullane; Tantallon Castle a few miles east of North Berwick on the A198.

Region #4 (Angus) - Glamis Castle at Glamis village (childhood home of Queen Elizabeth II) about eighteen miles north of Dundee.

Region #5 (Inverness/Dornoch) - Cawdor Castle between Inverness and Nairn (associated with Macbeth); Dunrobin Castle at Golspie (ancestoral home of the Sutherlands); Inverness Castle in the middle of town.

Region #6 (Northeast) - Dunnottar Castle at Stonehaven (associated with Franco Zefferelli's *Hamlet*); Slains Castle at Cruden Bay (19th century - associated with *Dracula*).

Region #7 (Perthshire) - Blair Castle near Pitlochry; Scone Palace at Perth (where rests the Stone of Destiny and the throne of Scottish Kings).

Region #8 (Arran/Kintyre/Islay) - Brodick Castle at Brodick on the Isle of Arran.

Region #9 (South) - Castle Kennedy a few miles east of Stranraer; Caerlaverock Castle (14th century) eight miles southeast of Dumfries near Southerness GC.

Visiting a distillery requires a little more effort. They aren't around every bend in the road except up north in the Spey River Valley and on Islay. Golfers concentrating on high-profile golf in Fife, Ayrshire, East Lothian, and Angus (Regions 1-4), are rather limited to Glenkinchie (#1 on the map) and The Famous Grouse Experience at Crieff (#2). Glenkinchie is located near the village of Pencaitland about ten miles south of Haddington, so it is particularly easy to reach from a base in Gullane or North Berwick. Like most distilleries these days, Glenkinchie is owned by a multinational beverage conglomerate (in this case, Diageo). Glenkinchie has a good visitor exhibit hall and tour. Famous Grouse is a hugely popular, moderately-priced blended whisky. The site of the Famous Grouse Experience is the formerly independent Glenturret Distillery, a maker of premium single-malt whiskies with claim to being Scotland's oldest distillery. Drive time to Crieff from St. Andrews or Carnoustie is about one hour, fifteen minutes, making it a manageable and enjoyable day trip perhaps combining golf at either Crieff or nearby Gleneagles.

Dalwhinnie distillery, about 30 miles north of Pitlochry, is a popular stop en route to or from the northern Highlands.

Farther north along the A9 are two distilleries at Pitlochry (Edradour and Blair Atholl) and the Dalwhinnie Distillery (#5), another thirty miles north of Pitlochry. While within reasonable reach of the lowland golf areas, these more likely might serve as congenial rest-stops *en route* to or from the northern Highlands. Pitlochry is about halfway between Inverness and the airports at Glasgow and Edinburgh. Golfers following my Itinerary #3 ("Parkland to Seaside") may base in Pitlochry for a few days, in which case, Edradour is a particularly attractive choice, renowned as Scotland's smallest distillery (with weekly output of about 160 gallons). It sits in a pretty vale just off the A924 one mile past Moulin village.

Now we come to "Speyside," one of the two areas where distilleries *are* around every other figurative bend in the road. Branching off the A9 thirty miles southeast of Inverness, the A95 winds through the beautiful Spey River Valley and is the main highway on the official "Whisky Trail"—a signposted circular route encompassing some fifty whisky distilleries. On the accompanying map, I have cited seven of the labels best-known to North Americans. An eighth, Glen Grant (at Rothes) is not exported across the Atlantic—this, because it is the best-selling whisky in Italy! Glen Grant is included because it's an especially attractive distillery with extensive garden and forest walks available to visitors. For those continuing on up to the Dornoch/Tain area, Glenmorangie (#13 at Tain) is the logical choice. With a wide range of premium whiskies, Glenmorangie has been an aggressive marketer in the U.S. in recent years.

Next in line are the famous whiskies of Islay. Those on the southeast side of the island around Port Ellen display the pungent, "peaty" qualities associated with Islay whiskies. The four distilleries toward the northwest end of the island produce a lighter, though still powerful, expression. There's another distillery (Isle of Jura) on neighboring Jura and, for those golfers on a trip including Arran and Kintyre, there are small, but interesting, distilleries at Lochranza (#21) and Campbeltown (#22, Springbank).

Connoisseurs of whisky tend to be as obsessed with their favorite subject as are wine-lovers and golfers! Not surprisingly, then, informative websites abound. Some of them are industry sponsored (e.g., *www.scotch-whisky.org.uk*). To this eye, the most objectively informative website is *www.dcs.ed.ac.uk*. Managed by John Butler of the University of Edinburgh, it is also "the web's oldest malt whisky site (1994)." Others are *www.scotchwhisky.net* and *www.whisky.com*. The Islay Whisky Society has its own website at *www.islaywhiskysociety.com* and, of course, virtually all the distilleries have their own website.

One final note: during peak travel months, many distilleries are open to visitors for tours on weekends, but they are not operational. Also, during July or August, distilleries are "quiet" or "silent" (non-operational). This is the time when annually-scheduled maintenance is carried out and employees are given a chance to breathe some fresh summer air. To see an operational distillery, visit distilleries during the week and, in July or August, call your intended target to make sure it is not only open but operating.

Locations of Twenty-Two Whisky Distilleries

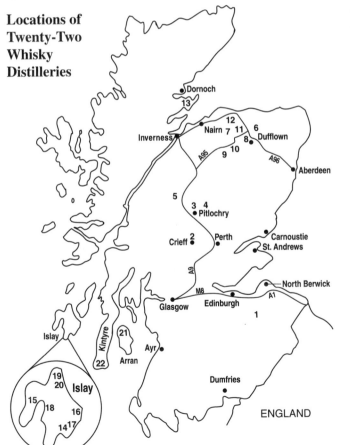

Lowlands and Southern Highlands
1. Glenkinchie
2. Famous Grouse
3. Edradour
4. Blair Atholl
5. Dalwhinnie

Speyside
6. Strathisla
7. Glen Grant
8. Glenfiddich
9. Glenlivet
10. Glenfarclas
11. Macallan
12. Glen Moray

Northern Highlands
13. Glenmorangie

Islay
14. Laphroaig
15. Bruichladdich
16. Ardbeg
17. Lagavulin
18. Bowmore
19. Bunnahabhain
20. Caol Ila

Arran/Kintyre
21. Lochranza
22. Springbank

PART III

THE DIRECTORY

OF

COURSES

Preparing for Play in Scotland

Linksland Golf

Many of golf's great writers, including Herbert Warren Wind and Bernard Darwin, have tried to define links golf—its unique qualities and history. Is it seaside golf?—yes. But is all seaside golf links golf?—clearly not. Is it always "out and back," like links in a string of sausages?—maybe in its purest form, but not always. If there are trees or an artificial lake on a course, is it a true links course? Questions like these propel discussion. Ultimately, the most interesting question is, "Is seaside golf in Scotland unique? Is it different than seaside golf in Florida, California, Spain, or Portugal?" Certainly, one can make the case that the environment is different—the air, the temperature, the precipitation— and these combine to make Scottish links golf qualitatively different than golf in other places. But then what about links golf in Ireland and England? Well, as you see, this topic can generate an essay or book—and it has.

To be brief, links golf in Scotland has both locational and qualitative aspects. Locational: yes, near the sea—in purest form a relatively narrow strip of sandy, non-arable lowland between settled and/or arable land and the sea. The narrow characteristic of linksland led to the familiar out-and-back design of many Scottish courses (e.g., Royal Dornoch, Nairn, Western Gailes, Brora, Cruden Bay)—basically two fairways wide.

The connection between sheep and golf could not be more clear.

But always narrow? No, exceptions abound. The key word in the previous paragraph is *low*land—lowland near the sea that, over centuries and eons, was subject to periodic inundation and continual sedimentary processes. Thus the land became sandy and non-arable—"waste land" fit mostly for grazing and, eventually, for golf. So, being seaside is not enough. Linksland might well extend some distance inland due to the character and geologic history of the land. And high ground near seaside, never subject to the ebbs and tides of sand and sea, may not be linksland at all (e.g., at Stranraer). The soil might be rich, giving rise to a great variety of plants, grasses and trees.

So, we come to the qualitative aspects: sandy soil that drains water and does not allow lakes to form; salt-water air and residues in the soil that prevent or retard the growth of trees; hardy grasses and plants capable of growing in sandy soil and salt air; dunes, hillocks, and depressions associated with the blowing and drifting of sand. The cumulative effect of these—along with those environmental aspects of mild temperatures, the likelihood of strong winds, and frequent rains—all add up to golf on a Scottish links course.

Does it add up to golf unique in all the world? Now we approach the literary territory explored with such effect by Wind and Darwin, Longhurst and Campbell, Finegan and Bamberger. Fortunately, you can go to Scotland and form your own opinion on this subject.

Parkland and Heathland Courses

Often these descriptors are used interchangeably though, in fact, they describe different conditions. It's another sticky wicket: generally, parkland and heathland (or moorland) courses are inland, away from the sea—though not necessarily far inland (e.g., Belleisle, Royal Musselburgh). The defining differences between parkland and heathland have to do with (a) soil and (b) vegetation supported by the soil. Parkland soil is relatively rich and retentive of moisture, giving rise to a variety of deciduous trees, wild grasses, and even lakes—in short, the kind of land associated with pastures and woods. Heathland has more in common with linksland—sandy, peaty soil, quick to drain, and relatively poorer in nutrients, thus supporting scrubby heather and evergreens but not much more. The best clues are in the rough: grass on the parkland courses; heather on the heathland courses. Most inland courses fall clearly into one camp or the other. Ladybank and Glasgow Gailes are heathland courses through and through, just as there's no doubt about the parkland status of Inverness Golf Club and the courses at Gleneagles. Others, like Panmure and Golspie, have qualities of linksland, heathland, and parkland. In these cases, in "The Directory of Courses," I've indicated that a course is a "hybrid." The most common hybrid combines linksland features with parkland features (e.g., Lundin Links, The Glen, Longniddry).

Handicap Certificates

Virtually every course will indicate in its statement of visitor restrictions, "handicap certificate required." Some courses are more specific: "Handicap certificate required - men 24, ladies 36." The St. Andrews Links Trust Management is even more specific: "All golfers wishing to play over the Old Course must be in possession of a current, official handicap which should be presented to the Starter on the day of play and the maximum handicap is 24 for men, 36 for ladies .... **Proof of handicap must be in the form of a handicap card or handicap certificate, a letter of introduction from a golf club is no longer acceptable as proof of handicap"** (their bold emphasis).

As a practical matter, most courses rarely ask to see proof of handicap. On the other hand, certain courses like Royal Dornoch and St. Andrews Old *require* that document and will check every time. Therefore, one should be prepared. Whether through a national association (USGA in the United States) or another handicapping service, registration is easy. See *www.usga.org* for more information on handicapping.

Buggies (Golf Carts)

The Scots call them "buggies." North Americans call them "carts." Whatever they're called, these machines constitute the most dramatic example of differing attitudes toward the game of golf.

In Scotland golf is still considered a *walking* game—a game encouraging quiet conversation with companions while taking a healthful stroll through natural terrain. I am not romanticizing anything here. This is the hallmark of golf in Scotland. Therefore, by and large, buggies are available only to those with a physical or medical condition that makes walking eighteen holes impossible. Furthermore, where buggies can be "hired," they are expensive—typically £20 to £25 ($35-45). Real estate sales and even enterprising profits are not much on the "radar screens" of most golf clubs in Scotland. They are mostly concerned with keeping the golf experience gratifying, yet simple, and keeping the club books balanced (to which end, they tend to gouge visiting golfers, but that's the worst one can say about the golf experience in Scotland).

> *In Scotland golf is still considered a walking game—a game encouraging quiet conversation with companions while taking a healthful stroll through natural terrain. I am not romanticizing anything here. This is the hallmark of golf in Scotland.*

This attitude contrasts sharply with the prevailing attitude at most golf courses in the United States where, under the influence of real estate developers, greedy professionals, and sheer laziness, "cart golf" has replaced golf as it has been played for centuries. This is the single biggest difference in the golf experience that visitors to Scotland will see and, of course, it has had its ultimate effect on course design. In Scotland, even at new courses that allow buggies (e.g., St. Andrews Bay's Devlin and Craigielaw in East Lothian), one will find the teeing grounds comparatively close to the greens. Clearly, this is to accommodate the walker, because this is the *preferred* way to play the game even where carts are available.

What does all this mean to the visiting golfer? Well, it suggests getting out of the cart and into walking shape. But, most important, it means one must be aware of cart availability and policy at each course. In "The Directory of Courses," I have indicated specific buggy policy and even the number of buggies available where that information could be gleaned. The following is offered in summation:

✓ *Some* courses do not allow buggies at all. Included in this category are all the current and historic "rota" courses—St. Andrews Old Course, Royal Troon, Prestwick, Carnoustie, Turnberry, and Muirfield.

✓ *Some* courses have a few buggies available to those with a *verifiable* medical infirmity or physical disability (e.g., Crail, Dunbar, Gullane). In a few cases, age alone may be a qualifier (e.g., St. Andrews New). Age and/or physical condition must be documented.

✓ *Many* courses have a few buggies available for general hire. This number rarely exceeds four; advance reservation is advised.

✓ A *few* courses have a stable of buggies available for general hire.

For whatever reason, if you must use a buggy to enjoy a round of golf, my advice is to plan ahead and/or include one or more of the following courses on your itinerary: *Craigielaw, Gleneagles' PGA Centenary Course, St. Andrews Bay - Devlin, St. Andrews - The Duke's,* and *Whitekirk.* At these courses, advance reservation of a buggy probably won't be necessary.

Practicing for Play on a Scottish Links Course

In North America, to my knowledge, a golfer cannot prepare for an encounter with the prickly gorse of Scotland or, for that matter, even the low-lying, tough, woody heather. Plenty of new "links style" courses feature hillocks and long, wispy grasses. But, to put them all together—with an admixture of wind and rain, blind shots, deep pot bunkers, and rolling fairways—I'm not sure there's any way to fully prepare for golf in Scotland. In bad weather, the courses can be positively brutal but, even in benign conditions, most visiting golfers will play five or six shots above their index. Someone who normally shoots in the high 80s probably will card scores in the 90s and low 100s. A mid-handicapper should be happy with scores in the 80s. The low handicapper may have his or her ego rearranged. In an interesting appendix to his report on a golf trip to Scotland (*Hallowed Ground: A Golf Trip to Scotland*), Tanner Stewart notes that, among the eight low-handicap golfers in his group, five of the eight averaged about five strokes over their USGA handicap indexes; the other three averaged six or more strokes over their indices. Having said that much, you can still go to your nearest practice range and get a jump start on good golf in Scotland. Here's what to do:

✓ Hit mid-iron (5,6,7) "knock down" shots to targets from 100 to 160 yards. This will help you prepare to play in the wind.

✓ Find an area of thin lies and practice with all clubs. The links fairways will tend to catch the leading edge of your clubs; you have to work on "nipping" the ball.

✓ Especially for the St. Andrews courses, practice the longest putts you can find; some of the double greens there are nearly as big as a football field. More important, you'll find plenty of opportunity to use the "Texas Wedge" from well off the greens.

Wind is the wild card on Scottish courses. On occasion, conditions can be brutal.

✓ When you get a blast of lousy weather, think of it as a chance to practice for golf in Scotland. Grab your clubs and head for the course.

Equipment

To help my clients anticipate the equipment necessary for play in Scotland, I give them a "Golf Readiness Checklist" duplicated here in *Appendix A*. From that list, I want to emphasize three items:

✓ Unless you carry your golf bag, you will probably be using a pullcart or "trolley." If so, take two three-foot *bungee cords* to secure your golf bag to the trolley. If you don't you'll be cursing all day as your bag repeatedly falls off the trolley amongst the hillocks and uneven rough.

✓ If you wear glasses, the worst element to deal with in golf is rain. In Scotland, where rain is likely sometime during your trip, you'll be thankful you took a *washcloth* to tuck into a jacket or pants pocket. A washcloth is easier to handle and stow than a towel.

✓ *Dress in layers.* During the typical three to four-hour round of golf, dramatic variations in cloud cover, temperature, wind speed, and precipitation are common. Here's a good way to layer: start with a short-sleeve golf shirt and/or long-sleeve, lightweight jersey; carry a sweater, a windbreaker, and a rain jacket. In the spring and fall, I don't even bother packing short-sleeve golf shirts. Rather, I start with a long-sleeve pullover and carry a windbreaker, sweater, and rain suit for extra cover.

The author ready for play on a brisk day in March. Note the gloves, stocking cap, and bungee cords.

At the Course

✓ Call your scheduled course a day or two before play. This is the time to confirm your presence, change a tee time, request a caddie, or reserve a buggie. The Scots will appreciate your thoughtfulness. At some clubhouses the front door or locker room door will be locked. Don't take it personally. It just means this is a private club where only members and guests are allowed to use clubhouse facilities. *Protocol:* Go to the pro shop to register and pay your green fee or submit your voucher. You'll be given a code to punch into a keypad near the front door or locker room door. That's your pass to club facilities for the day.

✓ *Yardage Books.* Every course has some kind of "stroke saver"—a yardage book with schematic drawings of each hole. They vary in quality but are uniformly indispensable because you won't find yardage markers on most courses. Cost: about £2-4. It's the best scoring investment you will make and an inexpensive souvenir of your trip.

✓ *Caddies.* This is a thorny subject with objective and subjective facets. First, the objective: Top courses usually make a

Trolleys ("pullcarts") are universally available and cost about £3-4.

distinction between caddies and bag carriers—and charge accordingly. Bag carriers may be most available in the summer when school is out. Caddies typically cost between £25 and £35. Bag carriers typically cost £15 to £20. It's fine for two or three golfers to split the cost of a caddie. Four golfers may be pushing the issue a bit, but that's a negotiable point. You just need to make it clear the caddie is hired to advise more than one golfer and ante up for the additional service. Tipping? A £10 note is typical. Check with the caddymaster or pro.

Now, some subjective facets: First, there's no question a good caddie can add special dimension to a round at an historic course like Prestwick, Royal Troon, or the Old Course at St. Andrews. On the other hand, regular use of caddies will add significant cost to a trip—perhaps amounting to as much as lodging if caddies are not shared. Second, by definition, the presence of a caddie or caddies changes group dynamics. That may be good or bad, but it's a fact. Third, some golfers may feel uncomfortable pressure to "perform" for a caddie. Fourth, there are good caddies and bad caddies who create good experiences or bad experiences.

Here's the nut of my experience and opinion: Low-handicap golfers can benefit most from having a caddie because they can actually do what the caddie says to do; high-handicappers can expect to enjoy the "local color," but they shouldn't expect a caddie to take ten strokes off their game. Rather than reserve caddies far in advance straight through a trip, the best approach is to assess the caddie situation as a trip unfolds and *call ahead to your appointed course at least two days in advance* to reserve a determined number of caddies. This gives you a chance to make personal contact with the club, confirm your tee time, and perhaps ask for a "senior caddie" who may give you the best experience. Finally, most often I would hire a bag carrier before a caddie simply because the bag carrier might end up being a youngster who not only needs the money but who happens to be a very good junior golfer.

For my part, I'm content with a trolley and a yardage book. My objective is to look at a course, make an effort, and not be too concerned about a final score. Even if a caddie can save me four or five strokes on a round, I really don't care enough about that to pay £10 per stroke.

✓ If you don't hit consistently well with a driver, consider leaving it at home. Direction is more important than distance.

✓ From the heather and long grass, your first objective should be to get the ball back in play. Don't be a hero and don't hurt yourself. Take a firm grasp and swing smoothly through the ball; don't thrash at it. If your ball goes into the gorse and you haven't hit a provisional ball, take a penalty drop and play on unless you're playing in a competition.

✓ Use the toilet before teeing off. Most courses don't provide facilities.

✓ Take water with you. You won't find that on most courses either. And if you're used to a hot dog "at the turn," forget about it. In most cases, there ain't no "turn" anywhere near the clubhouse.

✓ Take your hat off upon entering the clubhouse. It's the Scots' second biggest complaint about Americans and they'll not be shy about reminding you of your manners.

✓ The biggest complaint?—loud conversation on the putting greens. Remember, in Scotland the tees are close to the greens. Sshhh!

Sixty-Eight Great Courses:
A Directory with Profiles

The sixty-eight golf courses profiled here constitute about twelve percent of Scotland's 550+ courses. Ergo, this is a highly selective directory. Of course, any selective list of courses is fraught with danger. The aficionado of Scottish golf will say, "But you've left out Ballater, Braid Hills, and Bruntsfield Links." And I would simply reply, ninety-nine percent of golfers visiting Scotland go to play a handful of courses; they don't go to play Ballater, Braid Hills, and Bruntsfield Links. Maybe they should, but my aim here is to provide useful information rather than to change the profile of Scottish golf tourism. The problem with most directories is that they are not sufficiently selective.

My emphasis is on seaside courses because that is what most visitors to Scotland want to play. In priority order, most first-timers to Scotland want to visit (1) St. Andrews, (2) the Ayrshire coast, (3) Carnoustie, (4) North Berwick/Gullane, and (5) Inverness/Dornoch. In those locations, they are interested mainly in about ten to twelve courses: St. Andrews' Old/New/Jubilee, Kingsbarns, Royal Troon, Prestwick, Turnberry, Carnoustie, North Berwick, Gullane #1, Royal Dornoch, and Nairn.

If I can get a visitor to Scotland interested in a second tier of lesser-known courses, either on that first trip or on a followup trip, I consider it a victory. These courses might include Lundin Links, Crail, or Elie in Fife; Western Gailes, Glasgow Gailes, and Irvine Bogside in Ayrshire; Montrose, Royal Aberdeen, and Cruden Bay along the northeast coast; Golspie, Brora, Tain, and the Boat of Garten in the north; Crieff, Blairgowrie, and Pitlochry in the middle of the country. In short, there's plenty of golf here for both the first-timer and the guy or gal who has played the big-name courses and is now ready to dip more deeply into the reservoir of great Scottish courses. A treasure-trove of information awaits the careful reader of these pages.

Notes on the Entries

At the head of each entry, all necessary data is presented to help you contact the right person and book a tee time at sixty-eight of Scotland's finest golf courses. It's all here: *address - phone - fax - email - website - key contacts - visitor policies - green fees - deposits.* Following are notes on some data elements and the overall layout of the directory.

• *Club Name and Date.* Each entry starts with the proper name of a club or managing entity. The date in parentheses (1897) is the year the club was formed or was thought to have been formed. This date may or may not be the year when a course was created.

• *Course Yardage: Middle Tees and Medal Tees.* Note that a range of yardage is usually given (5850-6177). The first number is yardage from the "visitor" or "middle" tees. The second number is yardage from the tees for members' competitions or "medal" tees. At most courses, tee markers for visitor and casual member rounds are yellow; the back tees for member competitions are white. Most courses have a set of forward tees (usually red) presumed to be for female golfers and usually referred to as "the ladies' tees." *Unless informed otherwise, a male visitor will be expected to play from the yellow tees.* The Scots are a bit finicky about this. If you would like to play from the whites, ask the starter or professional for permission. Most often the answer will be, "I'm sorry, we reserve the medal tees for member play." But it doesn't hurt to ask. A low handicapper might well be allowed to play from the back tees.

A note on Scotland's "short" courses: At first glance, most Scottish courses appear to be considerably shorter than courses in North America. Literally, that is true. But keep three things in mind before jumping to the conclusion that shorter means easier: First, par at most courses is 69, 70, or 71; a "standard" par 72 is unusual. This means fewer easily-reachable par 5s and par 3s and more long par 4s. Second, yardages usually are measured to the *front* of the green rather than to the center. Add about 270 yards to the total to arrive at a figure comparable to measuring conventions in North America. Third, the elements, particularly persistent winds, tend to have a lengthening effect on the courses. All this adds up to harder, not easier.

• *SSS: Standard Scratch Score.* Scotland's "SSS" is comparable to the USGA's course rating. Just as it sounds, the SSS rating on a course is what the scratch golfer should achieve relative to par. If the SSS is 73 against par 69 (e.g., Southerness), a tough round of golf is in store. If, on the other hand, the SSS is 68 against par 70 (e.g., Portpatrick), you're probably looking at something like a stroll in a lovely park.

• ***Booking Contact(s) and Secretary.*** Though this information is subject to frequent change, I have included it because I think it's nice to be able to make a call and know with whom you might be speaking. Generally, you will *not* speak with the club secretary but rather with a booking secretary or assistant or even the club professional. The best opening gambit is to simply say, "Hello, this is _____ calling from _____. Can you help me with making a visitor reservation?". The conversation will flow on from there.

• ***Phone - Starter/Pro Shop.*** This number is included because most course offices turn over their "diary" to the starter or pro shop within a week of play. To check in before your appointed tee time, this is the number to call.

• ***Fees.*** Generally these are high-season fees April through October. Some courses maintain their "winter rates" into April and return to them in October. When traveling in April or October, it's always a good idea to double-check rates.

• ***Profile.*** Following the club data is comment on each course. This comment often has as much to do with the location, the ambience and feel of a place as with course description. Detailed course descriptions of major courses are available in other books dedicated to that purpose. My aim here is to convey the flavor of a place, put it in perspective, and answer the questions, "Why should I want to play this course?" or "Why should I want to go there?". Area accommodations and nongolf activities are discussed throughout the profiles. Look here also for highlighted TRAVEL TIPS and DRIVE TIME sidebars. Websites noted throughout the profiles are cumulated in *Appendix B*.

• ***Arrangement and Indices.*** Course entries are numbered from one to sixty-eight. They are arranged *alphabetically* because most people are more familiar with course names than with their exact locations or the names of Scotland's political subdivisions. To help navigate the alphabetical entry, several indices preceeding the directory give guidance:

• First, there's a *geographic* index in directional order so that one can identify courses in relation to one another.

• Second, all sixty-eight courses are arranged by *price* from highest to lowest. To me, this is the most important index. If you play the courses at the top of the list you will have a good trip, go to places most tourists go, and spend a lot of money. If you play courses at the bottom of the list you will have a good trip, go to places most tourists do not visit, and spend a lot less. If you play courses in the middle bracket you will play top-notch courses often described as "hidden gems" and you will spend a middlin' amount of money. There are no wrong answers—only different budgets and different approaches to travel. Fully half the courses in the directory are priced between £30 and £50. Generally, these courses best combine quality and value.

• A third index lists the courses by *type* and, here, I've distinguished among (1) parkland/heathland courses; (2) links courses with sea views; and (3) links courses where the ocean is neither in play nor particularly visible. This sea-view distinction is worth making because, for example, many people don't realize they won't see much of the ocean when they play Carnoustie or the Old Course at St. Andrews. On the other hand, the golfer has magnificent sea views at courses like North Berwick, The Glen, and Kingsbarns. This may or may not be critical in choosing courses to play, but it is useful information.

• *Course architects* are recognized in the fourth index. The giants of Scottish golf architecture are Tom Morris and James Braid and it is remarkable how many of the courses listed here are either complete works of their expertise, their imaginative extensions of nine-hole courses, or their redesigns of existing layouts. Students of Scottish golf may find this index particularly rewarding because it suggests a way of organizing an itinerary—perhaps an all-Braid excursion or an all-Morris pilgrimage. Better yet, consciously combining the two may allow comparison and contrast in design philosophies.

A Note for Juniors and Golf Professionals

Most courses offer reduced rates for juniors, most often defined as persons aged twelve through seventeen years (under eighteen). Sometimes this is a flat rate applicable all week; sometimes it is fifty percent of the adult green fee. Handicap requirements are not necessarily waived for juniors; best to check with each course for their policies.

Members of a national professional golf association (e.g., PGA of America) normally qualify for "courtesy of the course" (no charge) or a reduced green fee. To take advantage of this benefit, professionals *must* observe every reciprocal courtesy, including a personal call, email, or letter to the head professional and/or secretary and presentation of a current association membership card.

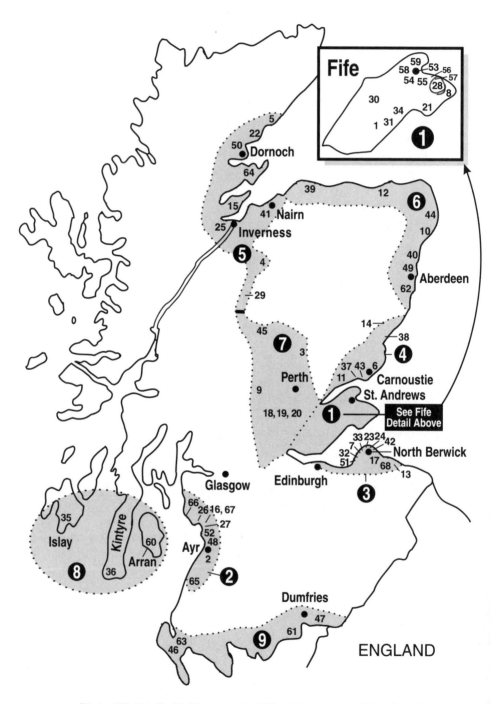

Fife

59
58 53 56
54 55 57
(28) 8
30
34 21
1 31
❶

5
22
50 ● Dornoch
64

39 12
❻
15 41 ● Nairn 44
25 ● 10
Inverness
❺
4 40
49
29 62 ● Aberdeen

45 14
❼ 38
3 **❹**
37 43 6
11 ● Carnoustie
Perth St. Andrews
9
18, 19, 20 **❶** See Fife
Detail Above
33 2324 42
7
32 ● North Berwick
51 17
Glasgow 68
13
66 Edinburgh
26 16, 67 **❸**
27
52
48
Ayr 2
❷
65

35
Kintyre 60
Islay Dumfries
36 Arran 47
❽ 61
❾
63
46 ENGLAND

Sixty-Eight Golf Courses in Nine Regions of Scotland

Index 1 - Geographic Arrangement of Golf
(located by number on map)
+ = British Open Qualifying Course
* = Current or historic venue for British Open

Region #1 - Fife (from Tayport, south along coast and back)
Scotscraig+ (59)
The Duke's Course (58)
St. Andrews Old/New/Jubilee (53, 54, 55)
St. Andrews Bay Torrance/Devlin (56, 57)
Kingsbarns (28) ✓
Crail (8)   CASTLE ✓
Golf House Club - Elie (21)
Lundin Links+ (34)
Leven Links+ (31)
Balbirnie Park (1)
Ladybank+ (30)

Region #2 - Ayrshire (north to south)
West Kilbride (66)
Irvine - Bogside+ (26)
Glasgow Gailes+ (16)
Western Gailes+ (67)
Kilmarnock - Barassie+ (27)
Royal Troon* (52)
Prestwick* (48)
Belleisle (2)
Turnberry - Ailsa* (65)

Region #3 - East Lothian (west to east)
Royal Musselburgh (51)
Longniddry+ (32)
Craigielaw (7)
Luffness New+ (33)
Gullane #1+ (23)
Honourable Company of Edinburgh Golfers - Muirfield* (24)
North Berwick - West Links+ (42)
The Glen - North Berwick (17)
Whitekirk (68)
Dunbar+ (13)

Region #4 - Angus/East Coast (Dundee to Edzell)
Downfield+ (11)
Monifieth+ (37)

Panmure (43)
Carnoustie* (6)
Montrose+ (38)
Edzell (14)

Region #5 - Inverness/Dornoch (south to north)

Kingussie (29)
Boat of Garten (4)
Inverness (25)
Nairn (41)
Fortrose & Rosemarkie (15)
Tain (64)
Royal Dornoch (50)
Golspie (22)
Brora (5)

Region #6 - Northeast/North Coast (south to north to west)

Stonehaven (62)
Royal Aberdeen (49)
Murcar (40)
Cruden Bay (10)
Peterhead (44)
Duff House Royal (12)
Moray Old (39)

Region #7 - Perthshire/Central (south to north)

Gleneagles - King's/Queen's/PGA Centenary (18, 19, 20)
Crieff (9)
Blairgowrie Rosemount (3)
Pitlochry (45)

Region #8 - Arran/Kintyre/Islay (east to west)

Shiskine (60)
Machrihanish (36)
Machrie (35)

Region #9 - South Coast (east to west)

Powfoot (47)
Southerness (61)
Stranraer (63)
Portpatrick (46)

Index 2: Courses by Price
(highest to lowest, weekday high season 2005)

Course	Course #	Price (£)
Royal Troon Old Course ✓ *Castle*	52	200* (incl lunch)
Kingsbarns ✓	28	145
Turnberry Ailsa - nonresident	65	130
Muirfield -single round	24	120
St. Andrews Old Course ✓✓	53	115
Gleneagles - all courses - nonresident	18, 19 ,20	110
Prestwick ✓	48	100
Carnoustie ✓	6	98
St. Andrews Bay - nonresident	56, 57	95
Western Gailes ✓	67	95 (incl lunch)
The Duke's Course	58	85
Gullane #1	23	80
Nairn	41	75
Royal Aberdeen	49	75
Royal Dornoch	50	72
Blairgowrie Rosemount	3	60
Kilmarnock Barassie	27	58
Cruden Bay	10	55
Glasgow Gailes	16	55
Murcar	40	55
North Berwick West Links	42	55
St. Andrews Jubilee	55	55
St. Andrews New	54	55
Golf House Club at Elie	21	50
Irvine	26	50
Panmure	50	50
Craigielaw	7	48
Luffness New	33	46
Ladybank	30	45
Dunbar	13	44
Scotscraig	59	44
Lundin Links	34	42
Southerness	61	42
Machrie - nonresident	35	42
Crail Balcomie	8	40
Machrihanish	36	40

Course	Course #	Price (£)
Monifieth	37	40
Moray Old	39	40
Montrose	38	40
Tain	64	38
Downfield	11	38
Longniddry	32	38
Leven Links	31	37
Machrie - resident	35	37
Balbirnie Park	1	35
West Kilbride	66	35
Inverness	25	33
The Glen	17	32
Boat of Garten	4	30
Brora	5	30
Crieff	9	30
Fortrose & Rosemarkie	15	30
Powfoot	47	30
Peterhead	44	30
Whitekirk	68	30
Royal Musselburgh	51	28
Edzell	14	28
Portpatrick	46	27
Duff House Royal	12	25
Golspie	22	25
Stranraer	63	25
Kingussie	29	25
Pitlochry	45	24
Belleisle	2	23
Stonehaven	62	18
Shiskine	60	15

*Royal Troon has a two-course policy that cannot be avoided (unlike at St. Andrews). Visitors pay for the companion Portland course whether or not they want to play it. Therefore, Royal Troon goes to the top of the list.

Index 3: Links Courses with Ocean in Play or in Sight
(alphabetical within each region)

Region #1 - Fife
Balcomie Links - Crail
Golf House Club - Elie
Kingsbarns
Leven Links
Lundin Links
St. Andrews - Jubilee
St. Andrews Bay - Devlin
St. Andrews Bay - Torrance

Region #2 - Ayshire
Prestwick
Royal Troon
Turnberry
West Kilbride
Western Gailes

Region #3 - East Lothian
Craigielaw
Dunbar
The Glen (North Berwick East Links)
Gullane #1
Honourable Company of Edinburgh Golfers (Muirfield)
Longniddry
North Berwick West Links

Region #4 - Angus/East Coast
Montrose

Region #5 - Inverness/Dornoch
Brora
Fortrose and Rosemarkie
Golspie
Nairn
Royal Dornoch
Tain

Region #6 - Northeast/North Coast
Cruden Bay
Moray Old
Murcar

Peterhead
Royal Aberdeen
Stonehaven

Region #8 - *Arran/Kintyre/Islay*
Machrie
Machrihanish
Shiskine

Region #9 - *South Coast*
Portpatrick
Powfoot
Southerness

Index 4: Links Courses - Minimal or No Ocean View
Glasgow Gailes
Irvine - Bogside
Kilmarnock (Barassie)
Luffness New
Monifieth
Panmure
St. Andrews Old Course
St. Andrews New

Index 5: Parkland/Heathland Courses
Region #1 - *Fife*
Balbirnie Park
Ladybank
St. Andrews - The Duke's

Region #2 - *Ayrshire*
Belleisle

Region #3 - *E. Lothian*
Royal Musselburgh
Whitekirk

Region #4 - *Angus/East Coast*
Downfield
Edzell

Region #5 - Inverness/Dornoch
Boat of Garten
Inverness
Kingussie

Region #6 - Northeast/North Coast
Duff House Royal

Region #7 - Perthshire/Central
Blairgowrie Rosemount
Crieff
Gleneagles - Queen's/King's/PGA Centenary
Pitlochry

Region #9 - South Coast
Stranraer

Index 6: Courses by Tom Morris, Sr. (1821-1908)
Crail (9 holes - 1895; 9 holes - 1899)
Dunbar (15 holes - 1856)
Luffness New (1894)
Moray Old (1889)
Muirfield (1891)
St. Andrews New (1894)
Scotscraig (1892)
Tain (1890)

Partially Designed or Expanded
Elie (1895)
Ladybank (1879)
Prestwick (12 holes - 1851)
Royal Dornoch (9 holes - 1887)
West Kilbride (9 holes - 1896)

Index 7: Courses by James Braid (1870 - 1950)
Belleisle (1927)
Boat of Garten (1936)
Downfield (1932)
Gleneagles - King's/Queen's (1919) with C.K. Hutchison
Irvine - Bogside
Powfoot (1903)
Royal Musselburgh (1926)
Stranraer (1950)

Remodeled or Expanded

Blairgowrie Rosemount (1934)
Brora (1920)
Carnoustie Championship (1926 - 1936)
Elie (1921)
Fortrose and Rosemarkie (1935)
Nairn (1938)
Prestwick (1918)
Royal Troon (1923)
Scotscraig (1904)

1. Balbirnie Park Golf Club (1983)

Region #: 1   **Category:** parkland
Architect(s): Fraser Middleton
Length: 6100-6400   **SSS:** 70-71   **Par:** 71

Address: Balbirnie Park, Markinch by Glenrothes KY7 6NR
Directions: off A92 N of Glenrothes

Reservations phone: 01592-752-006   **Fax:** 01592-752-006
Email: bpgc@aol.com
Website: balbirniegolf.com
Booking Contact(s): professional shop

Administrator: Steve Oliver   **Professional:** Craig Donnelly
Phone - Starter/Pro shop: 01592-752-006
Fee(s) (2005): wkday £35, day tkt £45; wkend £40, day tkt £55
Deposit (2005): £5
Visitor Policies: all week   **Buggies:** 4 - general hire

This is one of Scotland's finest Parkland courses. Everything but the price may remind one of the courses at Gleneagles. Thus, Balbirnie is also one of Scotland's best values.

Apart from its natural beauty, Balbirnie's most important asset is its location near Glenrothes just off the A92 at Markinch Junction midway between Edinburgh and St. Andrews (and on the rail line). This is a perfect location combining proximity to the golf courses of Fife with easy access to Edinburgh. Twelve minutes will get you to the coastal courses at Leven and Lundin; it's ten minutes to Ladybank; thirty to St. Andrews; and from Markinch Junction you can be in central Edinburgh on the train in forty-five minutes. This area also works well as a lodging base for those playing at both St. Andrews and Muirfield, cutting off about thirty minutes of drive time in each direction.

> *This is a perfect location combining proximity to the golf courses of Fife with easy access to Edinburgh.*

Situated in a huge woodland park, Balbirnie is a recent addition to Scottish golf. Among Fife's inland tracks, Ladybank may be the golfer's first choice. But, if you're staying in or near Glenrothes and looking for another break from links golf, there's every reason to make a date with this beauty created by Scottish designer Fraser Middleton. New teeing grounds constructed in 2004 at the second, ninth, and twelfth holes have added length and challenge to the course.

Lodging: The countryside surrounding Balbirnie is beautiful and offers up two outstanding "country house hotels" that cater to golfers and deserve special mention. One is the mid-priced *Balgeddie House Hotel* (01592-742-511; *www.balgeddiehouse.com*), located two miles northeast of Glenrothes just off

TRAVEL TIP
Look for some variation of
"Country House Hotel" in the
name of a hostelry and you
will usually find a uniquely
memorable lodging experience.

the A912. The other is the more expensive *Balbirnie House Hotel* (01592-610-066; *www.balbirnie.co.uk*) located right at Balbirnie Park. Each draws visitors from miles around to award-winning dining rooms. Together, they represent a type of establishment found throughout Scotland, typically transformed from a country

manor house to a modern hotel with character and class. These kinds of hotels can help make a trip to Scotland special, each in its own memorable way.

Barassie: *See Kilmarnock Golf Club*

2. Belleisle Golf Club (1927)

Region #: 2   **Category:** parkland
Architect(s): James Braid
Length: 6040-6431   **SSS:** 70   **Par:** 71

Address: c/o S Ayrshire Council, Burns House,
Burns SQ, Ayr KA7 1UT
Directions: 1 mi S of Ayr off A719

Reservations phone: 01292-441-258   **Fax:** 01292-442-632
Email: belleisle.golf@south-ayrshire.gov.uk
Website: no
Booking Contact(s): senior staffer

Sr. Staffer: Alan Thomson   **Professional:** D Gemmell
Phone - Starter/Pro shop: 01292-441-314
Fee(s) (2005): wkday £23, day tkt w/ Seafield £31; wkend £28, day tkt £35
Deposit (2005): £5
Visitor Policies: all week - public course   **Buggies:** no
Other: shorter Seafield Course adjacent

   Partisans of Fife may disagree but, arguably, Ayrshire on Scotland's southwest coast has the greatest concentration of important links courses in the country. Visitors from around the world flock to play Prestwick, Turnberry, and Royal Troon—three past and present sites of British Open history within a coastal span of less than thirty miles. Then there are the increasingly popular courses at Gailes, not to mention a half dozen other first-rate courses between Ayr and West Kilbride.

Against this constellation of stars, it's no wonder Belleisle is the Ayrshire golf course most overlooked and underplayed by visitors. In that sense, it qualifies as a true "hidden gem" among Scottish courses—one many consider the finest of Scotland's parkland courses.

And in that word "parkland" lies the truth of Belleisle's anonymity. Though less than a mile from seaside, this is not a links course. Through some quirk of nature, rich forest ground prevailed over sandy links turf in this spot just south of Ayr town center. The fairways are lush. Trees are full and present. Forest OB threatens. This is Belleisle—as full-bodied and robust a parkland course as you're likely to find. If it weren't for the occasional view of the Isle of Arran off in the distance (a *belle isle*), you might think you were miles inland, far away from the sea.

Apart from being one of the best bargains in Scottish golf, the main reason to visit Belleisle is to play a course that is pure James Braid, Scotland's most prolific golf architect. Much of Braid's work involved redesigning or extending existing golf grounds. At Belleisle, Braid was given a clean slate. The result was a "signature" parkland course with a look and feel of modernity. You'll find all the Braid trademarks at Belleisle—challenging par 3s to all points of the compass; long two-shotters that make or break the round; judicious bunkering to indicate the line of play. No tricks. No blind shots. Everything in full view. Is this James Braid's finest inland course? I'm not sure. I like to think of it as one of the "Four Bs"—the Braid quartet of Belleisle, Blairgowrie, Boat of Garten, and Irvine's Bogside. The setting of each course is different. Each is a gem.

Nongolf notes and lodging - Ayr: For those of literary bent, Ayr is the center of the Robert Burns industry in Scotland. That fact cannot escape when you are there. It's "Burns this and Burns that." Beneath the hype is the reality of Burns's primary place in Scottish cultural history. Burns enshrined the Lowland Scots dialect. He celebrated common people. He preserved and lyricised Scottish folk music. For all these reasons, "Robbie Burns" became and remains a national folk hero. His birthplace is an informative museum on Alloway's main street and is well worth a visit. On a broader scale, you can follow the "Burns Trail" through the villages and countryside of Ayrshire.

The Robert Burns Museum and birthplace on Alloway's main street are well worth a visit.

On and around the A719 in Alloway and South Ayr, between Belleisle and town center, you'll find a host of excellent small hotels, including *Fairfield House, Chestnuts Hotel,* and *Ivy House.* B & Bs and guest houses are listed by star-quality at ***www.ayrshirescotland.com***. Out in the countryside, at the village of Dunure, consider *Dunduff Farm* (Mrs. Agnes Gemmell, 01292-500-225; ***www.gemmelldunduff.co.uk***), a comfortable farmhouse set on a 650-acre estate.

3. Blairgowrie Golf Club (1889) - Rosemount

Region #: 7   **Category:** heathland
Architect(s): Tom Morris, Alister MacKenzie, James Braid
Length: 6229   **SSS:** 72   **Par:** 70

Address: Golf Course Rd, Rosemount, Blairgowrie PH10 6LG
Directions: A923 from Perth, turn rt at Rosemount sign; from A9, to Dunkeld and 1 mi S of Blairgowrie

Reservations phone: 01250-872-622   **Fax:** 01250-875-451
Email: admin@theblairgowriegolfclub.co.uk
Website: theblairgowriegolfclub.co.uk
Booking Contact(s): Melanie Collins

Mging Secretary: David Swarbrick   **Professional:** Charles Dernie
Phone - Starter/Pro shop: 01250-872-594/873-116
Fee(s) (2005): April & Oct £35, day tkt w/ Landsdowne £55; May-Sept £60, day tkt w/ Landsdowne £80
Deposit (2005): £10   **Buggies:** 8 - general hire
Visitor Policies: all wk; Wed, Fri, Sat frequent club competitions; hdcps - men 28, women 36
Other: Landsdowne companion course; caddies available

Carved out of a mature forest, each hole at Blairgowrie is lined with silver birch and pine, trimmed by borders of gorse, heather, and broom. It's always beautiful, but especially so in late May and early June. What I remember most about playing golf at Blairgowrie is the springy turf and the peaceful quiet of the forest. There's a peace here both auditory and visual—no housing developments, no golf carts—just you, your companions, and the forest. Even when the course is entirely filled, it can seem you are alone with the golf and the forest. The opening hole, "Black Tree," sets the tone: it's a long

> *There's a peace here both auditory and visual—no housing developments, no golf carts—just you, your companions, and the forest.*

par 4 requiring two powerful shots to a large, accepting green. Lots of bunkers, expertly placed by Alister MacKenzie and James Braid (at different times), add challenge and define the greens. A straight shooter can score well here. If you spray the ball, you're in for a long day and a lot of lost balls. The one-shotters are among the finest you will see anywhere.

TRAVEL TIP

Blairgowrie is a logical stopover for those making the scenic drive down the A93 from Aberdeen to Perth. A good three-star hostelry near the course is the *Rosemount Golf Hotel* (01250-872-604; www.rosemountgolf.co.uk).

A note on the Landsdowne course: the companion course to the Rosemount is not so highly regarded as the main attraction. But, at 6500+ yards, with narrow fairways and challenging greens, this was far more than a "relief course" designed by Peter Alliss and Dave Thomas during the 1970s. Recent changes to several holes have addressed perceived design flaws. A day ticket will get you on both courses for a reasonable fee. If you're up to thirty-six, I recommend this approach when the days are long and you can enjoy a respite between rounds. And, in the wake of an expensive renovation and expansion to the clubhouse carried out in 2004, that respite can take place in one of Scotland's finest golf properties. Blairgowrie is overlooked by too many visiting golfers.

4. Boat of Garten Golf and Tennis Club (1898)

Region #: 5   **Category:** heathland
Architect(s): James Braid (1931-2)
Length: 5650-5866   **SSS:** 69   **Par:** 69

Address: Boat of Garten, Nethybridge Rd, Inverness-Shire PH24 3BQ
Directions: 5 mi N of Aviemore, 2 mi E of A9; through town, turn left at Boat Hotel, then next rt

Reservations phone: 01479-831-282   **Fax:** 01479-831-523
Email: boatgolf@enterprise.net
Website: boatgolf.com
Booking Contact(s): Heather Bantick

Secretary: Paddy Smyth   **Professional:** none
Phone - Starter/Pro shop: 01479-831-282, shop mgr James R Ingram
Fee(s) (2005): wkday £30, day tkt £40; wkend £35, day tkt £45
Deposit (2005): £10   **Buggies:** 2 - general hire

Visitor Policies: all week; wkend between 10-4; no 4-ball on wkend
Other: 36-hole open championship 1st Sat in Aug (hdcp max - 14); deposit refundable if cancellation is 30+ days before play; participant in Drambuie Speyside Golf Classic late Sept

For me, the Boat of Garten brings to mind the old Sara Lee slogan: "Nobody doesn't like Sara Lee." A double negative equals a positive. There's nothing you won't like about "the Boat." Incidentally, the unusual name comes from Garten's history: the golf course sits above the place where in times past a boat ferried people, carts, and livestock across the River Spey. This is one of my favorite courses in all of Scotland.

Garten exemplifies two aspects of Scottish golf. First, this is a fine example of James Braid's approach to golf course design. Here you can see clearly how Braid used bunkers to indicate a preferred line of play. You can see how he so cleverly and sensitively routed holes through natural landscape to achieve changes of direction, visual appeal, and challenging golf. There's also a rhythm to this course in the sequence of the holes that, in no small measure, is due to Braid's genius. Second, the Boat of Garten is a case study in how a course can be short yet still challenging. Many moderns look at the yardage on a course like this and say something like, "It's only 5866 yards from the back tees. How can that be considered a real golf course?". But then you look at the details and realize there's only one par 5, most of the par 4s are long and difficult, and par is 69. This is not an easy course.

This is my idea of great golf (and life) in the Highlands . . . A little piece of paradise on Earth.

Some specifics: The course increases in difficulty as the round progresses. An opening one-shotter, unlike the rest of the course, plays over flat ground. From there, shots across banks of heather and shots from elevated tees to mogul-filled fairways and elevated greens give the feel of a hilly links course set in a stunning Highland forest. After a relatively easy go of it on the outward nine ("Avenues," #6, is a major exception), you encounter the inward nine featuring several doglegged par 4s where hitting a green in regulation can be accomplished only with two long, perfect shots (e.g., "Tulloch," #13, 422 yards, uphill, dogleg right). The locally-famous "Gully" (#15) requires a mid-iron tee shot to a plateau overlooking a gully, leaving 150 yards to a small green on the other side. To finish the challenge, "Road" (#18) is a punishing 426-yarder to an elevated green. Good luck. It's great fun.

Now for the rest of the Boat story: this is my idea of great golf (and life) in the Highlands. It's in a small town with a good hotel, a steam railway for atmosphere, and an incomparable natural setting in the beautiful Spey Valley.

It's reasonably priced, visitors are welcome all week, and the clubhouse and staff are unpretentious and welcoming. I can go to the Boat for a round of golf in the morning, have lunch in the attractive bar of the Boat Hotel (01479-831-258; *www.boathotel.co.uk*), then in the afternoon go for a hike with my wife in the nearby Abernethy Forest. It's a little piece of paradise on Earth.

Speyside and lodging: Boat of Garten is only one of many villages and towns within the greater Spey Valley, one of Scotland's great recreation areas for both warm-weather and cold-weather sports. Fishing, cycling, golf, hiking, skiing—you name it, it's all here. For the more sedate, "Speyside" is also a Mecca for birdwatching (Boat of Garten calls itself "The Osprey Village"). Finally, let us note, this is the region offering Scotland's most extensive network of whisky distilleries. The heart of Speyside is Grantown-on-Spey. Dufftown is the locus of the whisky trade. Aviemore is the ski town and one terminus of the steam railway. Just twenty-five minutes from Inverness, any of these locations makes a good base for Highland fun. First-rate lodgings throughout the area can be viewed at the excellent websites *www.boatofgarten.com* and *www.grantown.co.uk*.

5. Brora Golf Club (1891)

Region #: 5   **Category:** seaside links
Architect(s): John Sutherland (1891); James Braid (1924)
Length: 5854-6110   **SSS:** 70   **Par:** 69

Address: Golf Rd, Brora, Sutherland KW9 6QS
Directions: 5 mi N of Golspie on A9; 1st rt after bridge in village center

Reservations phone: 01408-621-417   **Fax:** 01408-622-157
Email: secretary@broragolf.co.uk
Website: broragolf.co.uk
Booking Contact(s): secretary

Secretary: Tony Gill   **Professional:** none
Fee(s) (2005): wkday £30, day tkt £35; wkend £35, day tkt £40
Deposit (2005): none
Visitor Policies: any time   **Buggies:** 2 - general hire

Brora is the northernmost course most golfers play when staying for several days in the Inverness-Dornoch area. This is as pure a seaside links as Scotland offers—nine holes out and nine holes back over rolling topography similar to that at St. Andrews and North Berwick rather than the dune-dominant terrain of

Cruden Bay or Royal Aberdeen. Add to that the genius of James Braid who came here in 1924 to re-work and extend a course already touched by Tom Morris of St. Andrews and John Sutherland of Dornoch. Finally, among Scotland's most famous courses, there is a pastoral quality unique to Brora: due to ancient grazing rights maintained to this day, this is the course memorable for its electric fences protecting the greens from wandering cattle and sheep, as well as the local rules that treat cow pies as "casual water." Brora is rural Scottish golf at its best.

As for individual holes, it's the usual Braidian stew—short, but challenging, and great fun. The Great One gives us par 3s pointing to all sides of the compass; only one par 5; and the usual "monster" two-shotters (five at 400+ yards). If you're a fan of courses by James Braid (count me in), you'll love this one. Another of those fans, golf writer Jim Finegan, cites Brora "among my dozen favorite seaside courses in Scotland . . . as fine an example of Braid's work at the sea as we are likely to find today." Appropriately enough, Brora is home to the James Braid Society, dedicated to preserving the memory and spirit of James Braid, especially, as they note in their charter, "by playing the lesser-known 'village' courses."

See also: Golspie, Royal Dornoch, Tain.

6. Carnoustie Golf Links (1842) - Championship *

Region #: 4   **Category:** seaside links - no view
Architect(s): Allan Robertson, Tom Morris, Willie Park, James Braid
Length: 6692-6941-7400   **SSS:** 74   **Par:** 70

Address: Links Parade, Carnoustie, Angus DD7 7JE
Directions: 3 blks off High St in ctr of town

Reservations phone: 01241-853-789   **Fax:** 01241-852-720
Email: info@carnoustiegolflinks.com
Website: carnoustiegolflinks.com
Booking Contact(s): Carol McKewan, Nan Hay, Kathleen Blair

Secretary: EJC Smith   **Professional:** Colin McLeod
Phone - Starter/Pro shop: reservations
Fee(s) (2005): £98 all wk; day tkt with Burnside £113; 17.5% VAT additional if booked by 3rd party (i.e., tour operators)   **Buggies:** no
Deposit (2005): 100% prepayment, non-refundable
Visitor Policies: wkdays; not Sat am or before 11:30 Sun; Carnoustie Golf Course Resort Hotel preference hrs: M-F 9-9:50; 1:30-2:20; Sat 2-2:50; Sun 11:30-12:20

Other: fairway mats in use mid November - April; course closed to visitors 1st wk in Sept for annual "Tassie" tournament; hdcps - men 28, women 36; participant in Carnoustie Country Dream Ticket and Carnoustie Country Classic mid-May; will host British Open in 2007

DRIVE TIME

St. Andrews: 40 min

Aberdeen: 2 hrs

Glasgow Airport: 2 hrs, 30 min

Visitors to Scotland usually mention Carnoustie somewhere in the same breath as St. Andrews' Old Course, Royal Troon, Turnberry, and Muirfield— the famous courses on the "rota" of the British Open. Particularly since the return of the Open to Carnoustie's hallowed ground in 1999, the Championship Course has risen in stature. Golfers want to play this course. They've heard about the legendary difficulty of Carnoustie. And, in 1999, they were able to watch on television as professionals flailed away in knee-high rough and as Jean Van de Velde imploded on the "Home" hole with the claret jug all but inscribed with his name. For years into the future, Carnoustie will see golfers taking photographs down in the Barry Burn and measuring their success on the infamous eighteenth against Van de Velde's brilliant flameout. After a period of relative decline since the Open was held here in 1975, Carnoustie has re-emerged as a place where golf history is made. Now the Open is scheduled to return to Carnoustie in 2007 and we anticipate a new chapter in Carnoustie's love affair with golf.

Among the Open rota courses, there is probably more misinformation about Carnoustie than all the others combined. What about Carnoustie's legendary level of difficulty? First, even more than most, this course is made difficult primarily by the vagaries of wind and weather. This part of the Angus coast does not get the "micro-climate" benefits of St. Andrews and North Berwick. Nasty weather just seems to cling to Carnoustie like a wet blanket. Second, you'll be playing off the visitor tees at around 6600 yards. That's not exactly a stroll in the park, but neither is it the "Tiger" championship tees that stretch to 7400 yards. To be sure, over 110 bunkers, punishing rough, and plenty of gorse, not to mention Jockie's Burn and Barry Burn, await the mis-hit ball. This course is no pushover under any conditions. But in fine weather, it's not the monster it's made out to be.

Many times I've heard Carnoustie called "boring," "a wasteland," "uninteresting." I would characterize those comments as hasty if not dead wrong. It's true that most of Carnoustie's middle fourteen holes are relatively flat. But a course cannot be labeled boring if it boasts at least a half dozen superb golf holes, flat or otherwise. And, in that category, I would put Carnoustie's #1 "Cup" hole at the top of my list of the Best Holes in Scottish Golf. It's a complete golf experience and, what's more, it's followed by another par 4, "Gulley," that would rank close to the top of that list too. To have such a strong start is unusual in

Scottish golf. And I don't think I need to say anything more about the now-famous closing holes at Carnoustie!

Now to the important part: How hard is it to get a tee time at Carnoustie? In recent years, an accommodations myth has grown up around Carnoustie—namely, that to get a tee time you have to stay at the Carnoustie Golf Course Hotel. *Not true!* Let me try to make the proverbial long story short: In 1998-9 the Angus Council put a lot of money into the big (and expensive) Carnoustie Golf Course Hotel & Spa Resort that sits behind the eighteenth green and first tee. The structure was "purpose built" to accommodate the Open in 1999 and put Carnoustie back on the map of international golf. After the Open, three to four hours of prime tee times were reserved daily for the hotel. If the times went unsold, they were to be returned to the Links Management *nine weeks prior to date of play* for release to the general public.

> **TRAVEL TIP**
> All "third parties" (i.e., tour operators) must pay a 17.5% value-added-tax on green fees at Carnoustie. Make a direct booking and save about $125 per foursome—enough to buy a nice dinner at one of Carnoustie's excellent restaurants.

Naturally, local hoteliers went ballistic. Meetings ensued. Hair was torn. Breasts were pounded. Lawsuits were threatened. But not to worry. After the Open, business returned more or less to its normal level in Carnoustie and the big hotel was left with lots of empty rooms and lots of tee times that had to be returned to the Links Management. Consequently, other hotels in town, late applicants, and freelancing golfers were able to secure tee times fairly easily.

Now the situation has improved still further—at least for golfers, if not for the hotel. Only two hours per day Monday through Friday are currently reserved for the hotel.

> *Carnoustie is the easiest "rota" ticket to get. This is essentially because visitors are welcome all week, including weekends, with only a few restrictions.*

Consequently, it is just about as easy to book Carnoustie as it was pre-1999—and that means Carnoustie is the easiest "rota" ticket to get. And this is essentially because visitors are welcome all week, including weekends, with only a few restrictions.

Nongolf notes and lodging: Carnoustie is not a particularly attractive town but, in some strange way, it grows on you. While its narrow, straight High Street is a monotonous slog of dingy buildings with little to excite, its sidestreets take you back to simpler times. As far as nongolf time goes, two days here will be plenty, though it makes a fine base for seeing the tourist sites of Angus. Scotland's fifth largest city, Dundee, is nearby and offers much to the discerning tourist (don't miss Discovery Point). And it's only a short skip to Glamis Castle, one of Scotland's major tourist attractions.

A real "birdie" for Carnoustie: there's value lodging at several mid-price hotels, including the *Carlogie House Hotel* (01241-853-185; *www.carlogie-house-hotel.com*), *Carnoustie Links Hotel* (01241-853-273; *www.links-hotel.com*), and *Lochlorian Hotel* (01241-852-182; *www.lochorian.co.uk*). *The Old Manor B & B*, operated by Margaret and Milroy Coates, (01241-854-804; *www.oldmanorcarnoustie.com*) is a fine four-star B & B with four elegant rooms and stirring views out to the sea over rich Angus farmground.

Luciano Ianetta preparing roasted red peppers in his kitchen at Ristorante Pizzeria Belmonte.

Moreover, dining in Carnoustie can be a gourmet treat. Folks come from miles around to be served by the Harris family at the *Lochlorian Hotel* in the heart of town at 13 Phillip St. A few blocks away, at *11 Park Avenue*, you'll find an award-winning restaurant of the same name (01241-853-336). Finally, at Burnside and High Street is *Ristorante Belmonte* (01241-853-261) and, I kid you not, this is one great Italian restaurant. Owner Luciano Ianetta and his wife, Maria, moved to Scotland some twenty years past and have been cooking up an Italian storm in Carnoustie ever since. Luciano works the front while Maria runs the kitchen. There's nothing pretentious or fancy here— just the freshest of ingredients cooked and presented with love and passion. Reservations recommended.

For all the foregoing reasons, I am enthusiastic about using Carnoustie as a primary base for "stay-and-play" trips. My enthusiasm has been shown already in Part II, Chapter 2, under the heading, "The Case for Carnoustie." I would reiterate here four main points: (1) Carnoustie is ideally situated for driving either north to Royal Aberdeen/Cruden Bay or south to St. Andrews; (2) lodging is cheaper than in St. Andrews; (3) Carnoustie has several restaurants as good or better than anything in St. Andrews; and (4) it's easier to get on the championship course at Carnoustie than it is to get on St. Andrews' Old Course. On top of all that, Panmure, Monifieth, and Montrose are only minutes away. In other words, the golf is just as good. As for the weather, well . . . .

See also: *Monifieth, Montrose, Panmure*

7. Craigielaw Golf Club (2001)

Region #: 3   **Category:** links with a view
Architect(s): Tom McKenzie (Donald Steel & Assocs)
Length: 6043-6601   **SSS:** 70-72   **Par:** 71

Address: Aberlady, E Lothian EH32 0PY
Directions: N side of A198, 3/4 mile W of Aberlady

Reservations phone: 01875-870-800   **Fax:** 01875-870-620
Email: info@craigielawgolfclub.com
Website: craigielawgolfclub.com
Booking Contact(s): starter - Gordon McLanachan

Club Manager: Derek Scott   **Professional:** Derek Scott
Phone - Starter/Pro shop: 1875-870-803
Fee(s) (2005): wkday £47, day tkt £70; wkend £65, no day tkt
Deposit (2005): 50%
Visitor Policies: after 9:30 am all wk   **Buggies:** 8 - general hire

If Craigielaw Golf Club had been set down somewhere in the southern United States of America, it might have been dubbed, "Y'all Come." The democratic spirit of Craigielaw is its most attractive asset. Craigielaw has combined some of the most appealing aspects of golf in America with traditional Scottish touches to create a first-rate, contemporary golf experience. So we have professional management; a grass range and practice area; a comfortable clubhouse with no "members only" areas; buggies if you want them; and, out on the course, 150-yard markers and a return to the clubhouse at the ninth hole. At the same time we are given an easily walkable course built on links grazing land framed by rock walls in the heart of Scotland's oldest stretch of golf ground—home to such leathered names as Musselburgh, Kilspindie, Longniddry, Luffness, and Gullane.

Craigielaw was founded specifically to appeal to all the women, juniors, and young men (particularly in Edinburgh) who could not breach the membership walls of all those august golf clubs mentioned above. And Craigielaw has been spectacularly successful. The membership rolls are filled to overflowing and the average age of the members is about thirty-five. Women and juniors comprise a significant share of membership and, in so many ways, the club is alive and bustling in a way that the older, nearby golf clubs simply can't imagine.

What about the golf course? It's an excellent golf course with lots of memorable holes well designed by the Donald Steel group. Craigielaw sits on high ground above a sand shelf (Kilspindie Golf Club is located directly below at water's edge). At length I could describe the merits of the opening gentle dogleg right, the daunting 424-yarder (#4) uphill into the prevailing wind, the well-bunkered par 3s, the challenging mix of par 5s exceeding 540 yards from the medal tees and, finally, the imaginative holes (#s 13 and 14) threading fairways through handsome old stone walls. It's all good stuff.

But, ultimately, the crux of Craigielaw comes down to the greens, for the greens—their sitings and severe undulations—are Craigielaw's main defense. The length of the course, even from the back tees, is not enough to deter obliteration of par by the big guys. But the greens—oh, that's another matter, for these are among the most severely undulating greens in Scotland. And, on this score, among all the courses described in this book, I see Craigielaw as most representative of a fundamental difference between modern golf course architecture and the "traditional" courses that evolved or were designed prior to 1970 (more or less).

In traditional golf course construction, the prevailing philosophy was that getting to the green should be the hard part—the golf equivalent of running the gauntlet or negotiating a mine field. Once on the green, the golfer would find a relatively flat (though perhaps huge) putting surface. This is essentially true of all the "classic" golf courses of Scotland, whether at Troon, Turnberry, Carnoustie, Aberdeen, Cruden Bay, Nairn, or St. Andrews.

At most modern courses the opposite is true: getting through the broad, manicured fairways seems the easy part; getting on and staying on the greens and getting the ball in the hole becomes the challenge. Elevated or crowned greens with sloped sidings reduce the real target area. And, once on a green, the golfer is often faced with severe undulations from all angles. At Craigielaw this description holds to such extent that some have complained about the course being "tricked up." I don't think this is quite the case. Par must be defended one way or another; this is the way they did it here.

At the same time, Craigielaw's setup does make one ponder course design. On the traditional courses of Scotland I can think of numerous short par 4s that can only be played by stroking the ball about 200 yards then playing to a well-protected green perhaps no more than 100 yards away. An easy par 4?—maybe, maybe not—but not susceptible at all to a 290-yard drive. Excepting its opening hole, most of Craigielaw lies at the mercy of the big hitter (weather permitting). Most of the action is at the green. Good design? I'm not sure. I prefer the traditional approach. But I know that Craigielaw is a good golf experience and I appreciate the club's ability to put it all together into an attractive package. So, "y'all come" to Craigielaw. It's a worthy addition to Scottish golf.

8. Crail Golfing Society (1786) - Balcomie Links

Region #: 1   **Category:** seaside links
Architect(s): Tom Morris (1895 - 9 holes, 1899 - 9 holes)
Length: 5453-5922   **SSS:** 69   **Par:** 67-69

Address: Balcomie Clubhouse, Fifeness, Crail KY10 3XN
Directions: well signposted 2 mi NE of Crail off A917

Reservations phone: 01333-450-686   **Fax:** 01333-450-416
Email: info@crailgolfingsociety.co.uk
Website: crailgolfingsociety.co.uk
Booking Contact(s): Margaret Hunter, Doreen Mayes

Secretary: David Roy   **Professional:** Graeme Lennie
Phone - Starter/Pro shop: 01333-450-278; 01333-450-960
Fee(s) (2005): £40 wkdays, £55 day tkt; £50 wkend, £63 day tkt
Deposit (2005): 50%   **Buggies:** 3 - med/phys
Visitor Policies: all wkdays; restrictions wkends - times available
Other: companion course - Craighead 6250 yds (1999) by Gil Hanse

I like to book clients at the Balcomie Links (pronounced Bal-COMB-ee) in Crail for three reasons: First, this is Fife's most scenic course. Second, at just under 6,000 yards, it's a throwback to nineteenth-century holiday golf—a shotmaker's course—that contrasts nicely with the brawnier tracks at St. Andrews and Kingsbarns. Third, a trip down the road to Crail from St. Andrews gets the traveler onto Fife's coastal route and into the pretty fishing villages of the "East Neuk" between Crail and Leven.

Crail village is ten miles south of St. Andrews. The Balcomie Links are situated another two miles along on the easternmost promontory of Fife where the shore makes its turn westward along the firth. Thus, Balcomie is not only the most scenic course in Fife, it's also the one most exposed to wind and rain from the North Sea. And, to put it mildly, this simple fact tends to have a lengthening effect on a rather short course.

Tom Morris came down here from St. Andrews to lay out nine holes for the Crail Golfing Society (Scotland's sixth oldest club) in 1895. In 1899, he came back to add another nine. This was some of Morris's last work, closing out a productive decade when, well into his seventies, he completed Muirfield, Elie, Luffness New, Scotscraig, and Tain. Balcomie's layout is odd, with the last four holes laid off on a terraced area east of the clubhouse a bit removed from the rest of the course. It's almost as if Old Tom laid out a perfect fourteen and then had to figure out how to cram another four into the picture.

The entire layout can be surveyed from high ground at Crail's simple but comfy clubhouse. The first hole, "Boathouse," plays down a slope leading to the sea for holes two through five. These latter are among the most stirring in Scottish golf and they will certainly remind one of Pebble Beach, particularly the #5 "Hell Hole," a brutal beauty playing

Crail's unusual hexagon-shaped pro shop

to 459 yards over the rocky shoreline. Holes six through fourteen play along an OB stone wall lending more atmosphere to the round. After fourteen, a hike of about two hundred yards takes you to the fifteenth tee to begin the homeward "terrace four." Throughout this layout you'll find the presence of Tom Morris in a raft of bunkers, testing par 3s, challenging greens, and one double green. In short, the Balcomie at Crail is a unique course designed by a unique individual in a unique setting—emblematic of all the reasons we go to Scotland to play golf.

LITERARY TIP

Upon leaving the #14 green, glance to the right on the hillside and you will see possible inspiration for "MacDuff's Cave," made famous in Michael Murphy's classic *Golf in the Kingdom* and Michael Konik's *In Search of Burningbush*.

Lodging - Crail and the East Neuk: For some, lodging in Crail or any of the villages in Fife's East Neuk will make an attractive alternative to busy and pricey St. Andrews. Two budget hotels for golfers are the *Balcomie Links Hotel* (01333-450-237; *www.balcomie.co.uk*) and *The Golf Hotel* (01333-450-206; *www.thegolfhotelcrail.com*). *The Hazelton* is a good B & B run by Karen and Jerry Dawe (01333-450-250; *www.thehazelton.co.uk*). Farther west along the coast at Anstruther you'll find the popular *Craw's Nest Hotel* (01333-310-691; *www.crawsnesthotel.co.uk*) and a four-star guest house, *The Spindrift* (01333-310-573; *www.thespindrift.co.uk*). For more about the East Neuk, see the website *www.eastneukwide.co.uk*.

See also: *Golf House Club (Elie), Leven Links, Lundin Links.*

9. Crieff Golf Club Ltd. (1891) - Ferntower Course

Region #: 7   **Category:** parkland
Architect(s): various, incl James Braid, Robert Simpson, John Stark
Length: 6052-6402   **SSS:** 72   **Par:** 71

Address: Perth Rd, Crieff PH7 3LR
Directions: 1 mi NE of Crieff town center on A85

Reservations phone: 01764-652-909   **Fax:** 1764-655-096
Email: davidmurchie@crieffgc.ssnet.co.uk
Website: crieffgolf.co.uk
Booking Contact(s): professional

Secretary: Scott Miller   **Professional:** David W Murchie
Phone - Starter/Pro shop: 01764-652-909
Fee(s) (2005): wkday £30, day tkt £48; wkend £40, no day tkt
Deposit (2005): none
Visitor Policies: all wk   **Buggies:** 4 - general hire
Other: nine-hole relief course, "Dornock," 4642 yds, SSS 63

DRIVE TIME
St. Andrews: 1 hr
Gleneagles: 20 min

Completed in 1980, only a few years before the PGA Centenary course at Gleneagles, neighboring Ferntower at Crieff offers golf over terrain similar to that at Gleneagles at about one-fourth the price. This is a good choice for the golfer on a budget or the golfer already familiar with Scotland's pricier tourist magnets. Replete with B & Bs, guest houses, and hotels, Crieff also is a good base for those planning to play at Gleneagles without staying there.

Directly north of Stirling, no more than an hour from the airports at Edinburgh and Glasgow, Crieff has long been a strategic crossroads on routes to and from the Highlands. The ancient feel of this attractive hill town is pervasive in its twisting streets and old stone buildings. When not on the golf course, visitors to Crieff can find historic sites, natural history at Loch Earn to the west, or the commercial history of Scotland's whisky trade at the Famous Grouse Experience (formerly the Glenturret Distillery).

The Ferntower Course plays east to west along the south-facing slope of a hill called the "Knock," a local landmark. From those heights, the golfer can enjoy superb views over the Strathearn Valley while hoping (usually in vain) for a level lie. Ferntower's three par 5s and four par 3s offer pleasing variety. Incidentally, the former pro at Crieff is John Stark, who gained a certain measure of immortality as the key figure in Michael Bamberger's delightful book, *To the Linksland*.

10. Cruden Bay Golf Club (1899)

Region #: 6   **Category:** seaside links
Architect(s): Tom Simpson
Length: 6022-6395   **SSS:** 72   **Par:** 70

Address: Aulton Rd, Cruden Bay, Peterhead AB42 0NN
Directions: 2 mi off A90 on high ground S of village

Reservations phone: 01779-812-285   **Fax:** 01779-812-945
Email: cbaygc@aol.com
Website: crudenbaygolfclub.co.uk
Booking Contact(s): administrator

Administrator: Rosemary Pittendrigh   **Professional:** Robbie Stewart
Phone - Starter/Pro shop: 01779-812-414
Fee(s) (2005): wkday £55, day tkt £75; wkend £65, no day tkt
Deposit (2005): none; 100% prepayment 30 days prior
Visitor Policies: not before 10 M, T; wkend pm only and not before 4:30 on club competition days   **Buggies:** no
Other: Closed wk of British Open for club event; visitors ok from white tees with appropriate handicap

DRIVE TIME
Aberdeen: 30 min
Nairn: 2 hrs, 15-30 min
Dornoch: 3 hrs, 30 min

Here's a measure of Cruden Bay's appeal: after my clients have finished a golf trip, I send a post-trip evaluation asking, among other items, for a ranking of courses played. In these post-trip evaluations Cruden Bay rarely ranks lower than #2. Usually it is #1—and that's compared to Carnoustie, Dornoch, Turnberry, Troon, and all the courses at St. Andrews. Pete Dye has cited Cruden Bay among his five favorite courses in the world! Readers of *Golf World,* as reported in *Best Courses in Scotland*, rank Cruden Bay sixth among Best Courses and fourth among Best Value Courses. For myself, I put Cruden Bay in my Top Five in Scotland with Machrie, Machrihanish, North Berwick, and Western Gailes (not to play favorites, in alpha order).

Many golf writers have described Cruden Bay in loving detail. Suffice to say here, the overwhelming impression made at Cruden Bay is that of a lunar landscape laid down on the gentle curve of an ocean bay. This is nothing less than pure links golf played on the wasteland between fertile soil and raging sea. The course, routed into the natural terrain by Tom Simpson (of the Carnoustie Simpsons), traces an elongated "figure-eight" from the elevated clubhouse to the equally elevated #10 tee at the far end of the course and back again. In between, it's, "Nelly, bar the door!"

Everything you want to find on a Scottish links course is here: long rough, gorse, burns, gullies, dells, dunes, blind shots, elevated tees, sunken greens, raised greens. Golf writer Jim Finegan summarizes: "One of the most awe-inspiring stretches of linksland in Scotland, indeed, in all of the British Isles." I would say Cruden Bay is simply *the* most dramatic duneland in Scottish golf. And, what's more, it's the most *fun* to play. It's so much fun, you hardly care about your score when you reach the comfortable nineteenth hole—incidentally, one of the finest in Scottish golf.

So, why isn't Cruden Bay played by more visitors? The obvious reason is that it's in the northeast corner of Scotland—not exactly the crossroads of most itineraries. At the same time, Cruden Bay has grown in stature as the golf experience there has spread by word-of-mouth from one visitor to the next. More and more golfers are making the pilgrimage to this special place.

Lodging: Cruden Bay lies about thirty miles north of Aberdeen, Scotland's third largest city, and ten miles south of Peterhead. If an urban base is the goal, one should stay in one of those cities where lodging is plentiful. For more information, see *www.agtb.org* and *www.peterhead.co.uk.* Cruden Bay, itself, is a tiny village offering few lodging options.

> *The overwhelming impression made at Cruden Bay is that of a lunar landscape laid down on the gentle curve of an ocean bay.*

Overlooking the golf course are two choices: the *St. Olaf Hotel* (01779-813-130; *www.stolafhotel.co.uk*) near the clubhouse is a family-run place with five rooms (Room #s 3 & 4 have golf course views). The *Red House Hotel* (01779-812-215; *www.redhousehotel.com*), a well-known stop for golfers, stands alongside the first fairway. At £45 per person in 2005, the Red House is a bit overpriced, but when you check into one of the rooms overlooking the golf course (Room #s 1, 2, or 5), the breathtaking view may compensate. Down in the village, under the direction of James and Shona Mutch, the *Kilmarnock Arms* has made a comeback in recent years (01779-812-213; *www.kilmarnockarms.com*). It's a gathering place for villagers when they're not at the golf course and, many years ago, this is where Bram Stoker resided while writing *Dracula*, said to be inspired by the ruins of nearby Slains Castle hovering over Cruden Bay on a promontory north of town.

11. Downfield Golf Club (1932)+

Region #: 4   **Category:** parkland
Architect(s): C K Cotton (expanded to 18 holes - 1969)
Length: 6247-6803   **SSS:** 70-73   **Par:** 70-73

Address: Turnberry Ave, Dundee DD2 3QP
Directions: NW of Dundee; Exit A923 off ring Rd; left on
Harrison Rd to T-junction; left to Turnberry Ave

Reservations phone: 01382-825-595   **Fax:** 01382-813-111
Email: teetimes@downfieldgolf.co.uk
Website: downfieldgolf.co.uk
Booking Contact(s): Margaret Stewart

Phone - Starter/Pro shop: 01382-889-246 **Professional:** Kenny Hutton
Fee(s) (2005): Apr & Oct wkday £32, day tkt £40, wkend £33; May-Sept wkday
£38, day tkt £47, wkend £40; no day tkt on wkends
Deposit (2005): £20   **Buggies:** 2 - general hire
Visitor Policies: not on Sat; Sun after 2:18 pm

Downfield is a course that visitors to Carnoustie or St. Andrews might
consider as a parkland respite from linksland golf. Situated in northwest Dundee,
midway between those two golf Meccas, the course is easily accessible in about
twenty minutes from either location.

Relatively new to Scottish golf, Downfield was designed in 1969 by C.K.
Cotton for the City of Dundee. At the time, it created a bit of a stir. Soon after its
opening, the club hosted the Scottish Open in 1972, the British PGA Match
Play Championship in 1974, and the Scottish Amateur in 1978. But, since those
halcyon years, Downfield's star has faded—not for the locals, but for the UK
golf establishment and the international visitor. Today, this condition makes it
all the easier to make a short-notice reservation or even walk on at one of
Scotland's finest inland courses.

The outstanding feature of Downfield is its forest setting with evergreen
and deciduous trees unmatched in their multifarious variety except perhaps at
Gleneagles and the Boat of Garten. The setting is usually described as "mature
woodlands," but that antiseptic description does not do justice to the beauty of
Downfield. This is rich, midland Scotland at its very best, and it's a good example
of why a parkland course should be mixed into an itinerary focused on linksland
courses. After playing golf at the links courses—never described as "pretty" or
"lush" or "graceful"—it can be a relief to visit a course where all those adjectives apply.

The irony and oddity of Downfield is that, if it's challenge you are seeking,
this is a course where you should relish playing off the yellow tees at 6250 yards

rather than the medal tees at 6800 yards. The reason: three relatively easy par 5s on the medal course become long, difficult par 4s on the shorter track. The medal par 73 (unusual in golf anywhere) is reduced to par 70 from the second tees. Fairways at #s 4, 5, 7, 15, and 16 are alleys cut through forest; landing areas are generous; and the course is always in "top nick." As golf writer Jim Finegan puts it, Downfield offers "good, honest golf . . . in an exquisite parkland setting, but it is no occasion for hat tossing and dancing in the streets." Well, yes, that's about right: Downfield may not be the highlight of your trip to Scotland. But it can be a welcome break from the links, and it's a lot less expensive than Gleneagles.

> *Downfield may not be the highlight of your trip . . . but it can be a welcome break from the links and it's a lot less expensive than Gleneagles.*

Nongolf notes: Dundee is Scotland's fourth largest city. Approaching from Fife, its setting is dramatic—on a high hill tumbling down to the Firth of Tay. In days past, jute, journalism, and shipbuilding made Dundee's reputation. Today, that reputation is associated with high unemployment and related maladies of the modern economy. Dundee has become the place where most visitors take a right turn at the north end of the Tay Bridge to get from St. Andrews to Carnoustie. Near that bridge is anchored Dundee's highest-profile tourist attraction. For a memorable experience, take a left (instead of a right) along the waterfront and you'll find Captain Robert Scott's vessel of Antarctic exploration, *The Discovery.* This ship is now a remarkable museum. It will leave you in awe of the indomitable spirit of the Scots. An audio-visual introduction precedes a tour of the ship. *The Discovery* is a useful reminder that the Scots were a seafaring people who built great ships and were willing to go places others feared to tread (or sail). This is one of the best nongolf expeditions I can recommend and its 5-star rating from VisitScotland corroborates my experience.

12. Duff House Royal Golf Club (1909)

Region #: 6   **Category:** parkland
Architect(s): James Braid (1910), Alister MacKenzie (1923)
Length: 5991-6161   **SSS:** 69-70   **Par:** 68

Address: The Barnyards, Duff House, Banff AB45 35X
Directions: 1 mi S of Banff on A98

Reservations phone: 01261-812-062   **Fax:** 01261-812-224
Email: duff_house_royal@bt.internet.com
Website: theduffhouseroyalgolfclub.co.uk
Booking Contact(s): Mrs. Janice Corbett

Secretary: Hamish Liebnitz   **Professional:** R S Strachan
Phone - Starter/Pro shop: reservations
Fee(s) (2005): wkday £25, day tkt 31; wkend £32, day tkt £37
Deposit (2005): £10   **Buggies:** 2 - med/phys
Visitor Policies: wkdays after 9:30; wkend after 11 am

Golf at Banff has a long history but, to make the proverbial long story short, Duff House has been part of that history only since 1910 when Alexander Duff, Duke of Fife, donated his parkland estate to the twin towns of Banff and Macduff. Prior to this magnanimous gift to Scottish golf, the game had been played on nine holes on linksland near the Moray Firth. Coincidentally, the duke was married to the daughter of the Prince of Wales, Princess Louise, who eventually became patroness at Duff House and secured the "Royal" appellation for the club.

To put an even finer point on the pedigree of Duff House Royal, the course we play today actually dates from 1923-5 when Alister MacKenzie was engaged by the club to give them a course worthy of the royal designation. As a last gesture before his relocation to America, where he created Augusta National, that's exactly what the master of wartime camouflage and great golf courses did. And, because Scotland boasts so few MacKenzie courses, Duff House Royal must be included in a selective directory of this sort.

Though not far from seaside, MacKenzie worked with flood plain parkland turf fronting the River Deveron. Here he created a challenging venue featuring huge, double-tiered greens protected by dozens of bunkers. Deceptively short at 6161 yards, the course has only one par 5, leaving us at par 68 against an SSS of 70. This kind of profile promises a collection of monster par 4s—a promise kept on the road home as we encounter #14 (434 yards), #15 (468 yards), and #17 (462 yards). Yes, I skipped #16: that's a 242-yard one-shotter reachable only by the power hitter. The eighteenth home hole will feel like sweet relief after playing this stretch of closing holes among the most punishing in Scottish golf.

Nongolf notes: For those traversing northeast Scotland's "Coastal Trail," Duff House Royal is situated about twenty-six miles west of Fraserburgh. It's just off the A98 where that highway returns to the coast at Banff-Macduff after an inland bend. Given some time and inclination, this is an area to savor and explore. For example, one can combine a day of golf with art at Duff House itself. The Georgian mansion designed by William Adam is now managed by Historic Scotland and is part of the National Gallery's network of "Country House Galleries" (*see **www.nationalgalleries.org***).

The inland attraction of the northeast corner of Scotland is the "Castle Trail." The seaside attraction is the collection of small fishing villages that dot the coastline. One of these is Pennan, twelve miles east of Banff-Macduff on the B9031. I mention this tiny village because scenes in a feature film, "Local Hero," starring Burt Lancaster were shot here. This is a movie I recommend to all travelers to Scotland. Written and directed by a Scot, Bill Forsyth, it captures a part of the spirit of Scotland without any of the usual clichés. It's a movie about North Sea oil and the transformation of a small village or, more precisely, how a small village manages to retain its character in the

> **When in Scotland, SLOW DOWN and enjoy the gift of life.**

face of "modernization." In the opening scenes of the movie, two American oil executives—buttoned-down, intense, and efficient—arrive in the small town to "make a deal" and get out as quickly as possible. By the end of the movie these fellows have shed their shirts and ties and are lazing about on the sand with an old beachcomber. I hope this is something like what happens to you on your trip to Scotland. The message: when in Scotland, SLOW DOWN and enjoy the gift of life.

See also: Moray Old.

The Duke's Course: *See St. Andrews - Old Course Hotel - Duke's Course*

13. Dunbar Golf Club (1856) +

Region #: 3   **Category:** seaside links
Architect(s): Tom Morris (1856)
Length: 6200-6426   **SSS:** 71   **Par:** 71

Address: East Links, Dunbar EH42 1LT
Directions: SE of town ctr off A1087

Reservations phone: 01368-862-317   **Fax:** 01368-865-202
Email: secretary@dunbar-golfclub.co.uk
Website: dunbar-golfclub.co.uk
Booking Contact(s): Shirley Fairbairn, Liz Thom

Secretary: Liz Thom   **Professional:** J Montgomery
Phone - Starter/Pro shop: 01368-862-086
Fee(s) (2005): wkday £43, day tkt £58; wkend £53, day tkt £75
Deposit (2005): £10
Visitor Policies: after 9:30 except Th   **Buggies:** 2 - med or phys

About twenty minutes southeast of North Berwick, just off the A1, at the attractive port/resort of Dunbar, golfers will find a classic links where the game has been played since at least the early seventeenth century. It's another course where the long hand of Tom Morris remains; the course has hardly changed since Morris laid out fifteen holes here in 1856. In 1880 three additional holes (the opening holes) were added to bring the course to the number made standard by that time.

You'll have no trouble recognizing the non-Morris three, for they have little to do with the rest of the course. Unusual in Scottish golf—or golf anywhere for that matter—the first two holes are par 5s. The first hole shoots straight away from the clubhouse and the second, like a boomerang, returns to place. Then #3, a par 3, makes a ninety-degree turn, heading straight to the ocean. After this quirky start, dictated by available land, the Morris holes proceed along a narrow strip of linksland, out and back, in classic fashion. Along the way exhilarating ocean views and a series of excellent golf holes are highlighted by a stone wall on the right side of the outgoing holes. This is no course for a slicer, for, once free of the outgoing stone, you'll have the ocean to deal with coming home. Back at the clubhouse you'll find no warmer welcome in Scottish golf. This is a down-to-earth golf experience—easily in my Top Ten list. And it will be abundantly clear why Dunbar is used as a qualifying course when the British Open is held at Muirfield.

> **TRAVEL TIP**
>
> Locals pronounce their town with the accent on the last syllable (i.e., Dun-BAR). Same with Inver-NESS, Aber-DEEN, and Dum-FRIES. On the other hand, it's LUFF-ness, so you never know.

Anyone interested in an additional eighteen holes will find the short but intriguing Winterfield golf course on the opposite (northeast) end of town. This course features a bundle of wild and woolly one-shotters (the first hole across a vast, grass gully is worth the price of admission), played first on the bluffs above the ocean, then out on a promontory fully exposed to the forces of nature. I know of only one other course in Scotland quite like this one and that is the promontory layout at Fortrose. Great stuff.

The town: Dunbar has always occupied a strategic position relative to England, so you'll see here a collection of castle ruins and historic buildings. Of greatest interest to many Americans is the birthplace of John Muir, the most influential conservationist of our nineteenth century and fountainhead of America's system of national parks. The John Muir Country Park is located outside Dunbar and his birthplace, now an excellent museum, is in the middle of town on the main street.

14. Edzell Golf Club (1895)

Region #: 4   **Category:** parkland
Architect(s): Bob Simpson
Length: 6042-6299   **SSS:** 71   **Par:** 69-71

Address: High St, Edzell, Angus DD9 7TF
Directions: 4 mi W of A90 on B966; left just past Edzell archway

Reservations phone: 01356-647-283   **Fax:** 01356-648-094
Email: secretary@edzellgolfclub.net
Website: edzellgolfclub.net
Key Contact(s): secretary

Secretary: Ian Farquhar   **Professional:** Alistair J Webster
Phone - Starter/Pro shop: 01356-648-462
Fee(s) (2005): wkday £28, day tkt £38; wkend £34, day tkt £48
Deposit (2005): £5
Visitor Policies: all wk, call on wkend   **Buggies:** 4 - general hire
Other: 9-hole relief "West Water" course, par 32, 2057 yds

For golfers in transit from north to south or visa versa, Edzell Golf Club is an elegant way to break up the drive. For 36-holers staying in Angus, this is a highly-regarded parkland course to pair with one of the historic seaside courses. Still another way to enjoy Edzell is to combine golf with a drive up Glen Esk on a narrow road that crosses the B966 about a mile north of Edzell. A twelve-mile jaunt on this road, through a broad, verdant glen, leads to the Glenesk Folk Museum, castle ruins, and abbey ruins on the rim of Loch Lee. A great place for a picnic! Back in Edzell are more castle ruins and gardens. Lots of fishing, hiking, and hunting in this area too. In short, Edzell is a good example of how a savvy traveler can combine golf

> **TRAVEL TIP**
> To see Scotland's most dramatic scenery, drive "the glens." Near Inverness try Glen Affric. At Ballater there's Glen Muick. In the south drive the "Waters of Moffat" (A708).

with excursions into the Scottish countryside in a way that will never show up on the typical tour. As for the golf, it's a challenge on a course planned by Bob Simpson of Carnoustie. Relatively flat and compact, Edzell is easy to walk despite its location at the foot of hills that rise to 1,000 feet. Pleasant views abound. The River West Walter plays a role here and out-of-bounds is a constant factor—in the case of #15, on both sides of a tight fairway. This one's a *real* hidden gem.

Elie - See: Golf House Club at Elie

15. Fortrose and Rosemarkie (1892)

Region #: 5   **Category:** seaside links
Architect(s): James Braid
Length: 5555-5890   **SSS:** 69   **Par:** 71

Address: Ness Rd East, Fortrose, Ross-Shire IV10 8SE
Directions: 12 mi N of Inverness; A832 at Tore roundabout;
rt at Fortrose police station, follow signs

Reservations phone: 01381-620-529   **Fax:** 01381-621-328
Email: secretary@fortrosegolfclub.co.uk
Website: fortrosegolfclub.co.uk
Booking Contact(s): secretary

Secretary: Michael MacDonald   **Professional:** none
Phone - Starter/Pro shop: 01381-620-733
Fee(s) (2005): wkday £30, day tkt £40; wkend £35, day tkt £45
Deposit (2005): no
Visitor Policies: all wk   **Buggies:** 3 - general hire

Golfers based in or near Inverness have their sights set clearly on Royal Dornoch, Nairn, and Tain—in about that order. Once those are played, this is a good course to squeeze into the itinerary, maybe on a quick morning or afternoon round but, better yet, on a day outing to the "Black Isle" (actually a peninsula) just a few miles northeast of Inverness. Incidentally, if lodging in a small town away from Inverness appeals, Fortrose is a good choice.

Fortrose and Rosemarkie is another James Braid design extended in 1935 from nine holes existing since the golf club was organized in 1888. At only 5555 yards from the visitor tees, with an SSS of 69, the course may remind one of the short but difficult track designed by Braid at Boat of Garten. But the setting here is dramatically different: the golf course is crammed into a promontory (Chanory Point) jutting into the Moray Firth. Just across the water, on another point of land, you'll see Fort George, a northern outpost of the English army (1769). These two pincerlike points of land aimed at one another form a natural harbor wall between Inverness and the sea.

Golf tour operators like to promote the "Hidden Gems" of Scotland. The trouble is, most of them are not hidden at all. Fortrose and Rosemarkie is an exception and an exceptional hidden gem. It's also one of the best bargains in Scottish golf.

16. Glasgow Golf Club (1892) - Glasgow Gailes +

Region #: 2   **Category:** seaside links - no view
Architect(s): Willie Park, Jr. (1892)
Length: 6323-6539   **SSS:** 70-72   **Par:** 71

Address: Glasgow Golf Club, Killermont,
Bearsden G61 2TW (Glasgow)
Directions: 2 mi S of Irvine off A737; 4 mi N of Troon town center

Reservations phone: 0141-942-2011   **Fax:** 0141-942-0770
Email: secretary@glasgowgailes-golf.com
Website: glasgowgailes-golf.com
Booking Contact(s): Margaret Stygal, Mary Syme

Secretary: David Deas   **Professional:** J Steven
Phone - Starter/Pro shop: 01294-311-561
Fee(s) (2005): wkday £55, day tkt £70; wkend £60, no day tkt
Deposit (2005): £15   **Buggies:** 3 - general hire
Visitor Policies: after 10:30 and 2 pm; wkend after 2:30
Other: reservations at Glasgow office; white tees for hdcp 6 and below; participant in Ayrshire Open Qualifier discount program

Glasgow Gailes is among the "dazzling dozen" that line the Ayrshire coast from West Kilbride to Turnberry. A common thread among them is the coastal railway that made the courses easily accessible to residents of Glasgow in the late nineteenth century. The Glasgow Golf Club opened its course at Gailes in 1892 to relieve member pressure on its home course at Alexandra Park in Glasgow. Willie Park, Jr., was asked to design the course and he did a magnificent job of it.

TRAVEL TIP
Directly east of Glasgow Gailes and adjacent to American Golf, find the North Gailes Country Club for a lighted range, two 9-holers, and spa facilities.

Western Gailes is situated on the west side of the rail line between the railway and the sea. Glasgow Gailes lies away from the water, on the east side of the line and a little to the north across a service road. In 2004 Glasgow Gailes was joined on the east side of the rail line by the private, Loch-Lomond-owned Dundonald, designed by Kyle Phillips (of Kingsbarns fame). The two easterly courses are on relatively flatter ground, without Western's seaside dunes and sea views.

The courses at Gailes will not likely supplant the royal triumvirate of Turnberry, Troon, and Prestwick on the golf traveler's list of priorities any time soon. But, for those who have extra time to give to the Ayrshire coast, this is the place to go. Western Gailes certainly has gained in international notoriety, having appeared on many "Best of Scotland" lists. Glasgow Gailes is in that middle ground of Scottish courses with places like Blairgowrie, Boat of Garten, and Irvine that deserve more attention than they get from visitors.

My recommendation: If you are up to thirty-six holes, make a day of it at Gailes. I particularly like the combination of Western and Glasgow, not only for the proximity of the courses, but for the variety they offer in such proximity. Playing Glasgow Gailes is a little like relaxing with Debussy after struggling through the Wagnerian experience offered across the road at

The classic red stone clubhouse at Glasgow Gailes

Western Gailes. Another special attraction of a day at Gailes: the clubhouses are handsome and warmly welcoming, with particularly fine views from the elevated lounge at Western. The Glasgow clubhouse is a classic.

See also: Western Gailes

17. The Glen (1906) - (North Berwick East Links)

Region #: 3   **Category:** seaside links
Architect(s): James Braid (1906), Philip Mackenzie Ross
Length: 5791-6043   **SSS:** 68   **Par:** 69

Address: East Links, Tantallon Terrace, N Berwick EH39 4LE
Directions: E of town center off Beach Rd

Reservations phone: 01620-892-726   **Fax:** 01620-895-447
Email: secretary@glengolfclub.co.uk
Website: glengolfclub.co.uk
Booking Contact(s): Rita Wilson

Administrator: Kevin Fish   **Professional:** none
Phone - Starter/Pro shop: 01620-894-596
Fee(s) (2005): wkday £32, day tkt £42; wkend £44, day tkt 54
Deposit (2005): £15
Visitor Policies: all wk 9:30-noon and after 1 pm; Sat after 2 pm; Sun 9:30-11 and after 2:30 pm

Among the most scenic courses in Scotland, this track on the opposite end of town from the historic "West Links," is worth a visit either in its own right or paired with the West Links on a day of 36-hole golf.

On a crisp fall day alternating between sunshine and a Lothian burst of showers, I played a round of golf at The Glen with then Club Captain John Wellwood. Briefly stated, I have never played a more enjoyable eighteen holes in Scotland. The reasons? Apart from the presence of good company, first, The Glen is a course that can be fully enjoyed by the average golfer. The mid-to-high-handicapper can play this course without feeling like a lightweight boxer thrown into the ring with a heavyweight. Though you'll find plenty of challenge here, no great banks of gorse or heather lie in wait to swallow up errant balls. Second, even if you're not playing well you'll still enjoy panoramic ocean views encompassing the coastal south, monumental Bass Rock, and The Kingdom of Fife to the north.

When not admiring the scenery, you'll find a collection of memorable golf holes—all consistently good, some outstanding. In the latter category, I would include all the one-shotters, particularly the signature #13, a 144-yarder where a blind shot leads to a green set in a hollow (with beach to the right) in a gully some one hundred feet below the level of the teeing ground.

The Glen's well-worn starter box and shop. May it stand forever as a monument to the simple side of golf in Scotland.

Number fourteen, at 370 yards, requires a solid drive across the aforementioned gully to achieve position for a clear second shot to a small green. Back to the beginning (and the end), the par 4 #1 hole ("The Haugh") plays straight out about 220 yards, then up a steep hill to a blind green. Number eighteen ("Jacob's Ladder") traverses the same ground in the opposite direction, plunging from the hilltop to a broad fairway and a narrow, deep green at the home hole.

Back at the old whitewashed clubhouse you'll receive a warm welcome in simple surroundings—at least for a little while longer. With their centenary celebration approaching in 2006, the folks at The Glen are celebrating in style with a spiffy new clubhouse setting the members back some £1.5 million. It will be a beauty, with wraparound glass on a second story dining and bar area looking out to golf course and sea. Visitors may see rates creep from the bargain range into the middle range of Scottish golf, but that's ok—The Glen is worth it.

See also: North Berwick - West Links.

The Courses at Gleneagles

18. King's Course   **19. Queen's Course**

20. PGA Centenary Course (formerly Monarch's)

Region #: 6   **Category:** parkland
Architect(s): James Braid, C.K. Hutchinson (King's, Queen's);
Jack Nicklaus (PGA Centenary)
Length: King's 6125-6790; Queen's 5660-5965; Centenary 5605-7081
SSS: King's 73; Queen's 70; Centenary 71-73
Par: King's 68-70; Queen's 68; Centenary 72

Address: Auchterarder PH3 1NF
Directions: well signposted 3 mi S of Auchterarder off A9

Reservations phone: 01764-694-469   **Fax:** 01764-694-387
Email: visitor.golf@gleneagles.com
Website: gleneagles.com

Professional: Russell Smith
Phone - Starter/Pro shop: 01764-694-362
Fee(s) (2005): Apr & Oct hotel guest £75, visitor £95; May-Sept hotel guest £90,
visitor £110; 3-5 p.m. £55 & £70, after 5 p.m. £40
Deposit (2005): hotel residents - none; visitors 100% prepay
Visitor Policies: 14-day cancellation ok
Buggies: Centenary - plenty; med/phys on
King's, Queen's with driver-caddie
Other: Scottish PGA annually early July on
Centenary; will host Ryder Cup 2014; Gleneagles
pays tour operators 15% on bookings

DRIVE TIME
St. Andrews: 1 hr, 15 min
Glasgow Airport: 1 hr, 30 min
Pitlochry: 50 min

Gleneagles can be described in the plainest of words: This is an international resort with three superb golf courses. But to put it that way is a little like describing the Empire State Building as a large edifice.

So, let's start over. Gleneagles is *the* finest international resort hotel in Scotland and, very likely, among the half-dozen classiest golf hotels in the world. With its amenities and grounds, Gleneagles puts Turnberry a bit in the shade. And the beauty of the place is not just in the stately granite walls of the main building or its incomparable natural setting on the edge of the Scottish Highlands. The contemporary beauty of Gleneagles lies in its relatively democratic spirit. This is a place accessible and welcoming to all—rich or not-so-rich, resident or non-resident.

As for the golf courses, it might suffice to say that the two courses by James Braid and C.K. Hutchinson (King's and Queen's) and the one course by Jack Nicklaus (PGA Centenary, formerly known as Monarch's) are at or near the top of the list of Scotland's best inland courses. But that would be putting it too plainly also—especially when golf writers have worn their thesauri thin from looking for words to describe these courses in this lovely land. In *Blasted Heaths and Blessed Greens,* Jim Finegan waxes positively rhapsodic in describing the Gleneagles courses as "no less than wonderful, a collection of arresting golf holes painted with bold brush strokes on a canvass of hills and valleys, of heather and bracken and gorse, of majestic hardwoods and equally majestic evergreens." I'll leave the Gleneagles poetry to those who have done it so well over the years. The visiting golfer will appreciate more pedestrian information from me.

First, if you are looking for traditional Scottish course design, you'll want to choose the King's Course or the Queen's (vintage1919). The King's Course features half-a-dozen par 4s in the 400+ range and par ranging from 68 to 70 depending upon the tees used. Braid offers *no* par 5s on the 6115-yard track. At 5965 yards, the Queen's Course is the shorter of the two. But don't be fooled. The course has only one par 5. The Nicklaus PGA Centenary course is about what you would expect. No matter how you cut it—despite the setting and the fact that he did a great job—it looks and feels like a modern, American course. Distances between green and tee are considerable. Five par 5s make up for their absence on the King's and Queen's. Carved fairways, bunkering, water, and undulating greens are all "Jack." So, if that's your cup of tea, then the Centenary Course should be your choice.

Second, no handicap or gender restrictions apply here. With five sets of tees on both the King's and Centenary courses, and with four on the Queen's, there's a track for golfers of every level of ability and strength. And, if you're ready for a buggy, the Nicklaus course offers carts and concrete paths (the first such in Scotland and still a bit offensive to traditionalists).

Third, though hotel guests have tee-time priority, Gleneagles is open to all. In fact, because golf holes abound, it's normally fairly easy to book a time at Gleneagles on *one* of the courses—even on short notice. And you won't be disappointed in any of the choices.

Fourth, relative bargains can be had at Gleneagles if you go at the right time or play at the right time. In April and October rates are reduced at the hotel as well as on the courses. From May through September, rates at the golf courses drop after 3 p.m. To learn more, see the hotel's exhaustive website ***www.gleneagles.com.***

21. Golf House Club at Elie (1875)

Region #: 1   **Category:** links-heathland hybrid
Architect(s): evolution w/ help from Tom Morris (4 holes - 1895/6)
Length: 6000-6273   **SSS:** 70   **Par:** 70

Address: Elie, Fife KY9 1A5
Directions: signposted near town center off A917

Reservations phone: 01333-330-301   **Fax:** 01333-330-895
Email: secretary@golfhouseclub.org
Website: golfhouseclub.org
Booking Contact(s): Moira Lawrie or secretary

Secretary: Graham Scott   **Professional:** Ian Muir
Phone - Starter/Pro shop: 01333-330-955
Fee(s) (2005): wkdays £50, day tkt £70; wkend £60, day tkt £80
Deposit (2005): 50%   **Buggies:** none
Visitor Policies: wkdays after 10 am; wkend - flexible; call

When I think of Elie, the phrase, "Sherman's March to the Sea," springs to mind. None of the typical links "out and back" along a coast line here. At Elie you start perhaps three-quarters of a mile from seaside at the clubhouse and then you *march*—albeit, to and fro—for six holes before approaching the water. Even then, it's back and forth until, finally, three exquisitely

Elie's starter house and "Excalibur," the periscope for viewing the first fairway

challenging holes present themselves for play along the rocky shore (#s 11, 12, and 13). And, yet, the sea is never out of sight. It's out there—tantalizing and omnipresent. You know you're at a seaside links, but it comes and goes like a lover pursued, then found, then lost. With the holes twisting and turning to all points of the compass, I like this layout at Elie enough to put it in my Top Twenty among links courses in Scotland. The rhythm of the course—from heathland to sea and back to heathland—is thrilling and fulfilling.

Now, if you've ever wondered where James Braid acquired his preference for the testing two-shotter, look no farther than Elie. This is where Braid was born and raised and, by no mere coincidence, the golf course here has *no* par 5s and only two par 3s! If it weren't for the imagination and variety applied to the par 4s, this could get plain boring. Elie provides the key to understanding Braid: length—incidental; tough but fair; above all, imaginative and fun.

The course at Elie is loaded with memorable features. First, there's the opening blind drive up the #1 fairway ("Stacks") over a sharp rise—but even more memorable, a periscope mounted at the starter house to view play over the rise. You'll only tee off after getting the call, "Play away!" from the starter. This periscope, vintage 1938 and called "Excalibur," came to the club in 1966 and has become a beloved landmark in Scottish golf. Next, you'll be struck by the proximity of town buildings along the fourth, fifth, and sixth fairways—among them, the Golf Tavern, once the meeting site of golf clubs, near the fourth tee. Farther along, memorable is the only way to describe Elie's three seaside holes that begin at the precipitously perched teeing grounds at #s 11 and 12 and follow the coast to "MacDuff's Cave"—a mountain cliff rising above the 190-foot-wide green at the #13 "Croupie."

Starter Ken Murray surveys the first fairway before giving the call to "play away."

In a flight of hyperbole, James Braid called this severely testing seaside two-shotter "the finest hole in all the country." And who are we to quarrel? Not done yet, you'll remember the narrow neck of land, two fairways wide, joining the four holes near the clubhouse to the twelve holes nearer the sea. No surprise, this odd feature has its history too: this was a part of the linksland contested by a landowner on one side and the town golfers on the other. It became the subject of an important legal decision adjudicated in favor of the golfers in 1822 after many years of squabbling—important because it helped establish case law supporting public access to linkslands. Finally, the newly-renovated clubhouse with its banks of plate glass windows looking out over the course will leave its impression too. In a word, *memorable*—an important word when it comes to judging golf courses.

See also: Crail, Leven Links, Lundin Links.

TRAVEL TIP

Attention, hikers! Try Elie's "Chain Walk." More a climb than a walk, this challenging hike skirts the golf course on the beach, then affords panoramic views from high ground above the course. Recommended to those of sturdy constitution.

22. Golspie Golf Club (1889)

Region #: 5   **Category:** links-parkland-heathland hybrid
Architect(s): James Braid (1905); revisions made in 1967
Length: 5677-5863   **SSS:** 68   **Par:** 68

Address: Ferry Rd, Golspie, Sutherland KW10 6ST
Directions: 10 mi N of Dornoch on the A9;
S end of town, hard rt at playing fields

Reservations phone: 01408-633-266   **Fax:** 0148-633-393
Email: secretary@golspie-golf.co.uk
Website: golspie-golf.co.uk
Booking Contact(s): Catherine McKay

Fee(s) (2005): wkday £25, day tkt £40   **Deposit (2005):** £10
Visitor Policies: all wk   **Buggies:** 2 - general hire
Other: participant in the Drambuie Highland Classic early May

Golspie lies ten miles north of Dornoch on the A9. Golf at Golspie and neighboring Brora is for travelers who have decided to spend a few days based in the Dornoch-Tain area while exploring the northern reaches of Scotland. Golspie is the least among this quartet of northern courses, yet it is a delightful track well worth playing. At 5677 yards from the visitor tees, the course is among the shortest included in this book. Yet, due to its pedigree (another James Braid design), its location, and its unique composition, Golspie deserves its place here, for this is the only Scottish course that so clearly breaks into an even six holes each of links turf, heathland, and parkland pasture. After the opening holes along the shore, you turn inland and only re-emerge at the close of the round. If your trip has included Braid's creation at Boat of Garten, Golspie's #9 ("Paradise") will remind you of the testing doglegs there. Paradise is followed by a fine par 3, "Lochy," playing across a deep hollow to a two-tiered green. Still more enjoyable golf follows in the strong closing three. Braid gave Golspie two challenging par 3s followed by the "Drum Brae" par 4 at 445 yards—a typical Braid home hole that says to the golfer, "You think this course is so easy? Try making par here."

Nongolf notes: Another reason for making the trip to Golspie is to visit Dunrobin Castle, home of the Dukes of Sutherland since at least the fourteenth century. One of Scotland's oldest, continuously-inhabited castles, Dunrobin's stately rooms and formal gardens make a great half-day diversion from golf. For information on area attractions, see *www.highlandescape. com.*

See also: Brora, Royal Dornoch, Tain.

23. Gullane Golf Club - Gullane # 1 (1882) +

Region #: 3   **Category:** seaside links
Architect(s): various
Length: 6077-6466   **SSS:** 72   **Par:** 71

Address: East Lothian EH31 2BB
Directions: W side of village on A198; highway bisects the golf courses

Reservations phone: 01620-842-255   **Fax:** 01620-842-327
Email: gullane@compuserve.com
Website: gullanegolfclub.com
Booking Contact(s): Margaret Robertson

Secretary: Nigel Watt   **Professional:** Alasdair Good
Phone - Starter/Pro shop: 01620-842-255
Fee(s) (2005): wkday £80, day tkt £100; wkend £95, no day tkt
Deposit (2005): £15   **Buggies:** 4 - med or phys only
Visitor Policies: wkday 10:32-noon and
2:30-4 pm; wkend - 7 times each day

Other: hdcp - men 24, women 30; combo tkts
with Gullane #2 & #3;

DRIVE TIME
Aberdeen: 3 hrs, 30 min
Carnoustie: 2 hrs
St. Andrews: 1 hr, 45 min
Troon: 2 hrs, 45 min

Gullane Golf Club is at the epicenter of golf along the coastline and countryside east of Edinburgh. Arguably, this swath of land called "East Lothian" offers Scotland's densest concentration of golf courses—and that's saying quite a lot. Within ten miles of Gullane village lie some twenty golf courses of varying price and quality—all good, some great. Now, with the development of a private club and courses on the Archerfield links between Muirfield and North Berwick, virtually all of the accessible coastline between Musselburgh and North Berwick is utilized for golf.

A year in the life of this rich Lothian land, with golf and Gullane at its center, is described in an evocative book *Playing Through* by Canadian writer Curtis Gillespie. And now, with the help of Mr. Gillespie, we might get to the root of one of the most burning issues in Scottish golf—i.e., Is the name of this town properly pronounced GULL-an or GILL-an? Having previously reported the pronunciation of Mrs. Sheila Montgomery, former booking secretary at Gullane ("There are no gulls in Gullane"), I have since learned that Mrs. Montgomery perhaps did not tell the whole story. As Mr. Gillespie reports, it seems the gentry who live on the hill overlooking the sea pronounce it GILL-an, while the common folk down on the flats call it GULL-an. Villagers whose Gullane ancestors extend to centuries past, often call the village by its ancient name, "GOOL-in." Mr. Gillespie suggests that, in striking up a conversation about Gullane with a local, the true diplomat will wait to hear how the local pronounces Gullane and then follow suit!

Now that we have that settled, I'd like to be able to say I favor the championship course at Gullane #1 as much as I like the town and its East Lothian surroundings—but I don't. There's no doubt that, at the seventh tee of Gullane #1, you can experience one of the most awesome panoramic views available on a Scottish golf course. To the north sits the Kingdom of Fife; off to the east lies Muirfield; and to the west, on a clear day, you can see all the way to the Forth Bridge on the west side of Edinburgh. There's also no doubt that my somewhat negative view of Gullane #1 has been influenced by the ferocious gales blowing off the North Sea whenever I've been there. I know it can't be like that all the time or no one would live in Gullane. Nevertheless, to my mind, this is the most overrated of Scotland's marquee courses.

> *I'd like to be able to say I favor the championship course at Gullane #1 as much as I like the town and its East Lothian surroundings—but I don't.*

I have my logical reasons too: First, the setting of the courses at Gullane, for all its promise near a pretty village, just past Aberlady (another pretty village), is remarkably pedestrian for its plain openness without the bracing virtue of views to the open sea. The main impediment to a sea view is Gullane hill where championship golf is played. Second, you have to climb that hill. And, rather than provide a graceful "switchback" climb of the sort found at Pitlochry, for example, the golfer is given a straight-away chute up a wind tunnel at #2 ("Windygate"), then a ski-slope ride back down to sea level at #17 ("Hilltop"). In between are fourteen holes routed around and through the crevices and flats of Gullane hill. The great views come at the aforementioned #7 "Queen's Head"—a hole that shoots practically straight downward for 400 yards. With a tailwind, a strong driver can reach the green, but I'm not sure that qualifies as great design. On the other hand, this is a tough, highly-regarded qualifying course when the Open is held at Muirfield, and golf has been played on these grounds for over three hundred years, so it can't be all bad. As I've said elsewhere, "I could be wrong. Go judge for yourself."

For the 36-holers out there, Gullane #1 is complemented by the more benign Gullane #2, a 6200-yard track that flanks #1 on the slopes of Gullane Hill and sweeps down toward Aberlady Bay before turning back toward the clubhouse. Management offers a day ticket on #s 1 and 2 for £95 weekdays and £100 weekends circa 2005. In Scottish golf these days that's a relatively good deal. There's still another eighteen-hole course to play (you guessed it, Gullane #3) and some locals think it's the most enjoyable of the trio.

Despite my personal distaste for the championship course, everything else about Gullane is great. The clubhouse, opened in 1993, is comfortable, modern, and efficiently run. Just behind the clubhouse is a nine-hole layout for kids (adults are not allowed unless accompanied by a child). The presence of this little gem serves as a reminder of how completely integral golf is to Scottish life. And near the children's nine sits the "Old Clubhouse," now a bar/restaurant not to be missed by any visitor to Gullane.

Speaking of golf, history, and culture, another not-to-miss attraction at Gullane is the small golf museum located next to the pro shop just off the first tee of the championship course. Here you can commune with the now legendary

Archie Baird, perhaps the most avid living collector and interpreter of Scottish golf history and memorabilia. But you can't just walk in on Mr. Baird. Tours of his museum are by appointment only. Phone him in advance at 01875-870-277. Make an appointment before or after your round and, if available, he'll meet you for a personalized tour. Nothing is behind glass.

Gullane's pro shop and adjacent golf museum run by Archie Baird

Archie will let you feel the weight and texture of old clubs, feathery balls, gutta percha balls, and Gene Sarazen's original sand wedge. He'll take you on a memorable tour through the history of golf.

Lodging and food in and around Gullane: Gullane village and the surrounding area are well stocked with quality lodging, including the five-star *Greywalls Country House Hotel* adjacent to Muirfield (01620-842-1444; *www.greywalls.co.uk*) and the ivy-clad *Golf Inn* on the main street (01620-843-259; *www.golfinn.co.uk*). Bargain lodging is available at two excellent B & Bs: *Faussetthill House* (01620-842-396) and *Hopefield House* (01620-842-191; *www.hopefieldhouse.co.uk*). Out in the countryside, nicely situated in Dirleton between Gullane and North Berwick, you'll find the four-star *Open Arms Hotel* (01620-850-241; *www.openarmshotel.com*). And, in nearby Aberlady, Edinburgh restaurateur, Malcolm Duck, has refurbished and reinvigorated the 17th-century vintage *Kilspindie House Hotel* (01875-870-682; *www.kilspindie.co.uk*).

Good food deserves special mention here, partly because it is unusual to have so much variety and quality in Scotland's village life. The aforementioned Kilspindie House is serving the same preparations that diners enjoy at Mr. Duck's reknowned *Le Marche Noir* in Edinburgh. At the Golf Inn, chef/owner John Burns is attracting diners from miles around with a consistently appealing menu. Across the street from the Golf Inn, *La Potiniere* (01620-843-214) thrives on the Scottish/French connection in fine cookery. Finally, the dining room at

Greywalls is open to nonresidents from 7:00 to 9:30 p.m. Add to these the ethnic and traditional restaurants in North Berwick's High Street and you have a cornucopia of quality to defy those who complain about food in Scotland.

See also: Craigielaw, Honourable Company of Edinburgh Golfers, Longniddry, Luffness New, Royal Musselburgh

The ivy-clad Golf Inn on Gullane's Main St.

24. Honourable Company of Edinburgh Golfers (1744) - at Muirfield, Gullane *

Region #: 3   **Category:** seaside links
Architect(s): Tom Morris (1891), Tom Simpson, Henry Colt
Length: 6601   **SSS:** 73   **Par:** 70

Address: Muirfield, Duncur Rd, Gullane, E Lothian EH31 2EG
Directions: through Gullane, left on Duncar Rd at edge of town

Reservations phone: 01620-842-123   **Fax:** 01620-842-977
Email: hceg@muirfield.org.uk
Website: muirfield.org.uk
Booking Contact(s): Secretary's Office/Anne McCarthy

Secretary: Alistair Brown
Fee(s) (2005): £120, day tkt £150
Deposit (2005): 100% prepayment   **Buggies:** no
Visitor Policies: Tues & Thurs, 8:30-9:50 am; four-ball and two-ball play in am; foursomes ("alternate shot") in pm; maximum of 12 in visiting groups; Mon & Fri - some times for residents of Greywalls Hotel
Other: hdcps - men 18, women 24; no cell phones on course or in clubhouse; jackets/ties in dining room; women may not lunch in clubhouse and must be accompanied by a man on the course; lunch - £20

DRIVE TIME
Aberdeen: 3 hrs, 30 min
Carnoustie: 2 hrs
St. Andrews: 1 hr, 45 min
Troon: 2 hrs, 45 min

One of the most difficult tee times to secure in Scottish golf is a tee time at The Honourable Company's course at Muirfield. This is the oldest golf club in the world (1744) and a certain exclusivity comes with the territory. Yet, to the club's credit, visitors are allowed to play at this historic course on Tuesdays and Thursdays. In addition, from April to September, about ten tee times per month for play on some Mondays and Fridays are granted to residents of Greywalls Hotel adjacent to the golf course (01620-842-1444; *www.greywalls.co.uk*). A comparison of this policy to the members-only approach at private clubs in the United States makes Scotland's most exclusive clubs look warmly welcoming.

With the coming of a new secretary in 2004, Muirfield took a giant leap into the modern age with the addition of credit-card processing and an excellent website where visitor bookings can be made online up to *fifteen months* prior to date of play (e.g., March 2005 for dates through June 2006, April 2005 for July 2006, etc.). This amounts to something like a revolution in Scottish golf.

To negotiate a tee time at Muirfield, it is important to know golf terminology as it is used in Scotland: "Four-ball" is a group of four golfers each playing their own ball. "Two-ball" is a group of two golfers each playing their own ball. "Foursomes" comprise two teams of two golfers, each team playing one ball—what Americans call "alternate shot."

TRAVEL TIP

For the surest shot at playing Muirfield, visit in March or October. Example: at this writing, fourteen of seventeen visitor times were available on both March 24 and October 25, 2005.

Here's how Muirfield works: In the morning, nine tee times are allotted for "four-ball" play off the tenth tee and eight times are allotted for "two-ball" play off the first tee. (If the four-ball times are taken, four golfers should indicate a willingness to split up into twos and apply for two of the two-ball times.) In the afternoon, after lunch in the clubhouse, all play is "foursomes" (alternate shot). You can buy either one round (a.m.) or a day ticket to include the afternoon foursomes. In either case, lunch costs an additional £20.

If you do get a tee time at Muirfield you will encounter a course quite unlike any other in Scottish golf. Though the turf is links turf and the sea is in sight, the course sits away from the sea in a vast field of billowing rough and gently rolling terrain. No strip of linksland here. Old Tom Morris had a lot of ground to work with at Muirfield. Applying his talent and imagination to that ground in 1891, Morris developed a uniquely creative layout in which the first nine, moving clockwise, encircles the second nine holes that run counter-clockwise. The result: constant shifts of direction and—unusual in links golf—a pattern that placed the #1 and #10 teeing grounds near the clubhouse. Given the relatively flat ground at Muirfield, all targets are in view. There are no blind shots. Challenge is provided by length; large, undulating greens; narrow fairways and unforgiving rough; and over 160 bunkers—most of them severely penal, with sides so steep the only play is up and out but not far forward. Most holes present at least eight bunkers for the golfer to avoid. This is by far the most heavily-bunkered course in Scottish golf.

Golfers great and not-so-great have applauded this design for over one hundred years. James Braid was so taken by the course that he gave the name Muirfield to one of his sons. This was Harry Colt's favorite course and, in the mid-1920s, he and Tom Simpson re-shaped the Morris original to achieve the course we have today. More recently, Jack Nicklaus named his most famous early project Muirfield Village. Tom Watson is another devotee of Muirfield. Among the rest of us mere mortals, when readers of the UK's *Golf World* were polled a few years back, they named Muirfield the best course in Scotland and third most difficult. One measure of the greatness of Muirfield is to note the winners of the British Open tournaments held at Muirfield since 1959. They are: Gary Player, Jack Nicklaus, Lee Trevino, Tom Watson, Nick Faldo, and Ernie Els. The British Open played here in 2002, when Tiger Woods fell away in the third round and Els triumphed in a four-way playoff, provided a level of drama only seen on the truly great courses—and, among those, Muirfield must be counted at the top rung with St. Andrews and Turnberry.

Accommodations: See *Gullane* and *North Berwick - West Links.*

25. Inverness Golf Club (1883)

Region #: 5   **Category:** parkland
Architect(s): members; bunkering by James Braid (1937)
Length: 5782-6256   **SSS:** 67-69   **Par:** 67-69

Address: The Clubhouse, Culcabock Rd, Inverness IV2 3XQ
Directions: From town center, follow B853 (Old Edinburgh Rd) to Culcabock Rd; E to clubhouse. From A9, exit B9006 (Old Perth Rd), 1.5 mi to clubhouse

Reservations phone: 01463-239-882   **Fax:** same
Email: secretary@invernessgolfclub.co.uk
Website: invernessgolfclub.co.uk
Booking Contact(s): secretary

Secretary: John Thomson   **Professional:** Alistair P Thomson
Phone - Starter/Pro shop: 01463-231-989
Fee(s) (2005): £33 all wk; day tkt £42
Deposit (2005): none   **Buggies:** no
Visitor Policies: 10-12 all wk, 2-4 M, T, W, Fri, after 10:30 Sun, call Th & Sat

DRIVE TIME 🚗

Glasgow Airport: 4 hrs

Aberdeen: 3+ hrs

Dornoch: 1 hr

St. Andrews: 3 hrs, 30 min

Let's be clear. Inverness Golf Club is a parkland course surrounded by residential Inverness. This is not the club profile most golf tourists are seeking when they go to Scotland. However, several years after having played at Inverness Golf Club, I can honestly say that at least a half dozen holes here have left a more lasting impression on my mind than any other half dozen holes in all of Scottish golf. That amounts to the strongest possible recommendation I can make for a golf course. This is simply one of Scotland's best—parkland or otherwise. My advice is to take a day's break from seaside golf and play this course. I guarantee you won't forget it.

As at Downfield in Dundee, Inverness Golf Club is tougher from the second (yellow) tees than from the back (white) tees. Two long par 4s from the yellows (#s 3 and 5) play at par 5 from the whites; yet the whites measure only thirty yards longer. This makes no sense.

That's about the only thing that makes no sense about Inverness—well, not quite. Let me set the stage: five of the holes at Inverness are on hilly land on the east side of Culcabock Road

> *A half dozen holes here have left a more lasting impression on my mind than any other half dozen holes in all of Scottish golf.*

(pronounced Cul-KAY-bock). This is an extremely busy urban thoroughfare with no walk light for the golfers! Trolley in hand, one must hope for a break in the traffic before making a mad dash for the safety of the other side. This makes no sense either. Pedestrian-controlled walk lights at that crossing would not bring the apocalypse to Inverness.

Enough with the complaining. After a placid start on Inverness's first two holes, the visitor encounters three attention-getting par 4s at 444+ yards over rather flat ground. Now the fun begins. From #6 straight through #15 we are given ten of the most consistently arresting holes in Scottish golf. Number six ("Wyvis"), at 291 yards, asks for a blind mid-iron layup before a second shot to a small, elevated green protected by a burn no more than five yards off the front of the green. Number seven ("Spion Kop") measures 169 yards to a green perched atop a steep, grassy embankment perhaps sixty feet above the level of the teeing ground. Number eight ("Meadows") is one of those short but perfect, doglegged par 4s that cannot be overwhelmed by a big hitter; instead, it requires a precise shot to the corner enabling a mid-iron second shot to a well-bunkered green. After a temporary finish on the west side of Culcabock Road at #9 and #10, we dash over to the east side for #s 11-15—five excellent holes, including two of the most difficult holes (#s 14 and 15) I have encountered anywhere in the wide world of golf.

These latter two holes deserve special attention. Number Fourteen ("Midmills"), the club's signature hole, is a diabolical par 4 dogleg right set at 435 yards from the yellow tees and 475 yards from the white tees. A huge poplar guards the right corner. A bunker guards the left corner at 220 yards. If this wicket is negotiated, the golfer faces a 200+-yard second shot to a long, narrow green through a funneling shoot bounded by OB on the right and a steep, grassy hill on the left. Making this shot with a golf club is akin to threading a needle with gloves on. A golf-ball-shooting rifle would be the better instrument. A professional golfer might make this shot, but the wise amateur will probably lay up. In this respect, Midmills has a lot in common with St. Andrews' Road Hole. It's just as tough.

Following Midmills, we come to "Curling Pond" or, to put a more American twist on the name, one might call it, "Bowling Alley." It's a 150-yard par 3 with a margin for error of perhaps fifty feet before one's ball is kicked off an embankment to OB on the right or swallowed up by bunkers and tall grass on the left side of a long, narrow green. Whew!—you should be sweating by now.

Now it's back to the west side of Culcabock Road for the closing holes featuring a 446-yard par 4 home hole sporting no less than nine bunkers! This is one that brings to mind that old saw, "It takes three good shots to get there in two." 'Nuff said; it's one of the toughest closers in Scottish golf.

If there were a beauty contest for bunkers ... the large, graceful bunkers filled with white sand at Inverness would surely win the contest.

Two other points of aesthetic interest that make Inverness such a memorable golf course: First, all but a few of the holes are thoughtfully framed by stands of pine, poplar, or tall flowering shrubs. This design element not only lends visual appeal to the course but also aids the golfer at approach. Second, if there were a beauty contest for bunkers (assuming bunkers may be thought beautiful), the large, graceful bunkers filled with white sand at Inverness would surely win the contest.

Lodging and nongolf notes: Inverness is the acknowledged capitol of the Highlands—a small city (population about 45,000) in a lovely setting. All major northern highways and rail lines converge at Inverness and it's loaded with accommodations in every price category. At last count, Inverness had more than two hundred B & Bs and at least fifty more hotels and guest houses. Tourism drives the local economy and, accordingly, lodging values abound in an atmosphere of fierce competition. Given such a plethora of accommodations, I am loathe to cite specific hostelries. Yet, as a starting point, I would mention the following where I can make a personal recommendation: at the upper end, *Culloden House* (01463-790-461; ***www.cullodenhouse.co.uk***) and the *Dunain Park Hotel* (01463-230-512; ***www.dunainparkhotel.co.uk***) are in the country on opposite sides of town. Another popular choice away from town center is *Bunchrew House* (01463-234-917; ***www.bunchrew-inverness.co.uk***). First-rate guest houses and B & Bs are *Silverwells Guest House* (01463-232-113; ***www.silverwells-inverness.co.uk***), *Moyness House* (01463-233-836; ***www.moyness.co.uk***), *Ballifeary Guest House* (01463-235-572; ***www.ballifhotel.btinternet.co.uk***), and *Lyndale Guest House* (01463-231-529; ***www.lyndale.dircon.co.uk***). All are centrally located and offer good value. An overview of Inverness lodging is at ***www.invernessaccommodationindex.co.uk***. The Inverness Bed and Breakfast Association has a website, ***www.invernessbedandbreakfast.co.uk***.

Since this is not a general travel book, I am also hesitant to open the subject of nongolf activities in this part of Scotland. Suffice to say Inverness is a logical jumping off point for compelling and uniquely Scottish tourist experiences— the beauty and mystery of Loch Ness, the Speyside whisky trail, the northern coastal fishing villages, the amazing subtropical gardens of the west coast, the barren reaches of the far north and the wild and lonely island chains of the Outer Hebrides and the Orkneys. Closer to home base, most tourists visit historic Culloden Battlefield where Bonnie Prince Charlie and Scotland's Jacobite supporters were defeated in 1746 in the last battle fought on British soil. Not far from Culloden, Cawdor Castle draws thousands of tourists annually to walk the beautiful grounds and re-visit the history and legend of MacBeth. In town, Inverness offers the best shopping and range of services to be found in the Highlands. The attractive High Street is restricted to foot traffic. There's a castle to tour on a high bluff overlooking the downtown, and the placid Ness River flows through the heart of the city on its way to the Moray Firth and the open sea. In short, Inverness is one of Scotland's enchanted places and you'll soon realize why so many people come up here to start their vacations in the country's northern Highlands.

> **TRAVEL TIP**
>
> For a scenic day trip, take the round trip train ride from Inverness to Kyle of Lochalsh on the west coast. It's two and one-half hours each way with a two-hour break in Lochalsh for lunch or sightseeing on the Isle of Skye.

 Telephone/Fax Calling Procedures

From the United States:
Dial 011 (international long distance), then 44 (country code), then the number in Scotland without the leading "0" (i.e., 011-44-1334-466-666).

26. Irvine Golf Club (1887) - "Bogside"

Region #: 2   **Category:** links - no view
Architect(s): James Braid
Length: 6408   **SSS:** 72   **Par:** 71

Address: Bogside, Irvine KA12 8SN
Directions: N of Irvine town center (A737), poorly marked road
nr Ravenspark Academy

Reservations phone: 01294-275-979   **Fax:** 1292-278-209
Email: secretary@theirvinegolfclub.co.uk
Website: theirvinegolfclub.co.uk
Booking Contact(s): secretary (a.m. only)

Secretary: WJ McMahon   **Professional:** James McKinnon
Phone - Starter/Pro shop: 01294-275-626
Fee(s) (2005): wkday £50, day tkt £60; wkend £60
Deposit (2005): £5   **Buggies:** no
Visitor Policies: M-F anytime; wkend after 3 pm
Other: participant in Ayrshire Open Qualifier Card discount program and the
Drambuie Ayrshire Classic early May

One might best think of Irvine's Bogside in league with the nearby courses at West Kilbride, Gailes, and Barassie. These courses offer alternatives to the more famous Ayrshire courses at Troon, Prestwick, and Turnberry. Understandably, most first-time visitors to the Ayrshire coast want to play the area's fabled trio. The returning veteran may well be looking for the next tier of courses and, in that tier, Bogside should be on everyone's must-play list.

At Bogside we experience another James Braid classic—perhaps most similar to Ayr's Belleisle in its expansiveness, changes of direction, and position relative to the sea (close but not at seaside). Here, Mr. Braid—Scotland's caped crusader for

BOOKING TIP
To book at Irvine, send a fax or email. The secretary works only morning hours.

the unforgiving two-shotter—showed his ultimate disdain for the stroke-saving par 5 and the pushover par 3. Bogside sports only two par 3s and one par 5. The remaining fifteen holes are two-shotters! Thus, what at first glance seems a course of average length, in typical Braidian style, turns out to be a bearcat where most golfers will not play to their handicap.

Visitors to Bogside applaud the remarkable variety of holes that Braid created on this expanse of links turf. Another striking feature: the silky-smooth, well-tended greens. This is a characteristic not only of Bogside but of all the courses along the Ayrshire coast. For whatever reason—probably the mild temperatures and wet weather—I think it's fair to say these are the best greens in all of Scotland, from West Kilbride and Irvine right on down to Turnberry and beyond.

Nongolf notes: Only twenty-six miles from Glasgow, near the mouth of the Firth of Clyde, Irvine reminds us that Scotland is a land of seafaring folk. We get that reminder at the Scottish Maritime Museum and at the impressive "Harbourside" Development, an

> *These are the best greens in all of Scotland, from West Kilbride and Irvine right on down to Turnberry and beyond.*

attractive urban renewal project that lends a modern interpretation to Scotland's coastal past. This is Burns country, so Irvine boasts a Robert Burns Museum. A few miles south of town, between Troon and Irvine, you'll find the ruins of Dundonald Castle, first home of Scotland's Stuart kings and Scotland's third most important castle site after the better-known (and better-preserved) structures at Edinburgh and Stirling.

See also: Belleisle, Glasgow Gailes, Kilmarnock Golf Club, West Kilbride, Western Gailes.

27. Kilmarnock Golf Club (1887) - Barassie +

Region #: 2   **Category:** seaside-heathland hybrid
Architect(s): various
Length: 6484-6817   **SS:** 73   **Par:** 71-72

Address: 29 Hillhouse Rd, Barassie, Troon KA10 6SY
Directions: follow signs at corner near oceanside where B746 (Kilmarnock Rd) turns into/out of Troon

Reservations phone: 01292-313-920   **Fax:** 01292-318-300
Email: secretarykbgc@lineone.net
Website: kbgc.co.uk
Booking Contact(s): Margaret Boyd

Secretary: Donald Wilson   **Professional:** Gregor Howie
Phone - Starter/Pro shop: 01292-311-322
Fee(s) (2005): play up to 36 holes M-F £58, wkend £60
Deposit (2005): £10 nonrefundable   **Buggies:** 4 - general hire
Visitor Policies: M, T, Th, Fri ; no Sat; Sun only after 2 pm
Other: participant in Ayrshire Open Qualifier discount card and Drambuie Ayrshire Classic; relief course 2788 yds - 9-hole Hillhouse Course

If you want to play "Kilmarnock," don't look for it in the town of Kilmarnock. You need to go to Barassie, adjacent to Troon, about ten miles westward. That's because this is a coastal course built in the late 1880s at Barassie by inland Kilmarnock merchants for their sporting pleasure. That was the time of the first big "boom" in golf—a time when outstanding golf courses were built along the railway running out of Glasgow down the Ayrshire coast. And these courses at West Kilbride, Irvine, Gailes, Barassie, Troon, Prestwick, Ayr, and Turnberry have stood the test of time. They're just as good today as they were then (or better).

The Kilmarnock course at Barassie will appeal primarily to the seasoned traveler who, having played the "rota" courses, is now looking for golf on new ground. It's interesting how the reputations within this second tier of courses seep through the international golf community. In this case, even though Barassie abuts Western Gailes, it is Western that has captured the attention of visitors. No denying the greatness of Western Gailes, but neither are the courses at Barassie, Glasgow Gailes, Irvine, and West Kilbride far behind.

At Barassie you'll find most of the course compactly wedged on rather flat ground between two converging rail lines. Barassie has everything you're looking for in a links layout—heather-lined fairways, pot bunkers, gorse, and those wonderful Ayrshire greens. All this, including the rail lines, might make you think you're playing Prestwick for half the price. Three par 5s, three par 3s, and twelve par 4s typify the Scottish approach to a "traditional" round with par at 72. In other words, this is tougher than your average par-72 track and, with a head wind off the water, the course can be severely challenging. With medal tees stretching to 6800 yards, it's easy to understand why Barassie is used as a qualifying course when the Open is held at Royal Troon. Most golfers will be quite adequately challenged from the yellow tees set at 6408 yards.

> *"Forget some of the 'name' courses and try this one." That advice could apply to about fifty of the sixty-eight courses in this directory.*

In sum, I would pass on the comment of a visitor who registered his observations on Barassie to the Scottish Travel Forum at the fine website *www.uk-golfguide.com*: "Forget some of the 'name' courses and try this one." That advice could apply to about fifty of the sixty-eight courses in this directory. And I'll say it again: to the extent a golf visitor to Scotland can disengage from the grip of the "name" courses, that visitor will have a less expensive, more interesting trip.

See also: Belleisle, Glasgow Gailes, Irvine (Bogside), Royal Troon, West Kilbride, Western Gailes.

28. Kingsbarns Golf Links (2000)

Region #: 1   **Category:** seaside links
Architect(s): Kyle Phillips, Mark Parsinen
Length: 6174-7126   **SSS:** 73   **Par:** 72

Address: Kingsbarns, nr St. Andrews, Fife K16 8QD
Directions: 8 mi S of St. Andrews off A917 just past village
of Kingsbarns

Reservations phone: 01334-460-861   **Fax:** 01334-460-877
Email: info@kingsbarns.com
Website: kingsbarns.com
Booking Contact(s): Donna Clark, Teresa Stewart, Ailsa MacDonald

Manager: Stuart McColm   **Professional:** David Scott
Phone - Starter/Pro shop: reservations
Fee(s) (2005): Apr-May £125 all wk, £185 day tkt; June onward £145 all wk, £215 day tkt
Deposit (2005): 50%; balance 1st day of month preceding month of play
Visitor Policies: all wk   **Buggies:** no
Other: closed Dec through March; host to Dunhill Cup late September; participant in Drambuie Fife Classic early June

From its entrance, straight through to the nineteenth hole, Kingsbarns Golf Links (not club) has the look and feel of a daily fee course where the owners are on site and really care about the product they are selling. For, make no mistake, there's a lot of selling going on here and the product is golf—not club memberships or horseback riding or tennis, but pure, unadulterated links golf.

While the American owners, Mark Parsinen and Art Dunkley, are not always on site these days, they once were and they still spend a lot of time here. In any case, their presence is felt in the businesslike attention to detail at Kingsbarns. First-rate staff carry out the owners' every wish and the result is a golf experience designed to be "world class" without the snobbery typical of many golf clubs in that category.

Kingsbarns and golf course architect Kyle Phillips fairly exploded onto the international golf scene in 2000—so completely that, within two seasons, the course had gathered up virtually every "Best New . . ." award there was to be had and had leaped to the upper tier of *Golf Magazine's* rankings of "World's Best Courses." In 2001 Kingsbarns joined the ranks of Carnoustie and St. Andrews' Old Course in hosting the annual Dunhill Cup, now played as a pro-am event—all pretty heady stuff for the new kid on the block.

Was all this hoopla and hype justified? In a few words: well, yes, probably. Kingsbarns is, indeed, a world-class course and, given four sets of tees, players of all levels can enjoy the challenge. The terrain at Kingsbarns has a wonderful rolling quality about it and sea views abound from every corner of the course.

The first tee and handsome stone clubhouse at Kingsbarns

Six holes skirt the rocky shore, offering a scene reminiscent of Pebble Beach, particularly at the 566-yard, doglegged par 5 twelfth hole that sweeps the shoreline *à la* Pebble, as well as the "signature" par 3 fifteenth hole playing from elevated tee to elevated green across a roiling inlet from the sea. There's not a weak sister in the bunch and modern routing returns the golfer to the clubhouse between nines. All this and more can be seen at Kingsbarns' excellent website.

Now for the bit of reservation you may have sensed in the previous paragraph. Kingsbarns came upon Scotland's golf stage at precisely the right moment—when the golf travel industry and Scots were starved for something new and bold and different, yet at the same time traditional. Scotland really had not turned out a new world-class venue since Mackenzie Ross reworked the Ailsa at Turnberry. Oh, there was the stray and underappreciated course like Craighead down the road at Crail. But Kingsbarns was something special and the world responded. This, we were told, might be the last and greatest seaside course ever built in Scotland. Praises and hosannas were fulsome and continuous.

A few years later, we have two new courses practically next door to Kingsbarns—the Torrance and Devlin courses at St. Andrews Bay, plus the newly-announced championship course to be located just south of St. Andrews and slated for play by 2007. Add to these the new course by Kyle Phillips at Dundonald Links and, in the context of all these new courses, Kingsbarns' newness does not shine quite so brightly as it did in 2000. I guess if Alan Greenspan were a golfer (and he may be, for all I know), he might suggest that the golf world reacted to Kingsbarns' arrival with a mild case of "irrational exuberance."

The other part of my reservation about Kingsbarns is the cost. There's no doubt a new course has startup costs that older clubs have put behind them—land costs, course construction, a clubhouse, etc.—and these costs justify above-average green fees. But, somehow, Kingsbarns has seen fit to raise the high-season visitor fee from £85 in 2000 to £145 in 2005—a tad under seventy-five percent in five years!

To my mind, a cost increase like this has a deadening effect in several ways on all of Scottish golf: first, by economic definition, it discourages untold numbers of golfers from playing a great course because it's just too darned expensive; second, by suggestion, it encourages other courses to raise their rates to "keep up with Kingsbarns"; third, it ensures that few visitors will ever play the course more than

> *If I can play four historic courses in Fife for the price of one Kingsbarns, you know what I'm going to do—and I think I'm pretty representative of a whole lot of golfers.*

once. Seems to me that's just the opposite of what Scottish golf should be doing.

I have seen increasing numbers of golfers passing on Kingsbarns because of the cost, and that is unfortunate because this is a great golf course. But, if I can play *four* historic courses in Fife for the price of one Kingsbarns, you know what I'm going to do—and I think I'm pretty representative of a whole lot of golfers.

29. Kingussie Golf Club (1890)

Region #: 5   **Category:** parkland
Architect(s): Harry Vardon - extended existing nine (1908)
Length: 5411-5615   **SSS:** 68   **Par:** 67

Address: Gynack Rd, Kingussie, Inverness-shire PH21 1LR
Directions: 1/2 mi N of town center off A78, turn at Duke of Garten

Reservations phone: 01540-661-600   **Fax:** 01540-662-066
Email: sec@kingussie-golf.co.uk
Website: kingussie-golf.co.uk
Booking Contact(s): secretary

Secretary: William Baird   **Professional:** no
Phone - Starter/Pro shop: 01540-661-374
Fee(s) (2005): wkday £22, day tkt £27; wkend £24, day tkt £30
Deposit (2005): no
Visitor Policies: all wk   **Buggies:** phys/med
Other: participant in the Drambuie Speyside Classic late September

The course at Kingussie (pronounced king-YEWsie) is included in this directory for two reasons: First, it was designed largely by the great Harry Vardon and that, alone, is cause for inclusion. Second, it is representative of the many "wee" courses found in the resort towns strung out along the A9 south of Inverness. In addition to the excellent course at Boat of Garten, you'll find eighteen-hole delights at Newtonmore (Kingussie's twin town just a few miles away on the A86), Aviemore, and Grantown-on-Spey. And little Carrbridge has its own nine-hole charmer. The common denominator here is not championship golf, but holiday golf in the Highlands—relaxed, scenic, invigorating, and plenty challenging to most golfers.

TRAVEL TIP

Look out for the lefties! This is "shinty" country, where kids learn to strike a ball from both the right and left sides. The upshot: Kingussie and Newtonmore share the prize for most left-handed golfers.

Like the Boat of Garten, Kingussie is more than a pleasant walk in pretty surroundings. Though quite short, there are no par 5s here. Thus, five of the twelve two-shotters extend well over 400 yards. Hilly terrain adds to the challenge. The Vardon emphasis is on shotmaking rather than length—and one could say, the "Scots emphasis" just as well, for this is a characteristic of most Scottish courses. Nevertheless, it's the scenery you'll remember as much as the golf. From high points on the course, the Monadhliath Mountains are visible to the west and the Cairngorms to the east. In between you'll marvel at the melange of soft colors and the crisp Highlands air.

Nongolf notes: The nongolf reasons for lingering in this lovely part of Scotland are just as compelling as the golf. Kingussie itself is widely known as the location of one of Scotland's most interesting "living museums;" that's the Highland Folk Museum located on Duke St. near town center. Here is assembled a collection of relics and reconstructed buildings, including a thatch-roofed

"Black House" modeled after those common on the Isle of Lewis ("black" because it was a smoky, windowless home to both animals and people). In the summer you'll find "citizens" of the village out tending the gardens and working at spinning wheels, all quite happy to welcome you into their homes and talk about their way of life. A larger companion Folk Museum is at Newtonmore.

The Black House at Kingussie's Highland Folk Museum

Before arriving at Kingussie, many people stop at the Dalwhinnie Distillery just a mile along where the A889 meets the A9. After Kingussie, one can spend hours or days exploring the forests and moors around Aviemore and Garten. Here, on the Rothiemurchas Estate and in the Glenmore and Abernethy forests you can walk quite literally for hundreds of miles on groomed trails. Rothiemurchas has Scotland's largest stand of ancient, native Caledonian or

"Scotch" Pine. A particularly fine display of this remarkable tree can be seen on the easy hike around Loch an Eileen. The visitor center for Rothiemurchas is on Ski Road, one mile from Aviemore. Railroad buffs will delight in the steam train that runs from Aviemore through Boat of Garten to Broomhill (see *www.strathspeyrailway.co.uk*). In short, lots to see and do in this territory twenty to forty miles south of Inverness.

See also: Boat of Garten

30. Ladybank Golf Club (1879) +

Region #: 1   **Category:** heathland
Architect(s): Tom Morris and others
Length: 6300-6601   **SSS:** 72   **Par:** 71

Address: Annsmuir, Ladybank, Fife KY7 7RA
Directions: From St. Andrews, 1/2 mi from Melville Lodges Roundabout off A92; driving toward St. Andrews, 1/2 mi on rt past town sign

Reservations phone: 01337-830-814   **Fax:** 01337-831-505
Email: ladybankgc@aol.com
Website: ladybankgolf.co.uk
Key Contact(s): admin. secretary

Admin. Secretary: Fraser McCluskey   **Professional:** Sandy Smith
Phone - Starter/Pro shop: 01337-830-725
Fee(s) (2005): wkday £45, day tkt £60; wkend £55, no day tkt
Deposit (2005): £20   **Buggies:** 2 - general hire
Visitor policies: wkdays 9:30-4 pm; phone wkends
Other: fairway mats used Nov-Mar; participant in Drambuie Fife Classic early June

Ladybank is a beautiful course in the heart of Fife. This flat, tranquil heathland course offers respite from the rigors of Fife's seaside links, yet presents its own challenge. Ladybank is a thinking golfer's course, requiring accuracy off the tee to stay clear of thick growths of heather, broom, and pine and birch forest. But beyond accuracy, it requires every shot in the bag.

Ladybank is all positive and popular with Fife residents. The course and clubhouse are well managed and manicured. There's a good practice area. Staff are helpful and friendly. It's an Open Qualifying Course and, though many changes have been made since its conception in 1879, Ladybank traces its roots to six original holes laid out by Tom Morris.

So, given its popularity and polish, why, on the gut level, does Ladybank disappoint ever so slightly? I can only think it's because this course is so much like dozens of superb American courses in forest settings. No single hole is truly memorable, yet none is entirely pedestrian either. The best measure I can suggest is against other great Scottish inland courses and, when I contemplate a comparison between Ladybank and Blairgowrie Rosemount, Belleisle, the Boat of Garten, or the courses at Gleneagles, Ladybank finishes second every time. In short, though it certainly is *Fife's* finest inland course, I don't think it is *Scotland's* finest inland course. As I've said elsewhere, "I could be wrong." Go experience Ladybank for yourself. You won't be sorry.

31. Leven Links Golf Club (1820) +

Region #: 1   **Category:** seaside links
Architect(s): Tom Morris, others
Length: 6500 yds   **SSS:** 71   **Par:** 71

Address: The Promenade, Leven, Fife KY8 4HS
Directions: off A915 from Leven town center; left on Church Rd, rt on Links Rd

Reservations phone: 01333-428-859   **Fax:** same
Email: secretary@leven-links.com
Website: leven-links.com
Booking Contact(s): secretary

Secretary: Ray Bissett   **Professional:** no
Phone - Starter/Pro shop: 01333-421-390
Fee(s) (2005): wkday £37, day tkt £50; wkend £45, day tkt £60
Deposit (2005): £10
Visitor Policies: all wk; call on Sat   **Buggies:** no

Literally cheek by jowl with Lundin Links Golf Club, Leven Links occupies the ground to the west of a stone fence ("Mile Dyke") separating the two courses. In many respects these courses are something like Siamese twins and, if you're playing one, it's easy enough to play the other.

Not surprisingly, the two clubs are joined (and were separated) by history. Leven is the older of the two, tracing its roots to the early 1800s and beyond. In the early 1800s golfers played eastward from Leven on nine holes. Then in 1868 Tom Morris laid out a new nine on the Lundin side of Mile Dyke. Until 1909, golfers played eighteen holes starting from opposite ends of the two nine-hole layouts! This amounted to the ingenious, but, as golf became more popular, it was neither practical nor very safe. Ultimately, the nines were split at the Mile Dyke and each club went its own way.

In terms of course design, what follows is the most interesting part of the history. When the nines were split, to achieve eighteen holes, there was nowhere to go but inland to the north side of the railway. Eventually the railroad went out of business leaving the rail embankment as an out-of-bounds waste area running the length of both courses. Lundin has left its rail embankment largely intact, while Leven has rather leveled its embankment. This is the sort of history that makes golf in Scotland—and these courses in particular—unique and fun.

See also: Lundin Links

32. Longniddry Golf Club, Ltd. (1893)

Region #: 3   **Category:** links-parkland hybrid
Architect(s): Henry Colt (1922), James Braid (1936),
Phillip Mackenzie Ross (1945), Donald Steel (1998)
Length: 5969-6230   **SSS:** 70   **Par:** 68

Address: Links Rd, Longniddry EH32 ONL
Directions: from A1, exit B6363 to town; off A198 (Main St), W of town

Reservations phone: 01875-852-141   **Fax:** 01875-853-371
Email: secretary@longniddrygolfclub.co.uk
Website: longniddrygolfclub.co.uk

Secretary: none 5/05   **Professional:** John Gray
Phone - Starter/Pro shop: 01875-852-228
Fee(s) (2005): wkday £37.50, day tkt £55; wkend £48, no day tkt
Deposit (2005): £10   **Buggies:** 2 - general hire
Visitor Policies: wkday, 9:30-4:30; wkend - call

I like Longniddry for its imaginative design crafted by four great golf architects. Like Royal Musselburgh, Longniddry is near the Firth of Forth but presents distinct parkland characteristics. Forested ground approaches the sea on this stretch along the south coast of the firth, giving the golf courses from Aberlady Bay to Musselburgh a lushness uncharacteristic of the courses from Gullane eastward. This makes for a visual treat with water in view but framed by woodlands. In this case, Longniddry is blessed with stands of Scotch Pine scarcely represented in the Scottish lowlands.

The design of Longniddry is, at once, traditional and modern. The course is essentially two fairways wide—out-and-back in classic links fashion—with a three-fairway bulge in the middle. But, instead of linking one hole to another in a relatively straight line, the primary designers, Henry Colt and James Braid, concocted exhilarating changes of direction on virtually every one of the outgoing nine holes. On return, along the shore, the course straightens but, even so, there's a twist at the end—for, just as at Western Gailes, the clubhouse here sits at the "finish line" of a racetrack routing.

Braid's influence on course design is seen also in the absence of par 5s at Longniddry. Naturally, this phenomenon was often dictated by available land. But that never stopped the man from designing an interesting course. The result here—no less than seven two-shotters of 400+ yards and an SSS of 70 against par 68. At 432 and 430 yards respectively, the home holes (#17 "Arthur's Seat" and #18 "Hame") will test your mettle.

33. Luffness New Golf Club (1894) +

Region #: 3   **Category:** links-minimal sea views
Architect(s): original layout Tom Morris, re-routing
James Baird (1924)
Length: 6122 yds   **SSS:** 70   **Par:** 69

Address: Aberdlady, E Lothian EH32 0QA
Directions: between villages of Aberlady and Gullane; clubhouse on E side of A198

Reservations phone: 01620-843-336   **Fax:** 01620-842-933
Email: secretary@luffnessgolf.com
Website: luffnessgolf.com
Booking Contact(s): secretary

Secretary: Grp Captn AG Yeates   **Professional:** none
Fee(s) (2005): £46, day tkt £66   **Buggies:** no
Deposit (2005): £20
Visitor Policies: M-F, not at wkend

It's easy to overlook Luffness New. I did it in the first two editions of this book. And yet the course is a major-leaguer in Scottish golf and has been for a long time. Its design pedigree traces directly to James Braid and Old Tom Morris, and it has been used as an Open qualifying course for Muirfield.

Luffness has still more in common with Muirfield: It's a "gentlemen's club" where ladies must be accompanied on the course and in the clubhouse by a member; foursome play ("alternate shot") is a popular format here; and the professional ranks of Edinburghian businessmen are well represented in the membership.

Luffness is literally easy to miss because, upon approaching Gullane village on the A198, one's eye falls upon a vast field of golf courses where it is quite impossible to tell where one course begins and the other ends. It's a case of not seeing the trees for the forest. Luffness is the first one on the right—and the left—for the course is bisected between its fifth and sixth holes by the A198. Five holes play to the east while thirteen holes play on the west side of the highway.

Over the years this simple fact of life at Luffness has led to some interesting re-routing of the golf course. What was once a rather conventional circular layout has given way to an unconventional series of three counter-clockwise loops that bring the fourth and twelfth holes near to the clubhouse. Consequently, it's not at all unusual at Luffness to find members playing a quick four, eight, twelve, or fourteen holes for some salutary exercise and a little practice on the links. How convenient. And all because the early routing had shots sailing back and forth over the highway. Those picky drivers of the horseless carriage!

The opening and closing holes at Luffness are classics. "Luffness Mill" starts the round on a gentle rise to a green only 332 yards away. Easy enough, one might say. But from the tee the view might lead one to think about hitting a shot into craters of the moon, for the green is shielded behind five deep bunkers completely blocking the fairway. It's a wonderful hole. The closing hole is a long par 4 (416 yards) featuring a wide fairway aslant to the teeing ground and a small green surrounded by a grassy embankment designed to keep balls from skipping OB onto the A198.

In between these beauties, Luffness plays over ground that, as the management likes to say, is "sensibly flat apart from minor undulations associated with seaside courses" (a wry dig at neighboring Gullane #1). I might put it a little differently, for, in my view, Luffness suffers from its location on the rather bland Gullane plain fronting Gullane Hill. Individual holes have merit and the greens at Luffness are superb but, overall, this is some of the least interesting ground in Scottish golf. Just one man's opinion.

The wild card at Luffness (and other courses at Gullane) is the brutal wind that frequently rushes off the North Sea, around the horn of Fife, and down the Forth estuary. The joker is the deepest, thickest, most luxuriant rough one could possibly imagine. At this time in history, only a grazing animal could *really* enjoy Luffness. Golfers might describe the experience as a "challenge" but, the fact is, you cannot wander even a foot or two off the fairway without the liklihood of losing a ball. This is one course where short and straight is the only way to play. Anything long and a little off line is most likely long gone.

I say "at this time in history" for an interestng reason—because, due to the removal of grazing animals from the land and the extermination of rabbits, the density of the rough here and at other East Lothian clubs has increased dramatically over time and has become a serious issue for golfers and club managements alike. A movement is afoot to thin the rough to maintain the traditionally "wispy" nature of their linksland grass. This reclamation work has been underway at Gullane Golf Club for several years and has been initiated at Luffness. In the meantime, if you are not a straight driver of the ball, I'd advise leaving the "woods" in the clubhouse and playing Luffness with the irons. You'll score better.

See also: Gullane.

34. Lundin Golf Club - Lundin Links (1868) +

Region #: 1   **Category:** seaside-parkland hybrid
Architect(s): James Braid (1908)
Length: 6394 yds   **SSS:** 71   **Par:** 71

Address: Golf Rd, Lundin Links, Leven KY8 6BA
Directions: From St. Andrews via A915; sharp left turn 3/4 mi W of Largo town center just past Old Manor Country House Hotel

Reservations phone: 01333-320-202   **Fax:** 01333-329-743
Email: secretary@lundingolfclub.co.uk
Website: lundingolfclub.co.uk
Booking Contact(s): Amanda Clunie

Secretary: Alistair MacDonald   **Professional:** D K Webster
Phone - Starter/Pro shop: 01333-320-051
Fee(s) (2005): wkday £42, day tkt £50; wkend £50
Deposit (2005): £10   **Buggies:** no
Visitor Policies: wkday 9 am-3:30 pm; Sat after 2:30 pm; Sun 12-2 pm

If I were playing golf regularly in Fife, I would sooner play at Lundin Links than on any course in St. Andrews. Why? First, the price is right. Next, looking over the Firth of Forth to North Berwick and Musselburgh, the setting is dramatic. Third, the course combines elements of seaside links and parkland terrain. And, finally, not a single hole disappoints and several will stay forever in your memory even if played only once: there's the stunning first hole that plays down to a broad fairway then back up to a tabletop green; farther along the seafront, moving away from the clubhouse, before the course makes a turn to the north, there's an impossibly difficult (often copied) 452-yarder to another elevated green set behind a burn and a steep embankment; the par 3, #12, takes you straight uphill to another tabletop green; then #14, advisedly named "Perfection," plunges back down Lundin's bluff to a green far below. Then it's on toward the clubhouse as each of the finishing holes becomes more demanding. "Home," at 442 yards into a prevailing wind, finishes the test with fittingly stiff character. It's no wonder Lundin Links is used as a qualifying course when St. Andrews hosts the Open.

But Lundin Links is a lot more than a test. It has *character*. True, Jack Nicklaus thought it pretty strange, for where else do you find out-of-bounds running through the middle of the entire course? This phenomenon is due to club history: the original nine holes, laid out by Tom Morris in 1868, utilized the linksland between the sea and a rail line; the course, like many in Scotland, was only two fairways wide. Later, the course was redesigned and extended to the other (north) side of the rail line, thus creating the parkland component of the course. When the railroad went out of business, the rail embankment was left alone. Consequently, the possibility of "OB" follows the golfer around Lundin Links, first on one side, then on the other, even in the middle of the course! Other qualities of Lundin Links: shared fairways, lots of bunkers, a few burns, and high ground (#13 and the teeing ground of #14) overlooking the entire course set against the Firth of Forth. All in all, simply grand.

Bronwyn and Brian Birrell welcome guests to Sandilands B & B in company uniform!

Lodging: Lundin Links is a great place to base while playing courses in St. Andrews and Fife. Several choice lodgings deserve special mention: at the upper end, the *Old Manor Country House Hotel* (01333-320-368; ***www.oldmanorhotel.co.uk***) overlooking Lundin Golf Club; in the middle, *Lundin Links Hotel* (01333-320-207; ***www.lundin-links-hotel.co.uk***); and, in the economy category, four-star *Sandilands B & B* (01333-329-881; ***www.sandilandsfife.co.uk***) at 20 Leven Rd. Incidentally, Sandilands is one of the best deals I've found in Scotland. It backs up on the town's "relief" nine-hole course and its rooms are the equal of hotels twice as expensive. Good four-star guest homes and B & Bs, rarely frequented by North Americans, are also available in Leven near the the golf club there.

See Crail, Leven Links, Golf House Club at Elie.

35. Machrie Hotel and Golf Club

Region #: 8   **Category:** seaside links
Architect(s): Willie Campbell (1891), Donald Steel (1978)
Length: 5964-6226   **SSS:** 70   **Par:** 71

Address: Port Ellen, Islay PA42 7AN
Directions: From Port Ellen ferry dock, 3 mi toward airport,
left off A846; from Port Askaig, about 15 mi, rt past airport

Reservations phone: 01496-302-310   **Fax:** 01496-302-404
Email: machrie@machrie.com
Website: machrie.com
Booking Contact(s): hotel staff

Hotel Mgr: Ian Brown   **Professional:** none
Fee(s) (2005): hotel residents £37, day tkt £47; non-res £42, day tkt £57
Deposit (2005): none   **Buggies:** 4 - general hire

Though it is possible to fly into Islay (pronounced EYE-*la*) from Glasgow (see *www.ba.com*), the best way to visit Machrie is on a leisurely sojourn encompassing the Isle of Arran and the Kintyre Peninsula. Starting by ferry from Ardrossan to Brodick on the Isle of Arran, allow at least five days to do justice to this wild and wonderful part of Scotland. On Arran you'll have an opportunity to play Shiskine, a twelve-hole throwback to the nineteenth century.

Kintyre and Machrihanish deserve two days before pushing on to Islay, where vacationers are drawn to the golf, the whisky distilleries, and the open spaces. Jura—home of one famous whisky distillery (The Isle of Jura) and about 200 permanent population—lies just northeast of Islay. Finished with this island-hopping and ready to return to the mainland, you will have passed through a total population of perhaps 15,000 souls. So, if you're looking to get off the beaten path, this is the way to do it.

"CalMac" car-ferries serve golf destinations on Arran, Kintyre, and Islay. The "Hopscotch 16" ticket allows four crossings at reduced rates to cover the three areas.

Whether such an island journey begins or ends at Islay, you will need to get familiar with the Caledonian MacBrayne ferry schedules available at their excellent website *www.calmac.co.uk*. Reservations can also be made by phone at 08705-650-000. The connection to Islay is at Kennacraig, a few miles south of Tarbert at the isthmus of the Kintyre Peninsula. Plan to reserve space well in advance during the busy summer months. General information about Islay can be had at *www.visit-islay.com*, and *www.isle-of-islay.com*. The Islay Whisky Society has its own site, *www.islaywhiskysociety.com*.

As at Turnberry and Gleneagles, the golf course at Machrie belongs to a hotel—in this case, the *Machrie Hotel and Golf Club* (*www.machrie.com*). Once in sad disrepair, the hotel was purchased by Malcolm King in 1995 and since has been restored to a level of comfort befitting its history and location.

With improvement comes increased cost. The Machrie Hotel is no longer a rundown "bargain." Circa 2005, rooms cost £54 per-person per-night double occupancy. On the other hand, high-season rates at fifteen self-catering lodges on the property are £180 (standard) or £310 (superior) for a typical two-night stay. Split the cost of a superior lodge four ways and a golf group is well housed at a reasonable £37.50 per-person per-night. Off-peak and golf packages can further reduce the cost of staying at the course.

But you don't have to stay at the Machrie Hotel to play the course. Near the golf course, there's the 4-star *Glenmachrie B & B* where, for £60, you can do bed, breakfast, and dinner with one of the best cooks in the land, Mrs. Rachel Whyte (01496-302-560; *www.glenmachrie.com*). At Bridgend there's the classic, ten-room *Bridgend Hotel* (01496-810-212; *www.bridgend-hotel.com*). I particularly like this Bridgend location because, from here, you can proceed in either direction on the forked main highways of Islay—either toward Port Ellen or toward Port Charlotte. At handsome and prosperous Bowmore, you'll find Mrs. Munro's classy *Bowmore House* right in the middle of town on Shore Street (01496-810-324). For more ideas see the general websites mentioned above. Jazz Fans!—for a special treat, plan to be on Islay in late August/early September for some of the best mainstream jazz available in the UK in memorable settings, including several of the local distilleries. Now for the course: Machrie is cut from the same cloth as Cruden Bay, Western Gailes, North Berwick, and Machrihanish. Here you'll find, as Jim Finegan puts it, "a bona fide relic . . . a priceless example of the way golf courses were once brought into being." And, as you might imagine, Machrie and those mentioned above are on a short list of my favorite courses in Scotland. Natural ground defines them all, with minimal sculpting from the hand of man; each presents a fair share of blind shots over dunes and hillocks to big, undulating greens; each is a bit quirky, carrying with it a piece of the nineteenth century and golf history into our time; each brings sheer fun to the golfer on a scale no modern course can approach; each is in a magnificent location relatively removed from the most heavily-traveled tourist trails.

TRAVEL TIP

Two events on Islay attract the multitudes. They are the Islay Malt and Music Festival in late May-early June and the Islay Jazz Festival in late August-early September. Book well in advance.

Late March to Late October Ferry Crossings, Kennacraig - Islay
Crossings take 2 hrs, 20 min and arrive at either Port Ellen or Port Askaig.
Check-in 45 minutes prior to departure.

(M, T, Th, F, Sat) - Depart Kennacraig
7 a.m., 1 p.m., and 6:00 p.m.
Return ferries from Port Ellen or Port Askaig:
9:45 a.m. and 3:30 p.m.

Wed - Depart Kennacraig
8:15 a.m. and 4:30 p.m.
Return ferry at 2 p.m. (also 5:30 a.m.)

"Brought into being"—that nicely-turned Finegan phrase—says a lot about the old process of coaxing a golf course out of the natural landscape; of giving life to a golf course already there, just waiting to be born; of finding the best green sites, then working back through the landscape to the most arresting teeing grounds. The gem at Machrie was brought into being in this way in 1891 by one Willie Campbell of Musselburgh. Campbell was a young and leading light in Scottish golf when he came to Machrie to lay out a championship course. He left for America soon after completion of his work at Machrie and became head professional at The Country Club in Brookline, Massachusetts, where he died way before his time in 1900. His wife, Geraldine, lived on to become a pioneering female golf professional.

Willie Campbell's purpose was to create a long and difficult course, challenging enough to bring golfers from the mainland to visit the Machrie Hotel and Golf Club. At more than 6000 yards, with no hole less than 200 yards, and with blind shots on virtually every hole, he succeeded. Within ten years, Machrie was attracting Scotland's finest golfers to compete for the Kildalton Cross Trophy and a prize of £100—at that time the highest stake in the world of golf. With such riches to be won in such a fine setting, Harry Vardon, James Braid, and J.H. Taylor came here to compete in 1901. Today the Kildalton Cross Trophy Tournament continues as an amateur open event held the first full week of August. Incidentally, the Kildalton Cross is Islay's prized historic relic: the only remaining Celtic "High Cross" in Scotland. It dates from the late eighth century and can be seen at the Kildalton Chapel five miles northeast of Port Ellen.

To bring the story of the golf course design up to date, in 1978 Donald Steel was asked to eliminate at least *some* of the blind shots imposed by Machrie's terrain and Campbell's brain. He did that mainly by shortening the par 3s and thereby lengthening the remaining two and three-shotters (only two of those). In common consensus, the result was an improved course—one more suited to the modern game while retentive of the spirit and character of Campbell's creation.

See also: Machrihanish, Shiskine.

36. Machrihanish Golf Club

Region #: 8   **Category:** seaside links
Architect(s): Tom Morris (1879); J.H. Taylor (1915);
Sir Guy Campbell
Length: 5960-6228   **SSS:** 71   **Par:** 70

Address: by Campbeltown, Argyll PA28 6PT
Directions: 5 mi W of Campbeltown on B843

Reservations phone: 01586-810-277   **Fax:** 01586-810-221
Email: kenneth.m.campbell@talk21.com
Website: machgolf.com
Booking Contact(s): professional

Professional: Kenneth Campbell   **Starter/Pro shop:** 01586-810-277
Fee(s) (2003): wkday & Sun £30, day tkt £50; Sat £40, day tkt £60;
Deposit (2003): 50%
Visitor Policies: all wk   **Buggies:** no

Machrihanish. Machrihanish. Mock-ri-
hon-ish. The syllables roll off the tongue,
conjuring visions of Celtic clans, pipers, and
warrior kings in some mythical medieval
kingdom. Out on the golf course you

> **DRIVE TIME**
> Glasgow Airport: 3+ hrs
> Inverness: 6 to 7+ hrs

encounter "Balaclava" (#6), "Bruach Mor" (#7), "Gigha" (#8), "Ranachan" (#9),
"Nocmoy" (#10), and Kilvian (#13)—and, at this point, you're likely to wonder,
"Where am I? And what language is this anyway?".

In this peninsular part of Scotland—not so far away from Glasgow as the
crow flies, but poles apart in spirit—Scotland's kinship to Ireland is more
apparent than in other parts of the country. Indeed, from the southernmost tip of
the peninsula—the Mull of Kintyre—the Emerald Isle is clearly visible (on
most days), no more than twelve miles away. Once connected by ferry service
to Ballycastle, Northern Ireland, residents of Kintyre continue to hope for a
resumption of oft-promised service. They've been waiting for five years.

The pastoral beauty of Kintyre, the romance of Celtic history, and the
reputation of the golf course at Machrihanish, have combined to make a trip to
this place something of a pilgrimage. Americans are starting to show up in
increasing numbers. Machrihanish is no longer a secret known only to the
cognoscenti of Scottish golf.

Actually, it's not so hard to get to Kintyre. Loganair (0845-773-3377;
www.ba.com), a "franchise partner" of British Airways, runs two flights daily
in and out of Kintyre from Glasgow. But that's not the best way to visit

Machrihanish because, remember, *getting there is half the fun*. That means by automobile on the A82 from Glasgow, up along the west side of lovely Loch Lomond, then down the west side of Loch Fyne to Tarbert at the isthmus of Kintyre. From Tarbert, forty miles southward on the A83 through stirring coastal countryside will get you to the promised land. Alternatively, one can ferry across from Ardrossan to Brodick (on the Isle of Arran), then on to Kintyre from Lochranza to Claonaig. Either way, plan on three to four delightful hours from Glasgow.

To my mind, the most satisfying way to make the pilgrimage to Machrihanish is within the context of an "island-hopping" trip through what I've designated as Region #8—encompassing the Isle of Arran, the Kintyre Peninsula, and Islay. This approach allows one to linger, to sink into the pace and pleasure of a magical landscape. At the course, it encourages one to *play more than one round*. For at both Machrihanish and Machrie, the golfer will encounter a host of "blind shots"—shots from tee and fairway to unseen landing areas. It's true, "The shots are only blind once," but to realize that truism, more than one round is required. I firmly believe the *only* way to play Machrihanish and Machrie is to leave time for multiple rounds.

Is the course at Machrihanish as good as its reputation? Is it worth the effort required to get here? How much of the allure of Machrihanish lies in its setting? All I can say, to paraphrase Julius Caesar, is that I came, I saw, and I went away convinced. There's magic in the air of Kintyre and, as with all great golf courses, the setting of the course is part of a total experience. Not only playing at Machrihanish, but *getting* there and *being* there, are among the most treasured memories of my trips to Scotland.

> **Not only playing at Machrihanish, but getting there and being there, are among the most treasured memories of my trips to Scotland.**

Kintyre and Machrihanish have had the same effect on others. Beatle Paul McCartney came here to vacation and ended up buying a farm, writing a song ("The Mull of Kintyre"), and recording that song with the Campbeltown Pipe Band. Golf writer Malcolm Campbell has concluded, "If there is a golfing heaven somewhere, then it is a safe bet that Machrihanish will have to be passed to get there." Not to be outdone, Michael Bamberger, in his modern classic *To the Linksland*, sought the mystery of the Scottish game and found it at Machrihanish, waxing rhapsodic with words like, "ambrosial," "exquisite," and "Nirvana" to describe the course and his experience. Bamberger finished, "If I were allowed to play only one course for the rest of my life, Machrihanish would be the place." That's a pretty strong endorsement.

So, what is it about this course that turns grown men to mush? The romance starts right at the first hole ("Battery")—universally regarded as one of the great experiences in Scottish golf. James Finegan calls it, "my favorite first shot in all the world." Battery is a 423-yarder requiring a drive over Machrihanish Beach to a fairway aslant to the line of play. It's a risk-reward setup—the more beach you risk, the shorter your second shot. Four bunkers are set to capture any ball hit through the fairway from 230 yards to 290 yards. This is a Tom Morris course, so, once in the vicinity of the green, the golfer will find broad undulations and devilish green-fronting swales.

Now it's on to the second and third holes and the first two of Mac's blind shots. The first one, from the #2 fairway, takes you across the Machrihanish Water (a burn running through the course to the sea) to another rolling green high up on a grassy knoll. The second, from the #3 tee, now changing direction toward the sea, requires a 200-yard carry over and through dunes to a sloping landing area. A good drive here is a must and is rewarded with a bird's-eye view of a green shaped like a jelly-bean set in a hollow below the fairway.

The fourth and fifth holes offer more exquisite links golf—first a short par 3 across a grassy swale, then a dogleg-left requiring two perfect shots to negotiate another route through dunesland. From here, the string of four two-shotters with the Celtic names begins: varying yardage at 315, 432, 337, and 354 likely will have you using every club in the bag. Thus ends what, in my experience, is the best "front nine" in Scottish golf.

Notice that the outward nine presents no par 5s and only one par 3. Now, on the inward nine, moving away from the sea to less dramatic ground, the pattern changes: here we have two 5s, three 3s, and four 4s—an entirely different arrangement lending spice to what must be described as the more bland of the two nines. Two holes are particularly memorable to me: first, #14, a 442-yard straightaway two-shotter over billowing ground; then, the extremely difficult 233-yard, par 3, #16 over wasteland to a smallish green protected by mounds and a deep bunker. Mac's two closing holes play over relatively plain ground and often are disparaged but, with OB lurking all the way down the left side, a good card can be easily ruined on "The Burn" and "Lossit" before the clubhouse door is reached.

When the clubhouse door *is* reached, you'll find a convivial place to while away a few hours with a good book, a pint or two, and an occasional glance through large windows to watch the golfers teeing off on Battery. Bamberger was right: this is Nirvana.

Lodging and nongolf notes: Good B & B choices can be found near the clubhouse at tiny Machrihanish village. These are *Ardell House* (01586-810-235) run by David Baxter and *The Warren* (01586-810-310) run by Judy and Bryan McClement. With golf the focus, this is the logical place to be if room is available. If not, Campbeltown offers lodging, though the old hotels in town center are marginal at best. I'm not aware of anything approaching luxury lodging on Kintyre, though *Craigard House* (01586-554-242; *www.craigard-house.co.uk*), one mile north of Campbeltown on the bay, comes closest. It's an eight-room guest house with singles starting at £45 and doubles at £30 per person. The best full-service lodging on the peninsula is at *The Hunting Lodge* (01583-421-323; *www.thehuntinglodge.com*) on the A83 at Bellochantuy nine miles north of Campbeltown. Formerly the Putechan Lodge, this sea-facing property was acquired in 2002 by one Stiubhard Kerr-Lidell, a true Scotsman who promptly assembled the finest whisky collection on the peninsula and perhaps in the country.

For some of the most dramatic scenery on Kintyre, take time to drive down to Southend, then westward along the coast on a single track as far as you can go. When the road dead-ends, you can walk another mile—sharply downward, then sharply upward—to a high point with views to a lighthouse on the coast far below and westward to Ireland and Islay. At the end of the trail is a memorial to servicemen killed in a Chinook helicopter crash that occurred off the coast in 1994.

Here at the bottom of Kintyre, you'll also find ancient ruins, cemeteries, standing stones, and the short but challenging Dunaverty Golf Course (4800 yards) where a sign suggests that you deposit your fee in an "honesty box" before starting play. On the course you will be joined mainly by four-legged creatures chewing the cud—another memorable experience available only in the remote regions of Scotland.

See also: Machrie Hotel and Golf Club and Shiskine.

37. Monifieth Golf Links - Medal Course +

Region #: 4   **Category:** links - heathland hybrid - no view
Architect(s): Allan Robertson, Alexander Pirie
Length: 6459-6655   **SSS:** 72   **Par:** 71

Address: Princes St, Monifieth DD5 4AW
Directions: N side of town off A930

Reservations phone: 01382-535-553   **Fax:** same as reservations #
Email: monifiethgolf@freeuk.com
Website: monifieth.co.uk

Secretary: Sandy Fyffe   **Professional:** Ian McLeod
Phone - Starter/Pro shop: 01382-532-767
Fee(s) (2005): wkday £39, wkend £49; no day tkt
Deposit (2005): 25%   **Buggies:** 4 - general hire
Visitor Policies: M-F after 9:32 am; Sat after 2 pm; Sun after 11 am
Other: participant in the Carnoustie Country Classic mid-May and the Carnoustie Country Dream Ticket

Monifieth is a brawny course well paired with the even brawnier Carnoustie Golf Links. In between the two, Panmure sits as a relatively delicate gem. These three, strung out along the A930 northeast of Dundee, encourage a prolonged stay based in Carnoustie. Less than an hour from St. Andrews, Monifieth also can fit into an itinerary based in that fair city.

The impression made at Monifieth—both around the course and on the course—is unique in Scottish golf. At bottom, the most important aspect of this part of Scotland is its working-class character. To me, Monifieth represents "lunch bucket" golf. There's nothing pretentious or ritzy here. This is a municipal course, flanked by another municipal course (the Ashludie). Situated between the coastal railway and the town in a remarkably plain

> **Monifieth represents "lunch bucket" golf. There's nothing pretentious or ritzy here.**

neighborhood of solid stone flats and commercial buildings, the links are played mostly by common folk. And that's the way it has always been at Monifieth, where one of Scotland's oldest clubs was organized by artisans and foundry workers in the mid-1800s. Lining the eighteenth fairway are no less than five golf clubhouses and assorted stone row houses, all equally stolid and nondescript. In short, you'll see nothing graceful or light or scenic at Monifieth. Just good, solid, affordable golf and sociability.

On the course, you arrive with knowledge that this is ancient golf ground. Public records show golf being played here for at least 450 years! Thus, at a course like Monifieth, the golfer sensitive to history can actually see and feel the evolution of a game. After several centuries of haphazard play along the links, nine holes were laid out in 1856 by Alexander Pirie and the legendary Allan Robertson of St. Andrews. In 1880, after institutionalization of the idea of eighteen holes for a "round" of golf, nine more holes were added. The course underwent other major changes in 1912, 1930, and 1968. Along the line, especially during the 1950s, long groves of pine trees were installed, creating a links course with lots of trees! Unfortunately, the trees look as if they were planted in rows all on the same day. So they stand like Wellingtonian brigades of soldiers lined up along one or another side of the fairways, particularly on the outgoing nine. Design modifications are not always positive. On the other hand, Monifieth boasts plenty of good holes. On balance, as golf writer Jim Finegan notes, "Monifieth has neither the weaknesses nor the strengths of Panmure." It's a straightforward, no-nonsense course with several long two-shotters, excellent one-shotters, and at least one great par 5 (#9). All said and done, you may not remember individual holes, but you *will* remember Monifieth's unique working-class setting and the long stands of pine trees lining the fairways.

See also: Carnoustie, Panmure.

38. Montrose Links Trust (1810) - Medal Course +

Region #: 4   **Category:** seaside links
Architect(s): evolution; Willie Park, Jr.; Tom Morris (1901)
Length: 6229-6495   **SSS:** 70-72   **Par:** 71

Address: Traill Dr, Montrose DD10 85W
Directions: N of town center off A92

Reservations phone: 01674-672-932   **Fax:** 01674-671-800
Email: secretary@montroselinks.co.uk
Website: montroselinks.co.uk
Key Contact(s): secretary

Secretary: Margaret Stewart   **Professional:** Jason Boyd
Phone - Starter/Pro shop: 01674-672-634
Fee(s) (2005): wkday £40, day tkt £50; wkend £44, day tkt £58
Deposit (2005): £10   **Buggies:** 1 - med/phys
Visitor Policies: all wk; Sat after 2:45 pm; Sun after 10 am
Other: relief course - Broomfield, 18 holes, 4830 yds; participant in Carnoustie Country Classic mid-May and Carnoustie Country Dream Ticket

On the east coast, situated halfway between Dundee and Aberdeen, about thirty-five minutes north of Carnoustie, Montrose Medal is in a bit of a no-man's land for the golf tourist. On a two-day stay in Carnoustie, it makes a good pairing with that great course—superior, in my opinion, to both Panmure and Monifieth. It's just a little farther away.

Montrose fits in well with any itinerary prepared to turn its back on the golf Meccas of Fife, Ayrshire, and East Lothian. For example, on a second or third trip to Scotland the now-seasoned aficionado of Scottish golf might focus on the east coast northward from the Firth of Tay. This focus would take you from the wealth of courses around Carnoustie, to Montrose and nearby Edzell, then on to the linksland north of Aberdeen. Montrose also fits well with any itinerary combining the Highlands and the east coast.

In any event, the reward is great when you get to Montrose. Golf history books will tell you about the ancient pedigree of this linksland that rivals all the better-known "homes" of golf. Records show golf being played here in the middle of the sixteenth century. The course is usually described as the fifth oldest in the world and its oldest associated golf club dates its articles of incorporation to 1810 with records of informal activity stretching much farther back into the eighteenth century. Until the idea of a golf round finally settled on eighteen holes during the 1870s, Montrose was famous for playing the game on twenty-five holes. While Prestwick was hosting the Open with twelve holes during the 1860s, in 1866 Montrose hosted its own Open played to all twenty-five holes! The winning score was 112 (quick math: that's about 81 for eighteen holes).

I like the Montrose course. It's a bit of a patchwork. On one hand, it's everything you expect from a seaside links—towering sandhills; long wispy beach grass; rumpled fairways; and deep, revetted bunkers. On the other hand, when the course veers off on the bias toward town for six holes, you get the distinct feeling you're on an entirely different course. That's not all bad. But, at Montrose, the change seems rather abrupt and you think there might be a story behind this routing. There is. I don't know it all, but I do know the Montrose golf clubs have had to fight more than once for their linksland and some compromises have been made along the way.

The important fact is that a lot of good golf awaits you at Montrose. In my view, the aptly named one-shotter, "Table" (par 3, #3), is as good as the famous "Redan" hole at North Berwick. From the teeing grounds at #s 2, 3, and 6, you have views of beach and sea equal in wild flavor to anything in Scottish golf. The holes, themselves, happen to be very good too, especially #6, "Sandy Braes," where I once finished with a "snowman" after landing in an innocent-looking bunker next to the green. The redeeming moment in that round was my par on the superb two-shotter, "Rashie's" (#17), where, it is said, "it takes three good shots to reach the green in two." Holes ten through fifteen are the ones that jut inland in a loop before the course resumes its more traditional links routing back to the clubhouse. You'll decide for yourself whether you like this configuration. Personally, I rather like the change in direction and character. Montrose should be on everyone's list of Top Twenty historic links courses in Scotland. It might creep into my Top Ten because it's a bit off the beaten path.

See also: Edzell.

39. Moray Golf Club (1887) - Moray Old

Region #: 6   **Category:** seaside links
Architect(s): Tom Morris (1889), Henry Cotton (1970)
Length: 6004-6643   **SSS:** 72   **Par:** 69-71

Address: Stotfield Rd, Lossiemouth, Morayshire IV31 6QS
Directions: well signposted from center of town

Reservations phone: 01343-812-018   **Fax:** 01343-815-102
Email: secretary@moraygolf.co.uk
Website: moraygolf.co.uk
Booking Contact(s): Mrs. McPherson

Secretary: SM Crane   **Professional:** A Thomson
Phone - Starter/Pro shop: 01343-813-330
Fee(s) (2005): wkday £40, day tkt Old £60; wkend £50, day tkt £70; combo day tkt with New Course £55
Deposit (2005): £10   **Buggies:** 4 - general hire
Visitor Policies: Sat after 2pm; Sun after 10am - call; flexible
Other information: adjacent RAF base is quiet on wkends; Moray New, a companion course - 6258 yds; Scotland's largest amateur open, "Moray Open," 3rd full week of July, played over Old and New courses

North and west of Cruden Bay, along northeast Scotland's "Coastal Trail," a remarkable array of courses awaits the visitor. Three of these courses are featured in this directory (Peterhead, Duff House Royal, and Moray Old). Other good eighteen-hole courses can be played (in order, east to west) at St. Combs, Fraserburgh, and Buckie.

A little farther along we come to Moray at Lossiemouth—a classic links course by Tom Morris (1889) and arguably the finest pearl in the strand. Situated twenty-five miles east of Nairn and six miles north of Elgin, Lossiemouth is about the last westward stop before the northeast coast becomes the western Highlands. This makes Moray Old a great course to combine with the championship course at Nairn and/or inland courses to the south (e.g., Boat of Garten, Grantown-on-Spey). This is also an excellent base for making a foray along Scotland's "Whisky Trail," a seventy-mile, signposted jaunt

> *There's much to remind one here of a course that came six years later in Morris's work—namely, the New Course at St. Andrews.*

encompassing most of the country's best-known, single-malt distilleries (including Glen Grant, Glenfiddich, Glenlivet, and Strathisla).

Moray Old is among those most classic of Scottish courses that begin in town (in this case, one block off the main street), proceed outward, then return to a handsome stone clubhouse overlooking a dramatic home hole. Thus, Moray Old stands in atmospheric league with St. Andrews' Old, Montrose, North Berwick, and Prestwick. Moray, in fact, is best known for its challenging 423-yard, par-4 finishing hole. Scots golf writer David Hamilton calls it "the noblest finishing hole in Scotland." With the Moray Firth and dunes to the left, and the clubhouse beckoning from behind a plateaued green (*à la* St. Andrews), golfers will return to town where, as Hamilton puts it, "a small, well-informed audience is usually present to watch futile attempts at the difficult second shot."

In some respects this is my favorite among the courses by Tom Morris. I know part of that judgment comes from Moray's northern location in a small town that sees relatively few visiting golfers from North America. But there's more to it: there's a beguiling, straightforward purity here that contrasts with

Morris's work at Dornoch. All the usual links features abound—deep rough, dunes, ocean views—but there are no blind shots, no severely-convoluted greens, no deep swales fronting greens. In fact, there's much to remind one here of a course that came six years later in Morris's work—namely, the New Course at St. Andrews: seven holes out, then a collection of holes featuring directional changes before the return to the clubhouse. Straightforward, no nonsense. I just love this northern setting on the relatively dry Moray Firth. And, excepting the noise from the jets flying in and out of the Royal Air Force base at Lossiemouth, you'll love it too. And what about that funny name "Lossiemouth"? Well, Moray and Lossiemouth are at the *mouth* of the River Lossie. This is literal Scotland.

  See also: Boat of Garten, Duff House Royal, Nairn, Peterhead.

  Muirfield - *see Honourable Company of Edinburgh Golfers*

40. Murcar Golf Club (1909)

Region #: 1   **Category:** seaside links
Architect(s): Archie Simpson (1909), James Braid,
George Smith (1930s)
Length: 5809-6287   **SSS:** 72   **Par:** 69-71

Address: Bridge of Don, Aberdeen AB23 8BD
Directions: from Aberdeen E at 3rd roundabout from River Don;
from A90 1st roundabout inside Aberdeen city limits (exhibition ctr); follow signs

Reservations phone: 01224-704-354   **Fax:** 01224-704-354
Email: golf@murcar.co.uk
Website: murcar.co.uk
Booking Contact(s): secretary

Secretary: Barbara Rogerson   **Professional:** Gary Forbes
Phone - Starter/Pro shop: 01224-704-370
Fee(s) (2005): wkday £55, day tkt £75; wkend £65, day tkt £85
Deposit (2005): £10   **Buggies:** no
Visitor Policies: all wk; Sat after 2:30 pm; Sun after 11 am
Other: 2684-yd, 9-hole relief course, "Strabathie," designed by James Braid;
participant in Aberdeenshire Golf Classic early September

  While traversing the humps and bumps of Murcar a couple of years back, I had the distinct feeling of playing golf inside a pinball machine. "The luck of the bounce" never had so much meaning as it has found at Murcar. With Royal Aberdeen and Cruden Bay, this must be among the most convoluted, crumpled pieces of duneland in Scotland. Of course these tracks all lie along the same stretch of coastline and, indeed, Murcar abuts Royal Aberdeen on the Royal's north side. This latter fact places Murcar and Royal Aberdeen among the best thirty-six hole combinations in Scottish golf along with the courses at St. Andrews, North Berwick, Gullane, and Gailes.

At #1 we're off to a gentle downhill start through a mogul-strewn fairway, but it's not until we reach the third hole, "Ice House" that the full impact of Murcar's duneland emerges. Here, over steeply falling ground strewn with mounds and hillocks and a pathway through the dunes, one can only hit and hope the golf gods are with you. To quote from the club's hole-by-hole guide, "The golfer on looking back from the rear of the green may be under the impression that he has just negotiated a lunar landscape."

> *Murcar is plain fun with lots of memorable holes . . . I had the distinct feeling of playing golf inside a pinball machine.*

Holes four through nine play along and through the coastal dunes in one of the longest stretches of great seaside golf in Scotland. Among these holes, Scottish golf historian David Hamilton rates the 423-yard #7 "Serpentine" among the finest eighteen holes in the country. And, with many elevated tees along this stretch, Murcar affords the best sea views among the great courses north of Aberdeen.

Playing away from seaside, the second nine inevitably fades a bit in comparison (rather like Royal Aberdeen in this respect too). Still, Murcar presents plenty of good holes to remember. Particularly striking are two more classics at #15 and #16—the first a short par 4 requiring a second shot across a burn to a green perched atop a steeply-embanked hill; then a peak-to-peak par 3 that plays across the fifteenth fairway (yikes!) to a severely undulating green protected front left by a heart-shaped bunker. Course architects today would not even dream of two holes like these—let alone in proximity to one another. This is course design from another time.

A further attraction of Murcar is an unassuming public face in the simplicity of its clubhouse and facilities. The staff could not be more warmly welcoming. All in all, it's a first-rate golf experience in the reasonably-priced class with Cruden Bay, North Berwick, Glasgow Gailes, and Kilmarnock Barassie. Certainly, if Royal Aberdeen is not available, the visiting golfer loses nothing (and retains a few quid) by making the stop at Murcar.

See also: Cruden Bay, Royal Aberdeen.

41. The Nairn Golf Club (1887)

Region #: 5   **Category:** seaside links
Architect(s): Archie Simpson, Tom Morris (1890),
James Braid (1910-26)
Length: 6472-6722   **SSS:** 73-74   **Par:** 72

Address: Seabank Rd, Nairn IV12 4HB
Directions: 16 mi E of Inverness; W side of town off A96

Reservations phone: 01667-453-208   **Fax:** 01667-456-328
Email: secretary@nairngolfclub.co.uk
Website: nairngolfclub.co.uk
Booking Contact(s): Wilma Kerr, Stephanie Otte-Witte

Secretary: David Corstorphine   **Professional:** Robin Fyfe
Phone - Starter/Pro shop: 01667-452-787
Fee(s) (2005): £75 all wk May-Sept; £50 April & Oct
Deposit (2005): £35   **Buggies:** no
Visitor policies: all wk; hdcp - men 28, women 36
Other: Open Amateur tournament usually last week of August

Most golf visitors to Scotland's northern Highlands have Nairn and Royal Dornoch at the top of a short list of priority courses. Invariably, Nairn is *second* on the list. In my view, that puts the two in the right order. The courses have a lot in common, including the long hand of Tom Morris.

DRIVE TIME
Inverness: 20 min
Dornoch: 1 hr 15 min
Aberdeen: 2 hrs 15 min

Both are attractive, out-and-back, seaside courses featuring difficult greens and dense banks of gorse and heather. But Nairn has neither the dramatic elevations of Dornoch nor Dornoch's spectacular setting on a crescent bay. Nevertheless, the Moray Firth is quite nice and it is visible from virtually every hole. The course is impressive in its own way and Nairn deserves to be on everyone's Top Twenty list.

This is a course where most ordinary golfers will lose a lot of balls and thus find a lot of penalty strokes. Tight fairways lined with gorse await the errant drive. More than one hundred bunkers dot the fairways and surround the greens. Once on the firm, silky greens, the average golfer can expect an unusual number of three-putt experiences. The greens are not so undulating as those at Dornoch, but they are bigger. In other words, getting *on* the green here is one thing; getting on the *right part* of the green is quite another. Bottom line: your normal stroke index won't mean much at Nairn; anything under 90 is a good score for most mortals.

Nairn's design pedigree is about as good as it gets. The course was conceived by Archie Simpson of the famous Carnoustie Simpson family. In 1890 Tom Morris was called in to extend and modify the course. Between 1910 and 1926, James Braid tinkered here, first in minor ways, then in major ways until the present design was achieved. Since then, to accommodate the longer modern game, new tees have extended the course to 6700+ yards.

Most golfers will remember Nairn for its gorse and its abrupt three-hole loop in the otherwise straightforward, out-and-back design. In the middle of the inward nine, #s 13, 14, and 15 make a jog inland, then back out again. Apart from that feature, there's a raft of memorable holes starting with all the first seven along the seashore and the closing three holes that follow the inland loop. My favorite among the closers is the par 4, #16. It's 418 yards of pure challenge first across a waste area to a rolling fairway, then across a burn fronting an elevated green surrounded by five

Major bequests from members have allowed Nairn to build one of the newest and finest clubhouses in Scottish golf.

bunkers. The next hole crosses another burn, then a brawny par 5 at 516 yards takes you to the clubhouse—incidentally, one of the newest and finest in Scottish golf. Nairn also sports a nine-hole "relief" course (The Newton) designed by James Braid.

Lodging and food: At the turn of the twentieth century Nairn made a transition from fishing village to Edwardian seaside resort and, in that respect, resembles North Berwick in East Lothian. In other words, the town is well stocked with both nursing homes and vacation lodgings. A first-rate small hotel run by golf-nuts (Rosemary and Andy Machan-Young) for golf-nuts is the *Claymore House Hotel* (01667-453-731; *www.claymorehousehotel.com*). Near the golf course, a step or two up in price are the "Swallow Hotels"—the *Newton* (01667-453-144) and the *Golf View Hotel* (01667-452-301; *www.swallow-hotels.com*). In the B & B category, one of the prettiest places I've found in my travels is the four-star *Glebe End* run by Angela and George Mackay (01667-451-659; *www.glebe-end.co.uk*). The hotels all have good food and bar operations and, on the main drag (Cawdor St), you'll find a classy but casual restaurant called *The Classroom* (01667-455-999). These properties and many more can be viewed at *www.visitnairn.com*.

North Berwick - East Links - *see The Glen.*

42. North Berwick Golf Club (1832) - West Links

Region #: 3   **Category:** seaside links
Architect(s): evolution
Length: 6033-6420   **SSS:** 71   **Par:** 71

Address: Beach Rd, North Berwick, E Lothian EH39 4BB
Directions: W end of town center, 1 blk off A198

Reservations phone: 01620-892-135   **Fax:** 01620-893-274
Email: secretary@ northberwickgolfclub.com
Website: northberwickgolfclub.com
Booking Contact(s): Norma Ogg

Mging Secretary: John W G Douglass   **Professional:** David Huish
Phone - Starter: 01620-892-666
Fee(s) (2005): wkday £55, day tkt £80; wkend £75;
Deposit (2005): £10   **Buggies:** no
Visitor Policies: all wk after 10 am; Sat after 3:30; Sun after noon

For North Berwick I'll go out on a limb: If I *had* to choose my favorite golf course in Scotland—a course to play day in and day out—it would be the West Links at North Berwick. Part of the reason for this choice is the golf course itself. North Berwick offers pure links golf on a beautiful stretch of emerald green ground bordered by the town on the south, grand homes and the Marine Hotel on the west, and broad ocean vistas to the north and east—if you will, a bit of St. Andrews with a view and the crowds long gone.

Another part of the reason is North Berwick's ambience and location. It's a small, attractive seaside town, rural and secluded, yet only thirty minutes by train from Edinburgh. And, since I like small towns *and* big cities, this combination means North Berwick is among my favorite spots in Scotland. The golf course cements the deal and its location puts it at the top of the list.

If I had to choose my favorite golf course in Scotland—a course to play day in and day out—it would be the West Links at North Berwick.

In the interest of persuasion, a few more details: First is the West Links' extraordinary setting one block off the town's main street. Just as at St. Andrews, golfers start at the first tee in town, play down the strand to the ninth, then return to town on the second nine. You'll find the eighteenth green no more than seventy-five yards from a road tracing the beach to the East Links (The Glen) about one mile away. There's a "connectedness" in this setting that, at once, exudes the history of golf and its central place in the social and cultural life of Scotland. Among Scotland's most venerable courses, only St. Andrews, Prestwick, Moray Old, and Montrose so clearly transmit this sense of history and unity with their town surroundings.

North Berwick is thirteenth on the list of Scotland's oldest golf clubs. The course is one of those designed more by evolution than by any individual. Historians indicate that, after several centuries of play along the links, club members settled on the current layout by about 1895—with little change since. Thus, there's an historic unity about the West Links surpassed only by that at the Old Course in St. Andrews.

As for individual holes on the West Links, there's not a weak link to be found. In fact, several are so striking as to be unforgettable. Start with "Point Garry (Out)," where a second shot is made to a black and white target perched behind an elevated green adjacent to rocks and beach below and to the right. Then come two long par 4s where, on the #3 "Trap," the first of North Berwick's famous stone walls makes its appearance. Next follows a 175-yard one-shotter called "Carlekemp" that should be called, "Precision" ("Perfection" comes later—that's #14). If all that weren't enough to announce a round of joyful challenge, bumps and humps and hollows follow over more exhilarating ground to close out the first nine.

Not to be outdone, the inward nine, if anything, exceeds the outward half in eccentric appeal. Here one finds, from the thirteenth to the eighteenth, a string of holes among the most famous in Scottish golf. Number thirteen, "Pit," is one of those you'll never forget—a 365-yarder whose sunken green is separated to the left side of the fairway by a low stone wall. Only a perfect second shot can find the green; more likely, you'll be laying up with the hope of getting close in three. Next comes the aforementioned "Perfection," where a second

Down in the trough of the tri-partite green on North Berwick's #16

shot toward the beach to a blind green requires just that. After ringing a bell to announce a clear green at Perfection, it's on to the par 3 "Redan"—one of the most copied holes in golf, sitting at an angle to the line of play across a grassy divide and pitched front to back. Par is a good score at the Redan. With no pause in the action, #16 ("The Gate") plays to the most unusual green in Scottish golf—a raised tri-partite tabletop with two large flats separated by a trough about three feet deep by nine feet wide! Number seventeen—"Point Garry (In)"—is another long two-shotter that once shared a green with Point Garry (Out). Finally, as at St. Andrews, the short home hole (274 yards) presents opportunity for heroics in front of onlookers ranged along the road and at the clubhouse windows. But wait! The green here, flat as a proverbial pancake, sits on a sharply-cut tabletop, surrounded by a grass moat. After a strong drive, a short pitch shot requires a deft touch to enable a closing birdie or par.

Does this sound like fun? Indeed, it is. I first played North Berwick in a rain storm only briefly interrupted by relative calm and glimpses of sunshine — yet it was among the most enjoyable rounds of golf in my experience. Since then I've had opportunity to play the West Links when it was possible to relax, look around, and savor the setting. Rain or shine, North Berwick delivers the best of what Scotland has to offer on a golf course. Silver-tongued Jim Finegan sums it up best: "For sheer golfing pleasure—a pleasure bred of variety, unpredictability, challenge, and proximity to the sea—few courses surpass North Berwick's West Links. Admittedly, it is old fashioned and, on occasion, even odd. But it is irresistibly old fashioned and irresistibly odd."

Back at the handsome stone clubhouse behind the eighteenth green, you can relax in the visitors' lounge and look out over the red-roofed town to the landmark Bass Rock—now a bird sanctuary but once home to political prisoners—and on to Dunbar on the eastern shore. It's a perfect end to a perfect round of golf.

TRAVEL TIP

Interested in spending time in Edinburgh? Stay in less expensive North Berwick and take the train into the city. Travel time: 32 minutes to city center - no parking, no hassles.

Lodging and nongolf notes: Despite its history as a seaside resort and golf magnet, North Berwick has been somewhat lodging-challenged in recent years. Hotels in various stages of decline have changed hands, while B & Bs have come and gone, but mostly gone. Now, in one of Scotland's hottest real estate markets, and with new levels of golf promotion underway, things are starting to look up. Of greatest import, in 2005, a long-awaited, desperately-needed £13 million refurbishment of *The Marine Hotel* (01620-892-406; *www.macdonaldhotels.co.uk*) began amid promises to turn this tattered old dowager into a raving beauty with luxury self-catering units, garden-level bedrooms, and a full-blown health club (aka "leisure center"). Locals have waited so long for this they'll only believe it when they see it. Many visiting golfers who prefer the high-priced spread will welcome the change, placing North Berwick's Marine on par with St. Andrews' Rusacks and Troon's Marine Hotel among the grand turn-of-the-century stone palaces overlooking Scotland's oldest and most famous golf courses.

Refurbished or not, my inclination is to use the public rooms of an expensive hotel but stay elsewhere. Better values can be had. Among these are John and Maggie Free's *Belhaven Hotel* (01620-893-009; *www.belhavenhotel.co.uk*) and

Tom and Emma Hill's *Golf Hotel* (01620-892-202; *www. thegolfhotel.net*). The Belhaven, at 28 Westgate, is really a guest house (no bar or restaurant). It's a two-star bargain in a five-star location within one hundred yards of North Berwick's eighteenth green. The Hills, former owners of the Open Arms Hotel in Dirleton, are restoring the 15-room Golf Hotel to some of its former glory on the main drag at 34 Dirleton Avenue. Prices are reasonable and, as the Hills say, the place is run "by golfers for golfers." Mid-town, two blocks south of the main

The Glebe House is North Berwick's classiest B & B and a bargain to boot.

street on Law Road, Gwen and Jake Scott preside over a walled Georgian mansion once attached to the church land in town center. Here, at *The Glebe House*, visual champagne is served in the form of an astonishing collection of fine furniture, prints, and paintings. It's North Berwick's classiest B & B (01620-892-608; *www.glebehouse-nb.co.uk*).

When not on a golf course or at your lodgings in North Berwick, the interesting streets of this attractive town beckon and, if the legs can tolerate another workout, you can climb nearby "North Berwick Law," an extinct volcano that rises to 613 feet and visually dominates the relatively flat Lothian coastal plain for miles around. North Berwick's Scottish Seabird Centre is fascinating and informative. Two enticing castle ruins—Tantallon to the east and Dirleton to the west—offer historic ramblings. With Dunbar only twenty miles farther east along the coast and vibrant Edinburgh only thirty minutes away by train, North Berwick has it all without the hoopla of St. Andrews.

See also: Dunbar, The Glen, Gullane, Luffness New, Whitekirk.

43. Panmure Golf Club (1899) +

Region #: 4   **Category:** links - parkland hybrid - no sea view
Architect(s): members
Length: 6085-6317   **SSS:** 71   **Par:** 70

Address: Burnside Rd, Barry by Carnoustie DD7 7RT
Directions: first village SW of Carnoustie on A930; turn left after crossing bridge over Barry Burn

Reservations phone: 01241-855-120   **Fax:** 01241-859-737
Email: secretary@panmuregolfclub.co.uk
Website: panmuregolfclub.co.uk   **Key Contact(s):** secretary

Secretary: Charles Philp   **Professional:** Neil Mackintosh
Phone - Starter/Pro shop: 01241-852-460
Fee(s) (2005): £50 all wk, day tkt £65; no day tkt Sat 3:30
Deposit (2005): £15   **Buggies:** 2 - general hire
Visitor Policies: Sat - call; Sun after 10:30
Other: participant in Carnoustie Country Classic mid-May and Carnoustie Country
Dream Ticket

After playing the championship course at Carnoustie, if one is inclined to
linger awhile, Panmure is a logical first choice for the next round of golf. For
half the price of its prestigious neighbor, Panmure offers a superb round of golf
on a delightful, challenging course. In fact, at a more reasonable length of 6085
yards from the visitor tees, the game here may be more enjoyable to the average
golfer than the test of strength at Carnoustie.

*Hogan went away trumpeting
the #6 hole at Panmure . . . as
one of the best two-shotters
in the world.*

Panmure has been characterized by
some golf writers as twelve great holes
surrounded by six holes of sheer banality.
Personally, I think it's more like fourteen and
four. Nevertheless, the critique bears some
truth. Panmure's opening three holes and closing three holes play over flat,
uninteresting pastureland. Yet this presumed weakness adds variety and
symmetry to the layout. The flat holes at each end bracket the hillocky, gorse-
laden interior. To me, that composition makes the course memorable; I like its
pace and rhythm.

Club historians remind us that this is where Ben Hogan practiced in secret
before winning the British Open in 1954 at Carnoustie—and that Hogan went
away trumpeting the #6 hole at Panmure (now called "Hogan's Hole") as one of
the best two-shotters in the world. As usual, he was right. Other memorable
holes include #8, where a flat green is guarded by a large, conical sandhill; #12,

a long par 4 requiring a precise
second shot over the Buddon Burn
to an elevated green; and the 234-
yard par 3 fifteenth hole.

Panmure Golf Club has a long
and proud history. Organized in 1845,
the club shared playing time at
neighboring Monifieth until its own
clubhouse and course were finished
in 1899. With its dormers and gables
and filigreed latticework, Panmure

*Panmure's classic clubhouse with filigreed
latticework in the gables.*

boasts one of Scotland's most attractive golf clubhouses. Lovers of historic
architecture can only hope the structure will be forever preserved.

44. Peterhead GC (1841) - Old Course

Region #: 6   **Category:** seaside links
Architect(s): Willie Park, Jr. (1891), Laurie Auchterlonie and
James Braid (1920s)
Length: 5758-6173   **SSS:** 68-71   **Par:** 69-70

Address: Riverside Drive, Peterhead AB42 1LT
Directions: N side of town; rt at T-junction of A90 and A198
(Waterside Inn); left at 1st roundabout, then left at 2nd roundabout

Reservations phone: 01779-480-725   **Fax:** 01779-480-725
Email: enquiries@peterheadgolfclub.co.uk

Website: peterheadgolfclub.co.uk
Booking Contact(s): secretary

Secretary: David Wood (a.m. only)   **Professional:** none
Fee(s) (2005): £30 wkday, £40 day tkt; £38 wkend, £48 day tkt
Deposit (2005): £5   **Buggies:** no
Visitor Policies: any time M-F & Sun; after 2 pm Saturday
Other: 9-hole relief course, 4456 yds (18 tees) by Laurie Auchterlonie (1923)
surrounds large practice area

More than most golf clubs in Scotland, Peterhead has experienced the ups and downs that come with the tides of history and the tides of the North Sea. Not to be too cute about it, but one of the ups and downs starts quite literally with the rather strange parking lot situated every bit of one-eighth of a mile from the clubhouse over a bridge crossing the Ugie River that flows around the linksland here into the North Sea. It's a long, uphill trudge.

More important, the club has struggled perennially with the tides of the local economy—first as an east coast center of the volatile fishing trade and, more recently, as one locus of the even more volatile oil industry. Founded in 1841, the club makes rightful claim to being the eighteenth oldest golf club in the world—as the club brochure notes, older than venerable Prestwick. Yet, some five decades passed before the club secured land adequate for a home and nine holes on the Craigewan links north of Peterhead. In 1891, two-time Open winner Willie Park, Jr., was commissioned to lay out those first nine. In 1908 the course was extended to eighteen holes. Still more land acquisition led to an additional eighteen designed by Laurie Auchterlonie in 1923 (thus Peterhead's "Old" and "New" tracks). But this promising configuration did not stand the test wrought by mid-century wars and economic dislocation. The New fell into disrepair to become a nine-hole relief course (and a very good one, by the way).

Fortunately, for the modern golfer who likes to practice and warm up a bit, much of that land became today's excellent practice area with target greens and a short-game facility—a rarity in Scottish golf. This history of economic insecurity seems to be reflected in the atmosphere of the clubhouse and club— in some respects, not quite up to the standard expected from the top ranks of Scottish clubs. For example, currently no professional is associated with Peterhead and the club's website has been "under construction" for way too long. One senses some economic problems.

Now we come to the more daunting tides of the sea. Among the great links courses along Scotland's east coast, Peterhead has the unfortunate distinction of having been most seriously affected by beach erosion. Since World War II, the Old Course's original sixteenth, seventeenth, and eighteenth holes have been lost to the sea. In fact, one can now stand on the sea-facing side of the clubhouse and look down on the abandoned site of the old eighteenth green. It's a sad sight—and not unique to Peterhead. Other great courses along this northeast stretch, including Royal Aberdeen, have had to deal with this formidable challenge from Mother Nature. It is a continuing storyline in Scottish golf.

And now for the course: Peterhead's experience with the power of the sea has led to significant changes to the original course (new holes) and re-routing. Three new holes were laid out in 1969 along the Ugie River and these, though they are fine holes, don't have much in common with the rest of the course. The first hole, "Ugie," is mildly reminiscent of the great first hole at Machrihanish— which means it's a pretty darned good hole. As for re-routing on the rest of the old ground, I sense a certain strain to make it all "work" and this leads to some awkward moments.

Nevertheless, it should be understood that Peterhead is an excellent course with duneland characteristics comparable to those at Cruden Bay, Murcar, and Royal Aberdeen. Elevated tees at many holes provide exhilarating sea views and Peterhead's remaining four holes that thread the seaside dunes are as good as any in Scottish golf. Relatively small greens and a persistent upward grade on the northward holes (usually into the wind) make this course play considerably longer than the official yardage might suggest.

Any golf party traversing northeast Scotland's "Coastal Trail" en route to or from Cruden Bay and Royal Aberdeen, will be rewarded by a stop at Peterhead. It's one of those historic, intriquing, and challenging courses too often overlooked by visitors.

See also: Duff House Royal.

45. Pitlochry Golf Club (1908)

Region #: 7   **Category:** parkland
Architect(s): Willie Fernie (1909)
Length: 5811   **SSS:** 69   **Par:** 69

Address: Golf Course Rd, Pitlochry PH16 5Q7
Directions: N of town off the A924 (Atholl Rd)

Reservations phone: 01796-472-792   **Fax:** 01796-473-947
Email: pro@pitlochrygolf.co.uk
Website: pitlochrygolf.co.uk
Booking Contact(s): professional

Secretary: DM McKenzie   **Professional:** Mark Pirie
Phone - Starter/Pro shop: 01796-472-792
Fee(s) (2005): wkday £24, day tkt £34; wkend £30, day tkt £42
Deposit (2005): none   **Buggies:** no
Visitor Policies: all wk; members only until 9:30 am

DRIVE TIME
Glasgow airport: 1 hr, 30+ min
Inverness: 1 hr, 45 min

I think I fell in love with Scotland at Pitlochry—the golf course and the town. It was the first course I encountered in Scotland and quite unlike anything I had seen in my part of the world. From the opening shot to a fairway split by a gully; then up a great hill for #s 2 and 3; then on to the blind shot at "Queen Mary's Rest" (#5); and the dramatically elevated teeing ground at #6 "Druid's Stone," here we have one of Scotland's most scenic courses, with spectacular views westward across the Tummel Valley. After playing holes #4 through #17 back and forth, round and about, on top of Pitlochry's graceful hill, the golfer descends to an attractive and welcoming clubhouse situated next to the #18 "Home" green. Not incidentally, among these eighteen holes, I would rank four as highly as any in Scottish golf for design brilliance and challenge (#s 1, 5, 10, and 16). As for the rest, they're all enjoyable, though, as a whole, they add up to only mildly-challenging golf. As golf writer Malcolm Campbell puts it, "Pitlochry is not the most testing golf course in the wide world of golf— and who is to say it is not the better for it—but it certainly is one of the most delightful to play." I would add that, since the arrival in 2004 of professional Mark Pirie, club operations and course maintenance have improved dramatically. At one time, I complained about the "furry" greens and the gruff old professional at Pitlochry. Such complaints are a thing of the past. The course is in "top nick," even though Pitlochry must deal with freezing and thawing more than most Scottish courses.

Nongolf notes and lodging: Equally delightful as the golf course is the town itself. About thirty miles north of Perth on the A9 (Scotland's main artery northward), Pitlochry is at the geographic center of Scotland and bills itself, "The Gateway to the Highlands." The town is a destination resort and has been since Victorian times. In summer the place can be crawling with visitors perusing the shops of the main street (Atholl Road). But don't let that scene get you down on Pitlochry. Off the main street, there's much to see and do here and the crowds can be avoided. This is an excellent base for making day trips throughout Perthshire and central Scotland. It's ideal for golfers playing the courses at Gleneagles, Blairgowrie, Crieff, Newtonmore, and Kingussie. Stirring, scenic drives meander westward from the A9 on narrow roads along Loch Rannoch, Glen Lyon, and Loch Tay. To the east, one of Scotland's most scenic highways,

> *I think I fell in love with Scotland at Pitlochry—the golf course and the town.*

the short A924 connecting the A9 to the equally-scenic A93, starts from Pitlochry in the middle of town. Just a few miles along the A924, at a leftward bend, as the narrowing road starts to climb, you'll find the entrance to Edradour Distillery, renowned as Scotland's smallest distiller of single-malt whisky (tours are free). A few miles to the north on the A9 lies Blair Castle, one of Scotland's most popular castle parks, and just a bit farther along is the House of Bruar, a prodigious gift emporium (***www.houseofbruar.com***).

But you don't have to leave town to have a good time. Pitlochry's winding streets invite exploration. Hiking and nature trails are close by (some surrounding the golf course). And the River Tummel awaits just below town where you'll also find the Pitlochry Dam and Fish Ladder and the Pitlochry Festival Theatre that draws visitors from miles around throughout the summer season (01796-484-626; ***www.pitlochry.org.uk***). Early booking advised.

Pitlochry is loaded with bargain accommodations. One of the best four-star finds I've made in recent years is *Beinn Bhracaigh B & B* run by Alf and Ann Berry (01796-470-355; ***www.beinnbhracaigh.com***). Beinn Bhracaigh is the unusual B & B where dinner is the main attraction. Ann's cooking is, in a word, spectacular. Another four-star entry in the B & B category is the *Dunmurray Lodge* operated by Tony and Irene Willmore (01796-473-624; ***www.dunmurray.co.uk***). Both of these establishments underscore my premise that one need never spend more than £35 to £45 per person per night for first-rate lodging.

The Moulin Hotel near Pitlochry is vintage 17th century with a modern brew pub attached.

Among the full-service hotels, on the north end of Atholl Road, the *Claymore House Hotel* does a good job with food and mid-price lodging (01796-472-888; *www.claymorehotel.com*). Three-quarters of a mile up the A924 (Moulin Road) you'll find the *Moulin Hotel* (01796-472-196; *www.moulinhotel.co.uk*), one of my favorite hotels in Scotland. The Moulin is an historic coaching inn (1695) with seventeen comfortable rooms, an attached pub, and its own microbrewery. The hotel pub is a hangout for locals as well as visitors. It's a great place to meet and be met.

46. Portpatrick Golf Club - Dunskey Course (1903)

Region #: 9   **Category:** seaside links
Architect(s): C W Hunter
Length: 5543-5913   **SSS:** 67-69   **Par:** 70

Address: Golf Course Rd, Portpatrick D69 8TB
Directions: signposted NW of village

Reservations phone: 01776-810-273   **Fax:** 01776-810-811
Email: enquiries@portpatrickgolfclub.com
Website: portpatrickgolfclub.com
Booking Contact(s): secretary

Secretary: John McPhail   **Professional:** no
Phone - Starter/Pro shop: 01776-810-273
Fee(s) (2005): wkday £27, day tkt £37; wkend £32, day tkt £42
Deposit (2005): £5 for groups of 8+
Visitor Policies: all wk   **Buggies:** 5 - general hire
Other: participant in Galloway Golf Classic mid-July

Tucked away as it is in the southwest corner of Scotland, few golf tourists visit the Dumfries-Galloway region. That's a good reason to consider a trip to this beautiful area. Beginning just south of Turnberry, that trip might include golf at Stranraer, Portpatrick, Southerness, and Powfoot with an admixture of inland courses at Newton Stewart, Selkirk, Roxburghe, and other "Borders" towns—all set in a paradise of rolling green hills and picturebook villages and towns perched beside sparkling rivers. Different from the rugged beauty found in the Highlands, the Galloway-Dumfries beauty is of the soft, green sort found in England's Lake District and in Ireland.

Among the southern courses mentioned above, Portpatrick is perhaps the most dramatically situated on the rocky coast of an anvil-shaped piece of land dead across the water from Belfast, Northern Ireland, just twenty miles away.

On a clear day you can see Ireland (#10 is "Erin View"), the Mull of Kintyre to the northwest, and the Isle of Man off to the south.

Wind, rain, and long, grassy rough are the main determinants of a golf score at Portpatrick. With few bunkers and no two-shotters over 400 yards, there's not much else to contend with. Given a day of benign weather, in fact, most will find this short course a lovely pushover and, in either case—blustery or calm—this is one place I would ask for permission to play from the medal tees at 5908 yards.

See also: Powfoot, Southerness, Stranraer.

47. Powfoot Golf Club (1903)

Region #: 9   **Category:** seaside links-parkland hybrid
Architect(s): James Braid (1903)
Length: 6010-6255   **SSS:** 70   **Par:** 71

Address: Annan, Dumfries-shire DG12 5QE
Directions: B724 off A75 at Annan, then 1/2 mi S of Cummertrees

Reservations phone: 01461-700-276   **Fax:** same
Email: par71@powfootgolfclub.fsnet.co.uk
Website: www.powfootgolfclub.com
Booking Contact(s): mgr

Office Manager: Claire McDeirment   **Professional:** none
Phone - Starter/Pro shop: 01461-700-327
Fee(s) (2005): wkday £30, day tkt £40; wkend £35
Deposit (2005): £10   **Buggies:** 4 - phys/med
Visitor Policies: M-F 9-11 am and after 1 pm; Sat-Sun 10:30 - 11:15 am and after 1 pm

Like Southerness, Powfoot lies near the border between England and Scotland and, thus, might be played most often by golfers traveling from England to one of Scotland's golf Meccas farther north. For all the reasons cited in my descriptions of Portpatrick, Stranraer, and Southerness, these courses and the beautiful Dumfries-Galloway countryside deserve more than a drive-through. Powfoot is another James Braid course, this one coming early in Braid's design career. For that reason, alone, Powfoot is interesting. Another point of interest: given the shape of available space, Powfoot is not a typical out-and-back links layout but, rather, a *series* of out-back patterns with several holes near the attractive clubhouse looking out over the course and the Solway Firth. I think all golfers will like the variety and changes of direction Braid drew out of the terrain.

Like most of the golf courses on Scotland's southwest coast, Powfoot was used as a military camp during World War II. The war left its marks on this course—in one dramatic and one less obvious way. You'll find the dramatic residue of the war at the #9 "Crater" hole where a mammoth depression created by a German bomb has been left as an "unnatural hazard." The less obvious legacy is the rather flat second nine played over ground leveled for military purposes. The last five holes, playing largely over parkland terrain, were reconstructed after the war. So, yes, this is Braid, but it's Braid put through a blender—nevertheless, well worth a visit.

See also: Portpatrick, Southerness, Stranraer.

48. Prestwick Golf Club (1851) *

Region #: 2   **Category:** seaside links
Architect(s): Tom Morris - 12 holes (1851); others
Length: 6544-6700   **SSS:** 73   **Par:** 71

Address: 2 Links Rd, Prestwick, Ayrshire KA9 1QC
Directions: From N on A79, 1 mi S of Prestwick Airport; rt at Station Rd (light); under rail overpass 400 yds toward beach. From S, left at Station Rd in Prestwick town center off A79 (Main St)

Reservations phone: 01292-671-020   **Fax:** 01292-477-255
Email: bookings@prestwickgc.co.uk
Website: prestwickgc.co.uk
Booking Contacts: Margaret Campbell, Morven English, Jane Kruse

Secretary: I T Bunch   **Professional:** David Fleming
Phone - Starter/Pro shop: 01292-479-483
Fee(s) (2005): wkday £100, day tkt £150; Sun £125
Deposit (2005): £50   **Buggies:** no
Visitor Policies: wkdays except Th pm; no Sat or bank holidays; limited play on Sun in summer
Other: hdcps - men 24, women 28

When my clients include the Ayrshire coast on an itinerary, I like to start them out at Prestwick Golf Club if possible. This is where you return to an older age of golf—to the nineteenth century and the historic days of the first Open championships. At Prestwick, on the course and in the clubhouse, you can soak in the aura and origins of professional tournament golf in an atmosphere little changed by the passage of time. And though its time has come and gone as a venue for the British Open, Prestwick remains among the most challenging courses in Scottish golf. And the word "challenging" really doesn't get to the heart of the matter. The course is also vexing, devilish, and entertaining in ways unique among the classic courses, past and present, on the Open "rota."

Between 1860 and 1925 Prestwick was the main venue for the Open Championship. No less than twenty-four of the first sixty-five Opens were held here. And, as testimony to the quality of Prestwick's course, those twenty-four tournaments were dominated by all the great names in the first two generations of Scottish golf: the Morrises from St. Andrews, the Parks from Musselburgh, the Simpsons from Carnoustie, and, later, Harry Vardon and James Braid. Tom Morris, Jr., considered the finest golfer of his day, won the Open at Prestwick three years in a row between 1868 and 1870 and thus was allowed to keep the original Open prize—a red Moroccan leather belt with silver buckle. Subsequently, a new prize was produced—the now famous "claret jug" engraved with the name of each winner of the Open since 1871.

Prestwick is another course where you will find the living presence of golf's nineteenth-century father figure, Tom Morris. Morris moved from St. Andrews to Prestwick in 1851 as a young man to lay out twelve holes, assume a position as Keeper of the Green, and, incidentally, raise a family. Today, much of that early layout remains, including seven of Morris's green sites. Morris returned to St. Andrews in 1864. Prestwick's clubhouse was constructed in 1868, and in 1883 the course was extended to eighteen holes. By that time the club was firmly established as one of the preeminent clubs in Scottish golf.

> *"You would like to gather up several holes from Prestwick and mail them to your top ten enemies."*
>
> *— Dan Jenkins*

When you step to the first tee at Prestwick you will be immediately struck by the vexing, devilish side of the place. A slicer of the ball will cringe, for tight up against the right side of the entire first fairway is a railroad embankment (OB). But, compensate too far leftward and you're into the gorse and rubble. The second shot isn't any easier. Prestwick's first lesson: accuracy will beat distance every time. The first hole, a mere 369 yards, will remind you, as Jim Finegan puts it, "this course may be a monument to the era of the gutta percha ball. But it is no tombstone. The golf here continues to be gloriously vital."

Now on to the attractively deceiving par 3 second hole before tackling the famous "Cardinal" par 5 with its strategically-placed, mammoth bunkers stretching the width of the fairway and lined with railroad ties. If this sight brings Pete Dye to mind, it's no coincidence. Pete came here to play in 1963 and went away a changed man. You can read about his Scottish epiphany in the book, *Bury Me in a Pot Bunker*.

Cardinal and Bridge (#4) play alongside the Pow Burn—a critical natural feature of Prestwick that cuts into the course behind the second green and then runs the full length of the layout. Thirteen of Prestwick's holes are crammed into the west side of the burn, while only five holes (#s 5-9) lie on the more expansive east side of the burn. This configuration gives the course a certain rhythm I like: tight at the beginning and end; open in the middle.

With all this excellent terrain covered in the first four holes, you can hardly expect it to get better—and, yet, it does—for now we approach the equally famous "Himalayas," a blind one-shotter (206 yards) over a 25-foot-high sandhill to a green surrounded by five bunkers. This is antique Scottish golf at its best.

Well, I could go on and on, hole after hole. Just two more: First, "Arran" (#10), is one of my favorite holes in Scottish golf. It's a 454-yard, par 4, dogleg right across the Pow Burn and then straight down a bunkered fairway aimed at the Isle of Arran off in the distance. Par is a good score, but the setting is so spectacular you don't care that much if you don't meet the test. Prestwick's most famous hole is the #17 "Alps" (one of the Morris originals). It's a 391-yarder with a drive up a hill, then a blind shot to a green fronted by a bunker so cavernous you need steps to get in and out (more Pete Dye material).

> *The line between Tom Morris . . . and Pete Dye, the most influential designer of the twentieth century, cuts right through Prestwick Golf Club.*

With the course largely unchanged in one hundred years, Prestwick stands as a living link between the past and present of golf course design. The line between Tom Morris, the most influential designer of the nineteenth century, and Pete Dye, the most influential designer of the twentieth century, cuts right through Prestwick Golf Club.

Back at the clubhouse you'll find a priceless collection of golf memorabilia, including a replica of Young Tom Morris's red Moroccan leather belt (the original is in possession of the Royal and Ancient Golf Club). Lunch is available 10 a.m. to 3:30 p.m. in the casual Cardinal Room. The more formal Long Room requires coat and tie and advance reservation (men only).

Lodging: Just south of Troon, Prestwick makes a good base for golf along the Ayrshire coast. There's a lot of lodging on and just off Prestwick's main drag. But that's the A79—a busy thoroughfare with a constant flow of traffic. The better choices are right at the golf course on Links Road. These are the "golf hotels," all suited up in row-house fashion. There's the *North Beach* at #7 Links Rd (01292-479-069), the *Prestwick Old Course Hotel* at #13 (01292-477-446), the *Golf View* at #17 (01292-671-234), and the *Fairways Private Hotel* at #19 (01292-470-396). None of these converted Victorians has more than twelve rooms, but they all have plenty of character and the personal attention of on-site owners. A little farther along is the *Parkstone Hotel* (01292-477-286; *www.parkstonehotel.co.uk*), a larger, more modern hotel with some rooms facing the sea. These hotels are all comparable and are reasonably priced considering their location. It doesn't get any easier than walking out your front door, then across the street to the first tee.

49. Royal Aberdeen Golf Club (1780) - Balgownie Course

Region #: 6   **Category:** seaside links
Architect(s): Willie Park, Sr., Robert Simpson, others
Length: 6104-6415   **SSS:** 70   **Par:** 71

Address: Balgownie, Bridge of Don, Aberdeen AB23 8AT
Directions: N of Aberdeen on A92; first rt at Links Rd N of Bridge of Don
Reservations phone: 01224-702-571   **Fax:** 01224-826-591
Email: admin@royalaberdeengolf.com
Website: royalaberdeengolf.com

Booking Contacts: Sandra Nicholson
Secretary: Fraser Webster   **Dir of Golf:** Ronnie MacAskill
Phone - Starter/Pro shop: 01224-702-221
Fee(s) (2005): wkday £75, day tkt £100; wkend £85; Apr & Oct - £50
Deposit (2005): 25%   **Buggies:** no
Visitor Policies: wkday 10-11:30 am, 2-3:30 pm; wkend after 3:30 pm
Other: limited caddie pool - limited # of pullcarts; hdcp - men/women 24

DRIVE TIME
Glasgow Airport: 3 hrs, 45+ min
Gullane: 3 hrs, 30 min
Inverness: 2 hrs, 30 min
Carnoustie: 2 hrs

If Royal Aberdeen's Balgownie Course were located in the lowlands of Scotland, undoubtedly it would be as well known as Muirfield, Troon and Scotland's other "rota" courses. The course is that good.

So it's just a matter of location, location, location. Scotland's northeast corner is a bit off the beaten path, but the wise traveler who finds it will uncover all the best the country has to offer: a vibrant city, castles, country house hotels, whisky distilleries, fishing villages, mountains, rich pastureland, and a variety of outstanding golf courses. It's no accident that this is the part of Scotland where England's royal family likes to hang out (i.e., at Balmoral Castle in the Dee Valley). They've been coming here for over a century.

Nor is it an accident that Royal Aberdeen and the great course at Cruden Bay are often considered in tandem. Only thirty miles apart, their moonscape terrains are cut of the same coastal cloth patterned by towering dunes and rumpled fairways in such extreme that they form a pair nearly unique in Scottish golf. Readers of *Golf World* ranked these two courses sixth (Cruden Bay) and seventh (Royal Aberdeen) in a "Best Courses" poll a few years ago. My guess is that they would rank even closer to the top if more golfers made the trek northward.

Despite its relatively short length (the championship tees stretch only to 6600 yards), the Balgownie is one tough customer. Golf writers, in virtual unanimity, acclaim the first nine among the finest in the country. Part of this acclaim derives from the first three holes that combine a 410-yard opener with a 530-yard par 5 and a 223-yard par 3. No "warm-up" typical of Scottish golf here! These are monsters that can wreck a scorecard before you know what hit you. A little farther along, the brutal 453-yard ninth hole, doglegging to the right as it falls off to the left, achieves star status: David Hamilton (*Scottish Golf Guide*) places it among the best holes in Scotland. In comparison, the inward nine may disappoint a bit but, played into the customary wind off the North Sea, it's no pushover even though 300 yards shorter.

A little history: One of the seven "royal" clubs of Scotland, Aberdeen Golf Club received its designation in 1903 when King Edward VII agreed to become Patron of the Club. Such was the momentary culmination of a proud history that began officially in 1780 but clearly stretched back to the middle of the sixteenth century when some form of golf developed along Scotland's eastern seaboard. In short, when the Society of Aberdeen Golfers formed in 1780 it became Scotland's fifth oldest golf club, joining the distinguished and defining company of clubs that played at Leith, Edinburgh, Musselburgh, and St. Andrews.

> *Golf writers, in virtual unanimity, acclaim the first nine among the finest in the country.*

In 1903, the Royal Aberdeen Golf Club had been at its current Balgownie location, about a mile north of Aberdeen, only since 1888. Prior to golf's explosion of popularity and standardization in the late 1800s, the club had played its golf along the linksland nearer town between the Rivers Don and Dee. Balgownie was just a suburban jump away to the north side of the Don and, there, several golf architects from Carnoustie's Simpson family (also involved at Cruden Bay) had the principal hand in creating one of Scotland's finest. Though Willie Park, Sr., was involved early on, it is Robert Simpson who is generally given credit for the Balgownie Course.

Finally, I should mention the Royal's splendid clubhouse—one of the woodiest in Scottish golf. It's another one of those overlooking the first tee and eighteenth green, thus providing continual entertainment for the members and guests within. It sports a priceless collection of golf memorabilia.

Nongolf notes and lodging: With a population of about 225,000, Aberdeen is Scotland's third largest city and is often called "the Granite City." Massive, gray stone buildings dominate the central part of town giving the place a stoic façade. But, beneath the gray aesthetics of Aberdeen lies Scotland's most contemporary and prosperous city, driven by North Sea oil and its related industries. Take a look at downtown Aberdeen and you'll see the High Street crawling with shoppers on a mission. Moreover, this is a university town—so, you'll sense all the modernity, promise, and energy of youth. If Edinburgh is

Scotland's history book and Glasgow is its warehouse, then Aberdeen is Scotland's "E-commerce" window on the future. It's an exciting little city with a personality all its own. For more information, see *www.agtb.org*.

Aberdeen presents a bit of a lodging problem for golfers. Most of the golf to be played is to the north of the city, while the best lodging is south and west of the city. Near town are the baronial *Ardoe House* (01224-860-600; *www.macdonaldhotels.co.uk*) and the five-star *Marcliffe at Pitfodels* (01224-861-000; *www.marcliffe.com*), both popular on high-end golf tours. More reasonably-priced and better located near Aberdeen's "ring road" (the A90) is *The Queens Hotel* (01224-209-999; *www.the-queens-hotel.com*). Set back from Queens Road, this is a handsome, family-run hotel with well-trained staff and first-rate food service.

Apart from the paucity of quality hotels and B & Bs on the north side of town, it's just not much fun to navigate Aberdeen's labrynth of busy streets that fan out in a welter of spokes from the city center. The solution?—get out of town to seek the countryside. Midway between Aberdeen and Cruden Bay, at the village of Newburgh, is the *Udny Arms* (01358-789-444; *www.udny.co.uk*) run by Guy Craig, his family, and staff. The Udny has a wide and well-deserved reputation as a first-rate "golfer's hotel." It's a solid three-star establishment giving attention to detail without being pretentious. Most important, with the Craig family's long history of culinary expertise, the Udny offers fine dining. If the idea of a farmhouse B & B appeals, you'll find *Savock House* near Newburgh, at Foveran village. This four-star find is operated by Pat and George Booth, club members at Cruden Bay (01358-789-602; *www.aboutscotland.com/aberdeen/savock.html.*)

See also: Cruden Bay, Murcar.

50. Royal Dornoch Golf Club (1877)

Region #: 5   **Category:** seaside links
Architect(s): Tom Morris (1891), Donald Ross (1900), John
Sutherland & J.H.Taylor - various yrs; George Duncan (holes 7-11)
Length: 6229-6514   **SSS:** 71   **Par:** 70

Address: Golf Rd, Dornoch IV25 3LW
Directions: 45 mi N of Inverness on A9; rt at town square,
left to clubhouse

Reservations phone: 01862-810-219   **Fax:** 01862-810-792
Email: rdgc@royaldornoch.com
Website: royaldornoch.com
Booking Contact(s): Donna Sutherland, Claire Riddell

Secretary: John S Duncan   **Professional:** Andrew Skinner
Phone - Starter/Pro shop: 01862-810-902
Fee(s) (2005): M-F, £72, wkend £82; day tkt w/ Struie £85 wkday & £95 wkend; no day tkt on championship course
Deposit (2005): £30
Visitor Policies: all wk; Sat after 2 pm   **Buggies:** 1- med/phys
Other: hdcps - men 24, women 35; participant in Drambuie Highland Classic early May; relief course - Struie - 5438 yds designed by Donald Steel

In 1886, when Old Tom Morris came up to Dornoch to help John Sutherland and friends lay out "nine proper golf holes" and plan nine more, he is said to have remarked, "The a'mighty had gowf in his eye when he made this ground." Of course, Tom Morris—not only the father of modern golf, but golf's greatest diplomat—said something like that about every course he planned. At Dornoch, there's every reason to think Morris meant exactly what he said. I am personally convinced that, when Morris saw this ground, he saw an opportunity to create the most difficult classic links course in his repertoire—classic in its "out and back" setup, two fairways wide; difficult in its elevation changes, its natural sitings for greens, and its susceptibility to every trick in the Morris bag.

If you can play good golf at Dornoch, you can play good golf anywhere. Leave some extra time. It's a course to play more than once.

Despite a host of alterations in ensuing years—first by Donald Ross in 1900, by John Sutherland over a long stretch of years, then by George Duncan in the 1940s—Dornoch is through and through a Morrisonian course, for its successive architects were decided followers of Morris. Dornoch native Donald Ross even went to St. Andrews to work with Tom Morris before returning to Dornoch to serve for a few years as its first professional and greenkeeper. Ultimately, of course, he emigrated to the United States where he became the most prolific golf course architect of the twentieth century. He returned to Dornoch in 1900 only to lengthen the course in response to introduction of the rubber-cored golf ball.

Thus, the hallmarks of Dornoch stand as a collective monument to Tom Morris and his disciples: large, severely-contoured, shaved greens sitting on plateaus; bunkers by the dozens; green-fronting swales; elevated teeing grounds; a few blind shots; tight driving areas often to aslant fairways. Natural phenomena add further difficulty to Dornoch: first, the wind, then the acres of ball-eating gorse. The net result: stroke for stroke, in my view, one of the two or three most difficult courses in Scotland. Also, one of the most beautiful. Indeed, in May and early June, at the elevated third, fourth, and fifth tees, set amidst thick banks of gorse in full yellow bloom stretching down the entire left side of the course, this is among the most breathtaking seaside vistas in all of Scotland.

Golf was played at Dornoch long before the nineteenth century. Public records dating to 1616 give Dornoch status as the third oldest locus of golf after St. Andrews and Leith (Edinburgh). True or not, the historical record is significant as an indicator that, by the seventeenth century, golf had secured a certain hold on Scotland over the entire length of the eastern seaboard—even in the most remote parts of the country.

After organizing as a club in 1877, Dornoch came into its own at the turn of the century, partly as a result of the area's association with Andrew Carnegie—CEO of U.S. Steel and library-builder *nonpareil*. Born in Dumfermline in Fife, Carnegie never left his Scottish roots entirely behind. He built Skibo Castle in the northern Highlands outside of Dornoch, and he learned to play golf on a course built for him there. In 1901 he presented the Dornoch Golf Club with a silver shield as reward to the winner of a tournament held annually ever since during early August. In 1903, the railway reached Dornoch, enabling vacationers to make an overnight journey from London to the far reaches of the northern Highlands. In 1906, Dornoch received its "royal" designation from King Edward VII via the patronage of the Duchess of Sutherland. In 1909, Carnegie paid for a clubhouse at the newly-christened "Royal Dornoch."

Despite this flurry of attention, until recent years Royal Dornoch remained largely unvisited by the international community of golf travelers. It was simply too far north—at least until 1985. That was the year new bridges spanning the Cromarty Firth and Dornoch Firth cut driving time from Inverness by about one hour. Suddenly, Dornoch became more accessible. Tom Watson and Ben Crenshaw came to Dornoch and went away raving (having left behind quotable tidbits). Then, adding fuel to the fire, golf writer Lorne Rubenstein's hymn to Dornoch, *A Season in Dornoch*, published in 2001, brought still more pilgrims to catch a glimpse of what Rubenstein and his wife experienced over a summer in this magical place. The upshot: these days Dornoch is one popular place to play golf. Book early.

I've expended more ink here on the history of Dornoch than on the course itself. But here's the bottom line: if you can play good golf at Dornoch, you can play good golf anywhere. Leave some extra time. It's a course to play more than once.

Nongolf notes and lodging - Dornoch/Tain: If Royal Dornoch is the only northern golf course on your itinerary and your time is short, your preferred base may be Inverness or Nairn. On the other hand, if one can linger awhile in the northern Highlands above Inverness, a logical base is the Dornoch/Tain area. There's plenty of golf to be played and, from here, one can explore the interior of Sutherland, Caithness, and Easter Ross. A stirring coastal route either by automobile or train will take you to Wick and Thurso and then on to John O' Groats—Scotland's "land's end" and northernmost ferry point to the Orkney and Shetland Islands.

FINDING SKIBO CASTLE
About 3/4 mile from the north end of the bridge over the Dornoch Firth, look for a sign for "Clashmore" and take the A949 in the direction of Bonar Bridge. About 1/4 mile along that highway, turn left at a small sign for the Carnegie Club. Take the first right on a single-track road marked "private." The castle is one and one-half miles along this straightaway.

A popular (but expensive) lodging choice in Dornoch is right at the golf course at the *Royal Golf Hotel* (01862-810-283; *www.swallow-hotels.com*). On the town's main street there's the historic *Dornoch Castle Hotel* (01862-810-216; *www.scotland2000.com/ dornochcastle*). But the best choice is the *Eagle Hotel* (01862-810-008; *www.eagle-dornoch.co.uk*). The key here is to ask for rooms in the "Bank House." Rooms in the Bank House are spacious and well appointed—among the best lodging bargains I have found in Scotland. For those (like Madonna) who want to indulge in Scotland's most extravagant splurge, I would be remiss not to mention *Skibo Castle* (01862-894-600; *www.carnegieclub.co.uk*). Skibo is a few miles outside Dornoch and, for a mere £472.50 per person (double occupancy 2005), visitors to the Carnegie Club can stay for one night, play golf on the newly-minted Carnegie Links (Donald Steel, 1995), and eat and drink all you want without seeing another tab. Such a deal!

Nearby Tain is home to the world-famous Glenmorangie Distillery and it also boasts two exceptional hotels. Perhaps the most popular hotel in the region, both for golfers and nongolfers, is the *Morangie House Hotel* (01862-892-281; *www.swallow-hotels.com*) where room rates start at £95 double occupancy. Competing with the Morangie House is the *Mansfield Castle Hotel* (01862-892-052; *www.mansfieldcastle.co.uk*). My favorite B & B in Tain is Sue and Bill McDougal's four-star *Golf View House* (01862-892-856; *www.golf-view.co.uk*). Set on two acres of land on a bluff overlooking Tain Golf Club, it's the best deal in town.

The best deal in town—the four-star Golf View B & B overlooks Tain Golf Club.

See also: Brora, Fortrose & Rosemarkie, Golspie, Inverness, Nairn, Tain.

51. Royal Musselburgh Golf Club (1774)

Region #: 3   **Category:** parkland
Architect(s): James Braid (1926)
Length: 6284   **SSS:** 70   **Par:** 70

Address: Preston Grange House, Prestonpans EH32 9RP
Directions: W of Prestonpans off A198

Reservations phone: 01875-810-276   **Fax:** same
Email: royalmusselburgh@btinternet.com
Website: royalmusselburgh.co.uk
Booking Contact(s): secretary

Secretary: Thomas Hardie (a.m. only)   **Professional:** John Henderson
Phone - Starter/Pro shop: 01875-810-139
Fee(s) (2005): wkday £28, day tkt £38; wkend £35, no day tkt
Deposit (2005): £10
Visitor Policies: wkdays except Fri pm   **Buggies:** 5 - general hire
Other: no credit cards

The courses at Musselburgh (pronounced *muscle-burra*) are situated between Musselburgh and Prestonpans on the estate of the Barons of Prestoungrange. In point of fact, the clubhouse of the RMGC—one of the finest in Scottish golf—is housed in a mansion the barons called home from the sixteenth century to the early twentieth century.

In the preceding paragraph, I have referred to "the courses" at Musselburgh because Royal Musselburgh is closely associated with the *Old Links at Musselburgh*, one mile east of Musselburgh town center. It was here, at the Old Links, that some kind of golf took root in Scotland—verifiably so by 1672 and probably as early as the 1400s. During the eighteenth century, four of Scotland's five oldest golf clubs played on the nine holes of the Old Links (in addition to the RMGC, this included the Honourable Company of Edinburgh Golfers, Royal Burgess Golf Club, and the Bruntsfield Golfing Society). Between 1868 and 1889 this ground was the site of *six* British Opens. And, when the last Open was played at Musselburgh in 1889, a chapter in the history of golf closed.

The starter house at the Old Links at Musselburgh—Scotland's oldest golf grounds, soon to be expanded from nine to eighteen holes.

The Royal Musselburgh Golf Club was the last major club to vacate the Old Links in favor of newer, more expansive digs—in this case, the club's current parkland site designed by James Braid in the early 1920s. Subsequently, the Old Links suffered from neglect but, today, efforts are being made to resurrect the old lady as a living museum of golf history. To enhance the time-machine experience, you can even rent a set of hickory sticks for your round. Since 1816, the course has been surrounded by a mile-long racetrack, making it not only the most historic but the most unusual layout in the country. For more information about the Old Links at Musselburgh, see *www. musselburgholdlinks.co.uk* (ph/fax: 0131-665-5438).

So, when discussing Royal Musselburgh, golf fans, we are talking *history.* We're talking about a golf club formed two years before the issuance of the Declaration of Independence, housed in a sixteenth-century mansion, with a history of play on ground dedicated to golf since the time of Columbus. For all these reasons, I encourage my clients to make a day of *the courses at Musselburgh* with a nine-holer on the Old Links in the morning, followed by lunch at the Royal Musselburgh clubhouse, before an afternoon round on Braid's twentieth-century creation. This combination makes for an unforgettable day of Scottish golf.

As for the course at Royal Musselburgh, this is a tree-lined beauty with heavy rough and a collection of imaginative holes designed by James Braid, with his usual emphasis on long par 4s, a mix of par 3s, and a de-emphasis on round-saving par 5s. Even though near the sea (and with occasional views out to the Firth), Royal Musselburgh sports parkland turf at a seaside setting reminiscent of Belleisle at Ayr (another Braid course). When in Edinburgh or East Lothian, don't miss it.

52. Royal Troon (1878) - Old Course *

Region #: 2   **Category:** seaside links
Architect(s): Willie Fernie (1888)
Length: 6201-6640-7175   **SSS:** 71-75   **Par:** 71

Address: Craigend Rd., Troon, Ayrshire KA10 6EP
Directions: terminus of B749 at corner of Craigend and Bentinck Dr

Reservations/starter: 01292-311-555   **Fax:** 01292-318-204
Email: bookings@royaltroon.com
Website: royaltroon.com
Booking Contact(s): Michael McCallum, Hamish Harkness, Douglas Bull, Tom Allen

Secretary: JW Chandler   **Professional:** R Brian Anderson
Fee(s) (2005): £200 (includes play on Portland Course & buffet lunch)
Deposit (2005): £50 within 21 days; balance 60 days before play
Visitor Policies: early May thru mid-Oct: M, T, Th only, 9:30-11 am & 2:30-4 pm;
no jrs under 16 on Old Course   **Buggies:** no
Other: Portland Course, 6289 yds, SSS 71; hdcp - men 20, women 30

The big news out of Troon in 2003 was a change of policy vis-à-vis the ladies. Women with a handicap of thirty or below were allowed to play the Old Course for the first time. Then came 2004 and the dramatic Open won by Todd Hamilton in a playoff over Ernie Els. Visitors flocked to Troon.

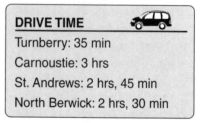

DRIVE TIME

Turnberry: 35 min
Carnoustie: 3 hrs
St. Andrews: 2 hrs, 45 min
North Berwick: 2 hrs, 30 min

Flush with success (and hubris), in 2005 Royal Troon's management committee saw fit to breach the "£200 barrier." Now, my prediction for 2006 and beyond: visitors will just start to say "no" and turn away from this venerable institution. Enough is enough.

The problem here is Royal Troon's inflexible two-course policy. The only option given visitors is a "day ticket" for play on the Old Course and the neighboring Portland Course (in other words, you *pay* for both courses regardless of whether you *play* both courses). For golfers who want to spend all day playing golf, this arrangement offers a certain kind of Nirvana—a perfect day in a perfect place. The setting is superb; the championship course is excellent; the Portland is good; the clubhouse is grand; the staff is first-rate. No complaints from the 36-holers.

The problem is that most people don't want to play two rounds of golf in one day. And, if they do, they might rather play the second round at Gailes, Prestwick, or Irvine. *About forty percent of those who book at Troon play only the championship course.* The net result: lots of disappointed golfers who end up paying the highest fee in Scottish golf for lunch and one round on a championship course—£200 (about $380) in 2005.

I say "disappointed" simply because that's the way a lot of golfers feel after visiting Troon. Troon, by itself, is simply not worth $380 (what golf course is?). It's a good and historic golf course. But it's not better than St. Andrews' Old Course, Muirfield, Turnberry, or Carnoustie. Indeed, I would put Troon at the tail-end of the "rota" list. St. Andrews' Old Course is more historic and structurally unique; Muirfield is more creatively unique; Turnberry is more uniquely beautiful; and Carnoustie is a tougher track. In short, the visiting golfer is likely to feel gouged by Troon's two-course policy. Perhaps at one time the management committee found friendly logic in the policy but, today, the only logic seems to be aimed at the pocketbooks of visiting golfers. In short, visitors are financing the posh venue of a very few privileged club golfers.

Despite the carping, Royal Troon is a great golf experience and, because visitors are accepted on only three weekdays, a tee time at Troon can be difficult to get in high season. In this regard, two important notes: First, unlike St. Andrews and Carnoustie, Troon will advance-book a single golfer. Second, if a date is booked up on your first call, it's a good idea to go onto the "waitlist" with the hope of filling a cancellation. Because full payment is not required until sixty days before play, Troon is the target of some speculative booking by tour operators; thus, cancellations occur as deadlines for payment come and go.

Once on the course, the golf pilgrim, if poorer in pocket, certainly will be richer for the experience. Royal Troon is a classic links course—out and back, counter-clockwise, first along a gently-curving bay; then, after meandering a bit at the turn, back to the clubhouse on an inland track. In this respect, among Scotland's Open courses, Troon is most similar to St. Andrews' Old Course, though with superior sea views. The course is essentially the work of Open champion Willie Fernie (1883) who came here in 1888 to serve as Troon's club professional and to extend an existing small course to eighteen holes. The main changes since then have largely involved adding bunkers and lengthening the course to a 7,200-yard championship stretch. Most visitors will play the course at a considerably easier 6200 yards. Single-digit handicappers may be allowed to play from the medal (white) tees.

In general, Royal Troon lacks the dune-filled drama found on the linksland at places like Cruden Bay, Aberdeen, and Dornoch. Requisite humps and bumps and wispy beach grasses are ever-present, but the terrain is relatively flat. Troon's six opening holes and six closing holes march in a rather straight line away from and returning to the clubhouse. It's the inside six holes (#7 through #12) that give the course its character and reputation. These holes feature constant changes of direction, doglegs to left and right (four of the six), a straightaway par 4 at 438 yards (#10, "Sandhills"), and one of the most famous par 3s in the world ("Postage Stamp," #8)—all in all, six of the best holes you will play on your trip to Scotland. The homeward nine is nearly three hundred yards longer than the first nine and, into the wind, can make for a rather trying experience.

Troon is the youngest of Scotland's "royals" but not the youngest of its Open venues (that honor goes to Turnberry). The royal designation was granted by Queen Elizabeth II on the occasion of Troon's centenary celebration in 1978. Open championships have been held here since 1923—testimony to the high regard given Troon by Scotland's "East Coast Establishment." Troon was the logical west coast heir to Prestwick's place in the Open rota. Indeed, as at all the Open venues, the quality of Royal Troon's challenge is reflected in its parade of champions. South African Bobby Locke won here in 1950. Since then, it's been an all-American parade. The winners have been Palmer ('63), Weiskopf ('73), Watson ('82), Calcavecchia ('89), Leonard ('97), and Hamilton ('04).

Nongolf notes and lodging: Troon is an ideal base for enjoying golf along the Ayrshire coast. The courses at Barassie, Gailes, Irvine, and West Kilbride all lie a few miles to the north. Prestwick and Ayr are the next towns south. Troon boasts five municipal golf courses, two of them comparable to Royal Troon's Portland (the Darley and Lochgreen). Most important, there's a relaxed, inviting air about Troon that you don't find on the busy streets of its larger neighbors. The town is big enough support a variety of shops and restaurants. There's easy access to the beaches and to a harbor where P & O ferries make two daily runs to and from Troon and Larne, Northern Ireland, about thirty-five miles north of Belfast. Thus, Troon can be a base for golf combining Scotland and Ireland. In 2005 ferry service was scheduled at varying times (one in a.m. and one in p.m.) between March 16 and October 3. See *www.poirishsea.com* for current schedule information.

Troon is short on B & Bs but is well served by hotels of varying size and distinction. A popular B & B about four hundred yards from the first tee at Royal Troon is Norma McLardy's *Copper Beech* at 116 Bentinck Dr. (01292-314-100; *www.copperbeechtroon.com*). The setting here is Tudor elegance.

Across the way at 117 Bentinck you'll find a classic Victorian called *Thorncroft House* (01292-312-457; *www.thorncrofthouse.com*). It's run by golfers (Caroline and Ken Rolph) for golfers and features spacious rooms with considerable style. A little farther along Bentinck at Darley Place is the *Glenside Hotel* (01292-313-677) operated by Stewart and

The four-room Glenside Hotel is one of Scotland's best bargains near a championship golf course.

Lynne Watt. The Glenside is one of Scotland's best lodging bargains in proximity to championship golf. With only four bedrooms and no restaurant, the Glenside is really a guest house—ideal for a golf party of four in singles. One long block away, on South Beach Road, the Watt family owns and operates a larger inn, the *South Beach Hotel* (01292-312-033, *www.southbeach.co.uk*), one of the most popular full-service hotels on the Ayrshire coast. The superior doubles here are spacious and the dining and bar facilities are popular with local residents—always a good sign. The classic *Anchorage Hotel* (01292-317-448; *www.anchoragehoteltroon.co.uk*) is a three-star choice with history as a coaching inn on Troon harbor.

Moving up the price scale, the massive *Marine Hotel* (01292-314-444; *www.paramount-hotels.co.uk*) overlooking the eighteenth fairway at Royal

Troon is a famous golf hotel in vintage comparable to Rusacks in St. Andrews and the Marine at North Berwick. Catty-corner from the Marine is the popular *Piersland House Hotel* (01292-314-747; ***www.piersland.co.uk***), the ancestral home of the Johnny Walker (whisky) family. Two establishments in the country-house category are *Lochgreen House* (01292-313-343) and *Highgrove House* (01292-312-511), owned and operated by master chef Bill Costley (***www.costley-hotels.co.uk***). The Lochgreen House is on the B749 about one-half mile from Royal Troon Golf Club. Highgrove House is a few miles east on the A759 at the "Loans" crossroads. Both hotels feature comfort in small-scale surroundings and "Four-Rosette" dining (the best).

    See also: Glasgow Gailes, Irvine, Kilmarnock, Prestwick, Western Gailes, West Kilbride.

The Courses at St. Andrews
53. The Old Course *
Region #: 1   **Category:** seaside links
Architect(s): evolution, Tom Morris
Length: 6566   **SSS:** 72   **Par:** 72

Address: St. Andrews Links Trust, Pilmour House, St. Andrews KY16 9SF
Directions: A91 to St. Andrews; 2nd left at Golf Pl

Reservations phone: 01334-466-666   **Fax:** 01334-477-036
Email: reservations@standrews.org.uk
Website: standrews.org.uk
Booking Contact(s): Isobel Barrett - Advance Reservations Office; Old Course application ok by fax or email; apply on or after 1st Wed in Sept for advance booking in the ensuing year

General Manager: Ewan MacGregor   **Buggies:** none
Fee(s) (2005): £115; PLUS 17.5% VAT on 3rd-party bookings
Deposit (2005): 100% nonrefundable prepay
Visitor Policies: closed Sun (see Part II, Chapter 3 for more detail)
Other: no trolleys in a.m.; hdcps - men 24, women 36

    So many thousands of descriptive words have been written about this storied, historic course there is no good reason for me to add to the word count. Most of what I have to say of a practical nature is in Part II, Chapter 3. All I want to add here is that,

DRIVE TIME	
Edinburgh Airport: 1 hr, 10 min	
Glasgow Airport - 2 hrs, 15 min	
Carnoustie: 40 min	
Gullane (Muirfield): 1 hr, 45 min	

A goal of every serious golfer: the first tee at St. Andrews' Old Course.

when people ask me, "Allan, what are your favorite courses?", I always start by saying, "First, the Old Course is in a class by itself." I really believe that. The moonscape setting, the huge double greens, the monstrous bunkers, and the grand scale of the Old Course are enough to distinguish it from all others. Layered on top of all that is the weight of history. And there's still another factor I find equally compelling about the Old Course: On no other course do I get such a clear appreciation for the interplay of skill and fate. Lady Luck plays a huge role here—for good and ill, just as in life. And, to me, that's why every golfer should play the Old Course at least once. It will keep you humble and appreciative of life (and of Tiger Woods).

54, 55. The New Course and The Jubilee

Region #: 1   **Category:** seaside links
Architect(s): New - Tom Morris (1895); Jubilee - various, Donald Steel (1988-9)
Length: New 5992-6604, Jubilee 6043-6805
SSS: New 72, Jubilee 73   **Par:** New 71, Jubilee 72

Address: St. Andrews Links Trust, Pilmour House, St. Andrews KY16 9SF
Directions: A91 to St. Andrews; 2nd left at Golf Pl

Reservations phone: 01334-466-666   **Fax:** 01334-477-036
Email: reservations@standrews.org.uk
Website: standrews.org.uk

Key Contact(s): Isobel Barrett /Advance Reservations Office
Secretary: Ewan MacGregor
Fee(s) (2005): New £55, Jubilee £55, PLUS 17.5% VAT on 3rd-party bookings
Deposit (2005): 100% prepayment
Visitor Policies: all wk
Buggies: New Course - a few - med/ phys and seniors (men 65+, ladies 60+)

I'm treating these two courses under one heading because the courses sit side by side and are often considered in tandem. The New and Jubilee are the options most golfers weigh when looking for play on another St. Andrews course. Then the question arises, "Which course is better?". Ask that question of twelve experienced St. Andrews golfers and you'll most likely get "six of one, half dozen of the other." At 6800 yards, the Jubilee is the longer of the two and is often cited as, "the toughest course in St. Andrews." Yet the New Course, not much changed since it was laid out by Tom Morris in 1895, is considered the natural heir to Old Course tradition. Appropriately enough, the New Course is positioned next to the Old Course, while the Jubilee occupies a narrower strip of land between the New Course and the sea.

Play on the New and Jubilee begins at the attractive Links Clubhouse overlooking the second fairway of the Old Course. This is where visiting golfers will find plenty of parking and all the information and service they are looking for: a reception desk, locker rooms, bar, restaurant, gift shops, practice putting greens, plus the starter office and first tees for both the New and Jubilee. An observation deck atop the clubhouse is an excellent place to get photographs and a panoramic view of the links layout.

In comparing the courses, one can only conclude that the similarities are more important than the differences. Obviously, they play over similar terrain. Given its position, the Jubilee offers more ocean views but, since there is really no high ground on the links at St. Andrews, this factor is negligible. Both courses are out-and-back classics. And, even in length, the 200-yard difference (New 6600; Jubilee 6800) is insignificant when spread over eighteen holes. Both courses feature great banks of gorse that line the fairways and frame the greens (a breathtaking canvass of yellow and green in the spring). Both courses have an astounding number of bunkers filled with soft St. Andrews sand. Both have large, undulating greens and one double green. Indeed, the similarities indicate a toss-up.

That much said, my own preference is for the New Course. Why? First, the New Course carries the indelible stamp of Old Tom Morris and thus sports a certain pedigree and integrity of design. The Jubilee, first opened as a twelve-hole course for women and children in 1897, has gone through several incarnations and, though Donald Steel brought championship length and wholesale redesign to the course in 1988-89, the course has a more layered history than the New. More important, land available to the two courses has had its effect. While the Jubilee is shaped like the sheath of a dagger, the New Course resembles the more graceful shape of a spoon. Five opening holes traverse the "handle" of the New Course, while three return to the clubhouse—all in a straight line. In the "bowl" of the spoon, Tom Morris exercised his imagination, creating ten varied holes with frequent changes of direction. In contrast, the

Jubilee rather resembles a forced march out (seven holes straight out), with a brief respite (six holes back and forth), before the return to the clubhouse (six holes straight back in). Admittedly, some figure-eight routing increases the angles, but, overall, I much prefer the greater variety and grace of the New Course.

A closing word in behalf of the Jubilee (and golf at St. Andrews): For high handicappers the Jubilee offers a set of Bronze Tees, shortening the course to 5674 yards. In other words, even a marginal golfer can enjoy St. Andrews linksland in proximity to the Old Course. St. Andrews provides golf for all ages and all levels of ability and, in the process, reminds us of the democratic roots of the game. In this respect, the town of St. Andrews is a model citizen—indeed, the First Citizen—in the world of golf.

See also: Part II, Chapter 3, for more detail on the courses at St. Andrews and Links Management policies.

The Courses at St. Andrews Bay (2002)
56. The Torrance   57. The Devlin

Region #: 1   **Category:** seaside "links-style"
Architect(s): Sam Torrance, Gene Sarazen, Denis Griffiths & Assocs (Torrance), Bruce Devlin, Denis Griffiths & Assocs (Devlin)
Length: Torrance 5509-7037, Devlin 5195-7049
SSS: Torrance 72, Devlin 74   **Par:** both 72

Address: St. Andrews, Fife KY16 8 PN
Directions: 3 mi S of St. Andrews on the A917

Reservations phone: 01334-837-412   **Fax:** 01334-471-115
Email: reservations@standrewsbay.com
Website: standrewsbay.com
Booking Contact(s): Graeme Dawson, Sonja Tait

Professional: John Kerr
Phone - Starter/Pro shop: 01334-837-023
Fee(s) (2005): same all wk and for both courses: Nov thru Mar resident £40, non-resident £45; April - May res £60, res combo tkt £100, non-res £70; June thru September res £75, res combo tkt £120, non-res £95. Combo tkt may be used over 1 or 2-day period
Deposit (2005): none   **Visitor Policies:** all wk
Buggies: Devlin - 36 for general hire; Torrance - none
Other: tour operators receive green fee discounts varying from £10 to £20; participant in the Drambuie Fife Classic early June

In the neutered world of golf guides where no one wants to offend, the tendency would be to describe the courses at St. Andrews Bay (SA Bay) in glowing terms and be done with it. However, my readers have come to expect more from me and, in the case of SA Bay, the devil is in the detail.

The background: These are the newest major courses in Scottish golf. And they are good—no question about it (I particularly like the Torrance). Opened in 2002 and 2003, the Torrance and Devlin are the main attractions at a monumental 209-room hotel intended to join Turnberry, Gleneagles, and the Old Course Hotel on the short list of Scotland's five-star international resorts with golf courses attached. SA Bay sits on 520 acres of rolling, high ground three miles south of St. Andrews on the coastal route (A917). It was developed by the American-owned Château Elán group led by Donald Panoz, inventor of the Nicotine Patch. Part monument to an ego, part mausoleum, the hotel has all the charm of a modern airport terminal. And not even one hundred years of maturity will embue the place with the character or class of either Turnberry or Gleneagles. As one might expect, this place is fully outfitted for conspicuous consumption—from internet hookups and in-room movie fare to several restaurants and five different "anti-stress" therapies available at the hotel spa. In other words, if you want to go to Scotland but feel like you're on a luxury cruise, or maybe never even left home, SA Bay may be the place for you. If you want to discover the real Scotland, I suggest you look elsewhere.

Part monument to an ego, part mausoleum, the hotel has all the charm of a modern airport terminal.

Moving on to more important advice: First, the visiting golfer should think of SA Bay as a daily-fee venue or even as filler on an itinerary. These courses are best reserved for (a) walk-on play; (b) Saturdays, when member clubs are not available; (c) Sundays when the Old Course is closed; and (d) when you're too pooped to pop and ready for a buggy on the Devlin. Second, note that the courses at SA Bay are £50 less expensive than Kingsbarns. With spectacular views out to the North Sea and greater proximity to the skyline of St. Andrews, SA Bay has every bit the visual appeal of Kingsbarns. Both feature modern course design on similar ground. In short, if Kingsbarns is seeming a bit pricey, but you still want to play a modern course in Scotland, SA Bay offers two good alternatives.

At the same time, keep in mind that, unlike Kingsbarns, this is not links golf. SA Bay sits well above the sea. It was developed on old farmground and is seeded with a grass mixture of thirty-five percent rye rather than the bents and fescues of traditional linksland. The ball sits up on these "American-style" or "links-style" fairways. On the Devlin this is particularly evident and there's barely a hummock or mogul to be found until we reach the tenth fairway. None of this is necessarily bad; it's just a fact.

Finally, visitors should be aware that SA Bay was slow to get off the ground. Locals and international visitors, alike, were generally underwhelmed with the development. The courses were slow to grow in and perhaps were opened a bit too soon. To compensate—to wedge their way into Fife's competitive golf market—SA Bay management has adopted an unfortunate policy of offering substantial "incentive discounts" (i.e., kickbacks) to tour operators in exchange for their bringing business to the hotel. So, when an operator extolls the virtues of SA Bay, just ask yourself: What's in it for him (or her)? Why should I want to stay at that hotel? Is that the best choice for me—on a high hill three miles outside of town? And why should I play one of these courses when I could play a traditional club in Fife for half the price? In other words, be suspicous. Go to St. Andrews Bay for the right reasons—for golf at the right time on good modern courses—but don't go because it is recommended by a tour operator.

58. St. Andrews - Old Course Hotel
The Duke's Course (1995)

Region #: 1 **Category:** parkland
Architect(s): Peter Thomson (1995)
Length: 6264-7371 **SSS:** 73-75 **Par:** 72

Address: Craigtoun, St. Andrews, Fife KY16 8NS
Directions: from town, Hepburn Gardens Rd 2 mi SW to Craigtoun Pk

Reservations phone: 01334-474-371 (Old Course Hotel)
Fax: 01334-477-668
Email: reservations@oldcoursehotel.co.uk
Website: oldcoursehotel.co.uk

Professional: Ron Walker
Phone - Starter/Pro shop: 01334-470-214
Fee(s) (2005): hotel residents - varying rates or incl in package rates - call hotel; nonresidents - April/May £50, June/Sept £85, Oct £65
Deposit (2005): no **Buggies:** 30
Visitor Policies: all wk

As if St. Andrews did not already offer an embarrassment of golf riches, in 1995 the five-star Old Course Hotel unveiled this gem by Peter Thomson, the celebrated Aussie who won the British Open five times between 1952 and 1965. Just two miles southwest of town, The Duke's occupies high ground affording excellent views over St. Andrews to the waters beyond and, on a clear day, off to Angus in the far distance. Usually billed as an alternative to links golf, the real beauty of The Duke's Course is that it is such a fine inland course in *proximity* to links golf. It's a rare combination. So, yes, The Duke's serves as an alternative to the St. Andrews links, but it happens to be an outstanding golf course worthy of play in its own right. A lot of Brits think so too, as evidenced in a recent poll conducted by *Today's Golfer*, a leading UK golf publication. Readers rated The Duke's "Best Parkland Course in the UK." High praise, indeed.

In expansiveness and length, The Duke's reminds us of Jack Nicklaus's PGA Centenary Course at Gleneagles. But that's about as far as the comparison goes, for Peter Thomson's idea of course design contrasts sharply with that of the Golden Bear. While Nicklaus never met a water hazard or forced carry he didn't like, Thomson eschews both, giving the golfer every opportunity to play the game along the ground as well as in the air. While both designers offer big greens, Thomson opts for relatively flat spaces in contrast to Nicklaus's approach that announces, "no straight putts here." This is not to say The Duke's is without challenge. With eighty bunkers scattered about and several "wee burns" to negotiate, along with punishing rough, there's plenty here to keep one's attention. Moreover, at 7110 yards from the championship tees, this is Scotland's longest inland course. Most male visitors will play the course at 6749 yards or even the next step down at 6264 yards. As with most modern courses, there's a track here for every level of ability and strength.

TRAVEL TIP

Want a taste of the Old Course Hotel without renting a room? All-day use of the hotel's spa facilities costs £25. After-round massage?—that's extra.

Since lines of ownership in St. Andrews can be confusing, let me reiterate: The Duke's Course is owned and operated by the Old Course Hotel, Golf Resort & Spa and is entirely independent of the Links Trust Management. Hotel residents receive priority treatment, but the course is rarely full up, so a visitor normally can secure a tee time with no problem. Another practical tip: this is a good course to play on Sunday when the Old Course is closed. As a daily fee course, it is easier to get on than many other courses in Fife.

I am not keen on places like the Old Course Hotel, but there's no questioning the hotel's quality or its superb setting overlooking the #17 "Road Hole" on the Old Course. Information on hotel facilities, rooms, and prices can be gleaned at *www.oldcoursehotel.co.uk*. Rates circa 2005 in high season *start* at £158 per person double occupancy. In the fall of 2004 the hotel was purchased by Herb Kohler, he of bathroom-fixture fame. Extensive refurbishments were launched in the spring of 2005.

59. Scotscraig Golf Club (1817) +

Region #: 1   **Category:** seaside links/heathland hybrid
Architect(s): Robert Simpson, James Braid (1904)
Length: 6303-6550   **SSS:** 72   **Par:** 71

Address: Golf Rd, Tayport, Fife DD6 9D2
Directions: from Dundee, E at Tay Bridge roundabout to Tayport town center, left on Elizabeth St; from St Andrews, direction Dundee, then 3 mi on B945, rt on Elizabeth St

Reservations phone: 01382-552-515   **Fax:** 01382-553-130
Email: scotscraig@scottishgolf.com
Website: scotscraiggolfclub.com
Booking Contact(s): Alison Harvey

Secretary: Barry D Liddle   **Professional:** John Kelly
Phone - Starter/Pro shop: 01382-552-855
Fee(s) (2005): wkday £44, day tkt £54; wkend £50, day tkt £60
Deposit (2005): £10   **Buggies:** 4 - general hire
Visitor Policies: M-F 9:30-11:28, 2:30-4:00; Sat 10-11 am and Sun after 2:30 pm

Scotscraig is an Open qualifier course and it pulls rank as the thirteenth oldest golf club in the world. Yet, this congenial club often gets overlooked in Fife's flurry of golf flak. When booking a course outside St. Andrews, visitors often choose Crail, Kingsbarns, or the courses at St. Andrews Bay—all to the south. Rarely do they consider driving ten miles north to Tayport on the Fife side of the Tay Bridge. That's their mistake. Tayport is a bedroom community for Dundee and a bit on the "other side of the tracks"—though in this case we're talking about the other side of the firth. No pretense here. Scotscraig is a solid, old-line golf club with a classic clubhouse. Nothing fancy on the course either. Here, you'll experience a

PLANNING TIP
Schedule low-deposit Scotscraig as a "fallback course" when balloting for play on St. Andrews' Old Course. If successful at the Old Course, cancel or reschedule Scotscraig.

challenge some people judge as demanding as that at Carnoustie. It's a seaside links with dashes of heather and trees. The course was essentially crafted by Carnoustie professional Robert Simpson and, later, James Braid—plenty of pedigree and plenty of good golf. If not on my list of Scotland's top twenty seaside courses, it's close—in a group with other Open qualifiers like Barassie, Irvine, and Monifieth.

60. Shiskine Golf and Tennis Club (1896)

Region #: 8   **Category:** seaside links
Architect(s): Willie Fernie (1896), Willie Park (1910)
Length: 2996   **SSS:** 41   **Par:** 42

Address: Shore Rd, Blackwaterfoot, Isle of Arran KA27 8HA
Directions: NW of village from either A841 coastal route
or B880 "String Rd"

Reservations phone: 01770-860-226   **Fax:** 01770-860-205
Email: info@shiskinegolf.com

Website: shiskinegolf.com
Booking Contact(s): Fiona Brown   **Professional:** none

Fee(s) (2005): wkday £15 (12 holes), 24 holes - £25; wkend £19 & 30
Deposit (2005): none   **Buggies:** 4 - general hire
Visitor Policies: all wk; time; July - Aug all reservations one day in advance

Shiskine is Scotland's wondrous twelve-hole attraction on the Isle of Arran just fifty-five minutes by ferry off the Ayrshire coast. While the least expensive course among the sixty-eight in this directory, Shiskine sits atop the list among those played for pure fun—with Machrihanish, Machrie, and Cruden Bay, These are the courses that evoke a time when golf was a quirky game of chance and skill played at seaside over natural, scruffy ground to greens hidden by hills and surrounded by burns and hollows—the places visited by the ghosts of Willie Fernie, Willie Park, Jr., and Old Tom Morris.

Two of those old Scots had a hand in Shiskine. Willie Fernie laid out nine holes for the new club in 1896. Some fifteen years later, Willie Park, Jr., was commissioned to alter and extend the course to eighteen holes. During World War I the linksland was commandeered for defensive puposes. After the war, parts of the course were neglected until the club found its identity in the twelve holes we have today.

Shiskine features seven par 3s, four par 4s, and one par 5. Seven of the twelve holes are blind. At the 368-yard #1 hole, we're off to a straightforward Scottish start with sea, beach, and OB on the left. Then it's on to "Twa' Burns" where the photocopied course guide advises that the target off the tee is a "**white tyre**." The #3 hole, "Crows Nest," is of a kind seen only in Scotland. It calls for a 130-yard shot up the grassy slope of an outcropping from the Drumadoon cliffs some seventy-five fee above the teeing ground. Somewhere up there is a green. From the tee the golfer sees only a white signal flag, meaning either "I surrender" or "all clear." What goes up must come down and that's what happens at the next hole, "The Shelf," featuring a seventy-five foot drop to the water's edge. By this time, anticipating "The Himalayas," "Drumadoon," and "Paradise," you're in thrall of magical stuff from another era.

Nongolf notes and lodging: In some cultures, a place like the Isle of Arran would be turned into a glitzy, glamorous getaway for the rich. But, bless the down-to-earth Scots, they're just not very impressed by glitz and glamor. Arran remains an affordable, unassuming place where thousands of Scots and English go to "get away from it all" for a few days or an extended stay. Arran's tourism moniker is "Scotland in Miniature," reflective of its rugged northern terrain and its rolling, green southern hills.

Standing stones on Machrie Moor—one of Arran's many attractions.

Brodick is the port here and is home to about 1,000 of the island's 5,000 citizens. Shops, restaurants, and hotels line Brodick's beachfront boulevard. Since tourism is Arran's main concern, lodging options abound (see *www.ayrshire-arran.com.*) I like the quiet northwest end of Brodick in the Glen Cloy precinct and can recommend *Glencloy Farmhouse* (01770-302-351) as a bargain retreat. Nearby, in the luxury category, is the *Kilmichael Country House Hotel* (01770-302-219; *www.kilmichael.com*), where good food is a special attraction. Speaking of good food, try *The Brodick Bar* (01770-302-169) on Alma Road in the center of town. A few miles south of Brodick, at Lamlash, you'll find the four-star *Lilybank Guest House* (01770-600-230) looking out across peaceful Lamlash Bay to the Holy Isle.

Elsewhere I have recommended Arran in the context of a peninsula-and-island-hopping trip encompassing Kintyre (Machrihanish) and the Isle of Islay (Machrie). But it's easy enough to make a daytrip to Arran from a base in Ayrshire. From March through October the first ferry out of Ardrossan is at 9:45 a.m. and the last ferry off the island leaves Brodick at 4:40 p.m. In between there's plenty of time for lunch and twenty-four holes at Shiskine. See *www.arran.net* or *www.calmac.co.uk* for the Ardrossan-Brodick schedule and prices. Whether for a day or for longer, the Isle of Arran is a special place well worth the time of a visiting golfer.

61. Southerness Golf Club (1947)

Region #: 9   **Category:** seaside links
Architect(s): Mackenzie Ross (1947)
Length: 6105-6566   **SSS:** 70-73   **Par:** 69

Address: Southerness, Dumfries DG2 8AZ
Directions: 3 mi S of Kirkbean off A710

Reservations phone: 01387-880-677   **Fax:** 01387-880-644
Email: bookings@southernessgc.sol.co.uk
Website: southernessgolfclub.com
Booking Contact(s): secretary

Secretary: I A Robin   **Professional:** none
Fee(s) (2005): wkday £42; wkend £52 - unlimited play
Deposit (2005): £10 UK residents; foreign visitors, none
Visitor Policies: M-F 10-12, 2-4; wkend 10-11:30, 2:30-4pm   **Buggies:** no

Travelers heading northward out of England on their way to the Ayrshire coast have a unique opportunity to stop along the way to play one of Scotland's finest linksland courses. For championship links golf at a reasonable price, there is none better.

But let's back up to get our bearings. On its approach to Scotland, England's M6 becomes the A74. Just inside the Scottish border at Gretna, the A75 branches westward twenty-five miles to Dumfries. Dumfries is a large town of considerable interest and good accommodations. That's the place to stop for a rendezvous with Southerness, situated on the coast of the Solway Firth fifteen miles south of town.

In this location, remote from the centers of Scottish golf, you'll find a course consistently ranked among the top twenty in Scotland. Some put Southerness comfortably in their top ten. Case in point: in the fall of 1999 I had the pleasure of playing a round of golf at Royal Dornoch with Neil Stott, a Southerness club member making his annual pilgrimage to Dornoch. Mid-round, in response to my complaints about Dornoch's "tricks" and tortuous greens, Neil said, "You ought to come down and play Southerness. It's tougher than this course but it's more fair. I think it's a better course."

So I did. And I can testify that Neil was right on at least one count: Southerness is even tougher than Dornoch. Whether it's better or not is in the eye of the beholder. At 6600 yards, Southerness plays more like 7000 due to the absence of par 5s (only two) and the presence of five par 3s. That leaves eleven two-shotters—virtually all 400+ yards. Note that SSS here is 73 against par 69. That's about as big a gap as you are likely to find in Scottish golf, rivaling Carnoustie's gap from the championship "Tiger" tees. And, yet, I found

Southerness fair enough. All the elements of links golf are present, but nothing is hidden from view. It's all in front of you and—surrounded by pastureland, the Solway Firth, and distant hills—it's all a visual treat. The only problem: average golfers will be hitting drivers and fairway metals most of the day on the long two-shotters and that gets a bit old.

The designer responsible for this southern gem was Mackenzie Ross, who resurrected Turnberry from its role as an air landing strip after World War II. Ross came to Southerness in 1947 to create what Malcolm Campbell has called, "arguably the only truly championship-standard seaside links to have been built on the British mainland since the Second World War." Though now we must make room for Kingsbarns and Dundonald in that assessment, Campbell's words are an extraordinary endorsement of a great golf course.

The birthplace of John Paul Jones—
American hero, British traitor.

Nongolf notes: Dumfries is a pretty town where Robert Burns died in 1796 and his wife, Jean Armour, lived until 1834. Burns and his wife are buried in St. Michael's churchyard in central Dumfries. Arbigland Gardens can be found at nearby Kippford and only one mile from Southerness you can see the birthplace of John Paul Jones—an American revolutionary war hero widely regarded as a traitor in Britain. Lockerbie, site of the infamous Pan Am bombing, is twelve miles northeast of Dumfries and well worth a visit. A moving memorial, "Garden of Remembrance," is located in a cemetery on the A709 at the edge of town.

62. Stonehaven Golf Club (1888)

Region #: 6   **Category:** seaside links
Architect(s): Artie Simpson (1897)
Length: 4804-5103   **SSS:** 65   **Par:** 67

Address: Cowie, Stonehaven AB39 3RH
Directions: 1 mi N of Stonehaven off A92

Reservations phone: 01569-762-124   **Fax:** 01569-765-973
Email: stonehaven.golfclub@virgin.net
Website: stonehavengolfclub.co.uk
Secretary: W A Donald   **Professional:** no
Fee(s) (2005): wkday £18, day tkt £25; Sun £24, day tkt £30
Deposit (2005): no   **Buggies:** no
Visitor Policies: M-F anytime; Sat after 4 pm

Located about fifty miles north of Carnoustie and fifteen miles south of Aberdeen, the golf course at Stonehaven, by any measure (4800-5100 yards), is not much more than an "executive" course. Apart from twelve-hole Shiskine, it is the shortest course included in this directory. Yet, Stonehaven is here because those 5100 yards pack quite a wallop perched atop perhaps the most dramatic seascape in Scottish golf.

Sited between the scenic coastal rail line and the sea, on steep cliffs above the North Sea, Stonehaven is also among the most exposed of courses to brutal winds and weather. A nasty day of wind and rain can make this course virtually unplayable. But a calm day will leave the golfer with nothing less than a golden memory of golf in an unforgettable location. In either case you'll be surprised to discover how challenging a short course can be.

Stonehaven town is an historic fishing village boasting population of about 10,000 hardy souls. It's a good place to poke around a bit after a stop for lunch in the attractive town center. Another reason to put Stonehaven on the itinerary: a mile or so south of town are the ruins and remains of Dunnottar Castle—like the golf course, perched dramatically atop a broad escarpment overlooking the sea. Dunnottar was used as the setting in Franco Zefferelli's treatment of *Hamlet* starring Mel Gibson.

My advice on Stonehaven: Make it a half-day stopover between points south and points north. With a price of £18 in 2005, it's not only a bargain but a scenic wonder to put in the mental scrapbook.

63. Stranraer Golf Club (1905)

Region #: 9   **Category:** parkland (seaside)
Architect(s): James Braid (1950)
Length: 6056-6308   **SSS:** 72   **Par:** 70

Address: Creachmore, Leswalt, Stranraer DG9 0LF
Directions: 3 mi NW of Stranraer on A718

Reservations phone: 01776-870-245   **Fax:** 01776-870-445
Email: enquiries@stranraergolfclub.net
Website: stranraergolfclub.net
Booking Contact(s): Olive Kelly

Secretary: Bryce C Kelly   **Professional:** no
Fee(s) (2005): wkday £25, day tkt £35; wkend £30, day tkt £40
Deposit (2005): £5   **Buggies:** 5 - general hire
Visitor Policies: all wk; 9:30 am-12:30 pm and after 1:30 pm
Other: participant in Galloway Golf Classic mid-July

Among the quartet of southern courses featured in this book—Stranraer, Portpatrick, Southerness, and Powfoot—Stranraer is the first in line along the coastal route southward from Turnberry (just 40 miles on the A77). Stranraer is a ferry port with service to Belfast (see *www.stenaline.co.uk*) and is also on the rail line from Glasgow. Competitive ferry service to Ireland departs from nearby Cairnryan (see *www.poirishsea.com*).

Stranraer sits at the south end of Loch Ryan, an inlet from the North Channel, at the neck of the anvil-shaped peninsula called the "Rhinns of Galloway." In this location, far from Scotland's golf Meccas to the north, James Braid created another fine golf course with a typically unusual combination of holes—this time only one par 5 and three par 3s, leaving fourteen two-shotters including three stretching beyond 450 yards! Of the rest, the golfer is given a pleasing variety of shapes and lengths in holes varying from 315 to 397 yards, all artistically and thoughtfully

Braid's Last	
Hole No.	18
Yards	336
Par	4
Stroke Index	15

The 18th at Stranraer—literally, James Braid's last contribution to Scottish golf in 1950.

framed by leafy backdrops of bushes, deciduous trees, and pine. It was James Braid's last creation before he died in 1950 (Stranraer Golf Club was formed in 1905, but the original course was abandoned when it became a military post during World War II). Since 1950, Stranraer has gained a sterling reputation for its excellent greens and general course conditioning and maintenance. This is attributable in part to the relatively mild gulfstream weather found in this part of Scotland. The rest of it is attributable to local pride in "Braid's Last" exemplified most recently in more than £100,000 spent on unseen drainage work on three holes susceptible to standing water during recent years of exceptionally wet weather in southwest Scotland. Though seaside, Stranraer is a parkland course positioned largely on high ground overlooking the sea. Several holes skirt the shoreline, but the rest of the course is inland and quite hilly. This one's a seaside beauty.

So, why visit Stranraer? First, it's an excellent course. Second, it's one of the few bargains left in top-tier Scottish golf. Third, getting there is half the fun. Fourth, if you're coming to Scotland from England, heading for the Ayrshire coast, it's not much out of the way at all. Fifth, at the clubhouse, newly-refurbished for Stranraer's centenary in 2005, you'll experience a particularly warm Scottish welcome; they don't see a lot of North American visitors here, so your presence will be noticed and appreciated. Need more reasons? I would add the attractions of southern Scotland. This is Clan Kennedy country and near Stranraer you'll find the magnificent 75-acre Kennedy Castle Gardens. Fourteen miles south of Stranraer on the Rhinns of Galloway is Logan Botanic Garden where you can see plants from the Southern hemisphere flourishing on a gulfstream coast.

See also: Portpatrick, Powfoot, and Southerness.

64. Tain Golf Club (1890)

Region #: 5   **Category:** seaside links
Architect(s): Tom Morris
Length: 6109-6404   **SSS:** 71   **Par:** 70

Address: Chapel Rd, Tain, Ross-shire IV19 1PA
Directions: signposted from ctr of town
Reservations phone: 01862-892-314   **Fax:** 01862-892-099
Email: info@tain-golfclub.co.uk
Website: tain-golfclub.co.uk
Booking Contact(s): admin secretary

Admin Secretary: Mrs. Joanna Bell   **Professional:** Munro Ferris
Phone - Starter/Pro shop: 01862-893-313
Fee(s) (2005): wkday £36, day tkt £44; wkend £44, day tkt £54
Deposit (2005): £10   **Buggies:** 5 - general hire
Visitor Policies: all wk; wkend after 11:30 am
Other: participant in Drambuie Highland Golf Classic early May

Golf writer Jim Finegan describes Tain as "golf in a minor key," and that says it pretty well. Tain simply lacks the grandeur of its near neighbor Royal Dornoch. It is always seen in the shadow of that magnificent course.

Having said that, let me quickly add that Tain, in its minor key, is one of the most unusual and enjoyable courses in the entire country. It's a Tom Morris layout, so it comes replete with penal bunkers, green-fronting swales, a few blind shots, and imaginative one-shotters. The first hole alone is worth the price of admission: from the first tee it looks straightforward enough but, out in the fairway, you realize you are about to make a blind second shot over a public byway *and* a fence to a tucked away, smallish green. Welcome to quirky Tain! Most of the front nine humps and bumps along *in extremis* before the ground smoothes out a bit on the inward nine. "Alps," a two-shotter (#11), is reminiscent of Carnoustie's "Spectacles" and two superb par 3s over a burn at #16 and #17 bring the round to an unusual close. The home hole is plain vanilla made venturesome only by the proximity of the green to the plate-glass windows of the attractive clubhouse built in 1998.

For some reason, a lot of pesky black flies inhabit Tain. In calm weather they can be annoying. You can hope for a stiff Scottish breeze. And a final note on the setting of Tain Golf Club: on Golf Road, a one-lane track leading to the clubhouse, you'll drive the length of a striking gothic cemetery and, if you're a golfer, you can't help but think, "Here lies the ultimate 19th hole." Indeed, Tain Golf Club leaves an indelible imprint on the mind.

65. Turnberry Hotel – Ailsa Course *

Region #: 2   **Category:** seaside links
Architect(s): Mackenzie Ross (1946-51)
Length: 6440-6976   **SSS:** 72 **Par:** 69-70
Address: Turnberry, Ayrshire KA26 9LT
Directions: rt at junction of A77 and A719

Reservations phone: 01655-334-135; main desk #01655-331-000
Fax: 01655-331-152
Email: turnberry.reservations@westin.com
Website: turnberry.co.uk
Booking Contact(s): reservations office for hotel and courses
Director of Golf: Paul Burley; 01655-334-300

Phone - Starter/Pro shop: 01655-334-048
Fee(s) (2005): hotel res £105 all wk; non-res £130 wkday, £175 wkend
Deposit (2005): none
Visitor Policies: all wk; hotel residents have
priority; non-res may book 2 wks prior to
date of play - call pro shop
Buggies: no; caddies only; no pullcarts (carry
or be caddied)
Other: companion course, the Kintyre
(formerly Arran), redesigned by Donald Steel,
opened 2001, £105 all wk

DRIVE TIME
Troon: about 35 min on the A77;
1 hr on the coastal route (A719)
Glasgow Airport: 1 hr, 15 min

    I'd love to wax poetic about Turnberry's incomparable location in South Ayrshire, for this is Robert Burns's romantic countryside where the Ayrshire coastal plain gives way to the rolling, green hills of Galloway. Above it all, the Turnberry Hotel sits majestically on a high bluff overlooking an expansive seascape encompassing two golf courses and views to the Isle of Arran, the Kintyre Peninsula, and, on a clear day, Ireland on the far-off southwest horizon. Ten miles offshore, the Ailsa

Situated on a high bluff overlooking the sea,
Turnberry is Scotland's premier seaside resort.

Craig—a tortoise-shaped volcanic rock (1208 feet high)—anchors the scene with primeval certitude. Here we have Scotland's premier seaside resort—indeed, one of the world's premier seaside resorts.

But this is a practical book. Travelers want to have less poetic information— like, "Do you have to stay at the hotel to play the golf course?" and, "If you stay at the hotel, how much does it cost?".

OK. *Do you have to stay at the hotel to play the golf course?* Technically, no. Because Turnberry is, in effect, a daily-fee course, one can usually get onto the Ailsa Course, even in high season, without staying at the hotel. The way to do that is to request a tee time *two weeks* prior to the desired date of play. Alternatively, one might simply call the course when in the area to determine if a tee time is available. Most visiting golfers who really want to play Turnberry are not willing to take that risk, in which case, the only option is to "pay the piper."

How much does it cost to stay at the hotel? That's the stopper for many people. Here's the damage, circa 2005: £375 ($580) per night, double occupancy, plus £105 for golf on the Ailsa. That's a hotel-golf experience of about $450 per person, per day. Which is not to say there aren't seasonal and package deals you can buy into. Turnberry is one Scottish hotel where tour operators do get rates well below the stated "rack rate." But, is Turnberry worth the cost at whatever price? Only you can decide.

Is Turnberry worth the cost at whatever price? Remember that classic bumper sticker: "We're not extravagant. We're just spending our kids' inheritance."

Like the great hotels of the Canadian Rockies, Turnberry Hotel was a product of the golden age of rail transportation. Built in 1906, it was owned and operated by a railroad company as a destination resort. Sitting atop the great bluff overlooking the linksland, with its russet roof and white façade, the building looks as if it might have been transferred wholesale from colonial America— maybe George Washington's Mt. Vernon on steroids. Edwardian or neo-colonial, in either case it's a classic—timeless in its appeal, yet a monument to times gone by. One can only hope it will continue giving visual pleasure and physical comfort for centuries to come.

The history of golf at Turnberry falls into two distinct periods: the War Years and the Post-War Years. Britain's engagement in the twentieth century's two world wars wreaked havoc at Turnberry. Twice within thirty years, the linksland was commandeered as an airstrip by the Royal Air Force. After World War I, James Braid and C.K. Hutchinson were hired to reconstruct the golf courses. With the coming of World War II, land was bulldozed and runways were built (fortunately, most of the damage was done a bit inland below the hotel, away from the seaside linksland). By 1945, Turnberry was as exhausted as the British nation.

Into this breach stepped a determined hotel director, Frank Hole, who would not allow his parent company to abandon the golf courses at Turnberry. Hole persevered and ultimately contracted with Mackenzie Ross to design a new course. Work began in 1946 and continued over a period of five years. When it was done, Ross had achieved a course widely recognized as a classic of championship quality equal to its setting—the first such course built in Scotland in many years and the first of the post-war period (ultimately, the only twentieth-century course included on the "rota" of the British Open).

Tournament golf found its way to Turnberry immediately, culminating, first, in its hosting of the Walker Cup in 1963, then in its designation in 1977 by the Royal and Ancient as the newest venue for the British Open. Turnberry arrived on the international golf scene as the stage for one of the two or three most dramatic tournaments in Open history—the famous "Duel in the Sun" between Tom Watson (the winner by one stroke) and Jack Nicklaus. In a literate introduction to one of the best yardage books in Scottish golf, architect Donald Steel tells the Turnberry story:

> Turnberry's graduation to the envied ranks of host to the Open championship was a dream in every sense. When, at last, the ultimate accolade was conferred upon the incomparable Ailsa course in 1977, it inspired one of the most memorable weeks in the long history of champion-ship golf.
>
> It was a week dominated by Tom Watson and Jack Nicklaus, the supreme players at the time; it was a week when the record books were rewritten, a week when the sun shone. As Watson and Nicklaus discovered, there are few more inspiring places to play golf than Turnberry, a true delight with spectacular ocean holes and views not exceeded anywhere.
>
> Polls now regularly acknowledge the Ailsa as one of Britain's top three courses, confirmation that gives it eminence worldwide. Together with a handsome new clubhouse and a magnificent new spa to augment the splendours of the hotel, its facilities are second to none.

Since 1977, Turnberry has hosted two additional Opens—in 1986 (won by Greg Norman) and in 1994 (won by Nick Price). Interesting, isn't it, how these Scottish tracks seem to bring the cream to the top! And the next Open at Turnberry? Infrastructure seems to be the problem here. If the Ayrshire Council comes through with improved road access to Turnberry, hotel management is hoping the Open will return in 2009.

A few notes on the Ailsa course: With its expansive layout, rolling terrain, and wispy, waving grasses, I like to think of Turnberry as "Muirfield with a view." Certainly this is one of the two or three most beautiful seaside courses in Scotland. Hole #s 4 through 11 play along the water in Scotland's finest stretch of sustained seaside golf—first, tacking leftward along Turnberry Bay to the promontory where the famous #9 tee is perched; then cutting ninety degrees to the right past Turnberry's landmark lighthouse.

These magnificent seaside holes are bracketed by superb inland combinations of (1) three parallel opening holes (par 4s of varying length) and (2) seven closing holes that feature imaginative changes of direction, length, and variety. There is simply no weak link here—all told, some of the most memorable holes in Scottish golf.

Now what do you think about forking over the money for Turnberry? It's not an easy decision, but remember that classic bumper sticker: "We're not extravagant. We're just spending our kids' inheritance."

Nongolf notes: Just north of Turnberry, south of Ayr, you'll find historic Culzean (pronounced Cull-LANE) Castle, the most visited of Scotland's "National Trust" properties. This perfectly-preserved Georgian mansion, built by Robert Adam, Scotland's leading architect of the eighteenth century, is surrounded by forest walks, expansive grounds, and formal gardens. It was an elegant office site for General Dwight Eisenhower during World War II and, despite the heavy traffic, should be seen when you're in the area.

An alternative to the pricey menu of food and drink at Turnberry: drive two miles north to the village of Maidens where you'll find *Cotter's Restaurant* at the Malin Court Inn (01655-331-457) and, nearby on a picturesque half-moon bay, *Wildings Hotel and Restaurant*. Wildings, in particular, is wildly popular with the locals. Reservations recommended (01655-331-401). For pub life, head the other direction on the A77 to Girvan.

66. West Kilbride (1893)

Region #: 2   **Category:** seaside links
Architect(s): Tom Morris (1893), Willie Fernie (1905), James Braid (1923)
Length: 5896-6452   **SSS:** 71   **Par:** 71

Address: 33-35 Fullarton Dr, Seamill WK, Ayrshire KA23 9HT
Directions: left toward sea at junction of A78 and B781 (Yerton Brae)
Reservations phone: 01294-823-911   **Fax** 01294-823-911
Email: golf@westkilbridegolfclub.com
Website: westkilbridegolfclub.com
Booking Contact(s): secretary for 8+ groups; otherwise pro shop

Secretary: Hamish Armour   **Professional:** Graham Ross
Phone - Starter/Pro shop: 01294-823-042
Fee(s) (2005): wkday £35; day tkt £45
Deposit (2005): none
Visitor Policies: M-F only   **Buggies:** no

West Kilbride Golf Club is best described with the word "most." This is the *most northern* linksland along Ayrshire's golf coast stretching some sixty miles from West Kilbride to Turnberry. West Kilbride sits about twenty-four miles north of Troon and five miles north of Ardrossan (where CalMac ferries embark for the Isle of Arran). Despite its pedigreed design history involving Tom Morris, Willie Fernie, and James Braid, West Kilbride is easily the *most overlooked* and *most underrated* of Ayrshire's great links courses. This is due in part to its location a bit removed from the golf magnet at Troon. Among all the golf courses of Scotland—not just those of Ayrshire—West Kilbride is among the *most exposed* to the open sea. Situated on a sand shelf below sharply rising bluffs, the course sits defenseless against whatever the western seas and skies care to unleash. Part and parcel of that siting, West Kilbride enjoys the *most panoramic views* to the open sea (at eye level) of any golf course in Scotland. With no hills or dunes to obscure the view, the water is simply there, visible from every hole, and, on the occasional sunny, calm day, there can be no finer place on God's green earth. Essentially three fairways wide, bounded on one side by the proximate sea and on the other by private property, West Kilbride presents the *most out-of-bounds* of any course I have encountered. Out-of-bounds is a factor on twelve of eighteen holes, including seven of the last nine. Finally, West Kilbride has the *most laid-back, classiest clubhouse* in Scotland. We're not talking ritz here, but down-home, comfortable digs with Louis Armstrong, Billie Holiday, and Sarah Vaughan on the sound system. It doesn't get any better than that.

67. **Western Gailes Golf Club (1897) +**

Region #: 2   **Category:** seaside links
Architect(s): Willie Park, Sr. and Jr., Fred Hawtree (1975)
Length: 6179-6639   **SSS:** 73   **Par:** 71

Address: Gailes, Irvine KA11 5AE
Directions: 8 mi N of Troon off A78 (2 mi S of Irvine)

Reservations phone: 01294-311-649   **Fax:** 01294-312-312
Email: enquiries@westerngailes.com
Website: westerngailes.com
Booking Contact(s): Vicky O'Dowd, Lynn Scott

Secretary: Ian Sproule   **Professional:** no
Phone - Starter/Pro shop: call reservations #
Fee(s) (2005): £95 wkday, £140 day tkt (incl buffet lunch M, W, F);
Sun £100, no day tkt   **Deposit (2005):** 50%   **Buggies:** no
Visitor Policies: M, W, F 9-12, 2-4:30 pm; Sun 2-3:30 pm

With Kingsbarns, Nairn, Cruden Bay, Royal Aberdeen, and Royal Dornoch, Western Gailes in recent years has formed a sort of second tier of elite courses increasingly familiar to golf tourists. This is due largely to its presence on some package tours and then the word-of-mouth buzz that follows such experiences. Certainly, if price is a measure of self-worth, Western Gailes has put itself in the company of Carnoustie and Prestwick and only a notch below St. Andrews' Old Course.

This is among Scotland's finest linkslands. It's in my personal Top Five . . . .

Is the reputation and price of Western Gailes justified relative to the rest of Scottish golf? In a word, yes. This is among Scotland's finest linkslands. It's in my personal Top Five list along with Cruden Bay, Machrie, Machrihanish, and North Berwick. That's a list that has as much to do with location, cost, accessibility, and clubhouse ambience as with the golf courses themselves. I like this northern part of the Ayrshire coast and, though Western is not in the bargain category, it is a uniquely satisfying place.

The great draw at Western Gailes, as at Cruden Bay, is the extraordinarily convoluted links terrain and the powerful challenge of golf on a characteristically windy venue. Here, a kaleidoscope of sandhills, hillocks, humps, bumps, depressions, marram grass, gorse, and heather present an ever-changing visual treat and persistent challenge to the shotmaker. Holes #5 through #13 play along the coast—one of the longest stretches of seaside play in Scottish golf. And it is here that the gales common to Gailes come so frequently into play, for this is a course fully exposed to the prevailing winds. And, though the visitor tees play to only about 6200 yards, these middle holes can often make you feel like

The elegant whitewashed clubhouse at Western Gailes—winner of award for the UK's "Best Dirty Bar" (casual lounge for golfers).

you're grappling with a 7000-yard monster. Certainly, the average golfer will be adequately challenged from the yellow tees; if you are allowed to play from the white tees (ask the starter), you'll fully understand why Western Gailes is used as a qualifying course when the Open is held at Royal Troon or Turnberry.

Western Gailes sits on a narrow strip of land between the coastal rail line and the sea. The course is basically two fairways wide—at first glance, a classic out-and-back links. The difference at Western is the position of its elegant whitewashed clubhouse. Rather than residing at one end of an out-and-back chain of holes, this clubhouse sits on high ground nearly at mid-point in the chain. Thus, the routing is a racetrack loop—off to the first turn (#1 to #5), down the backstretch (to #13), then on to the wire (#14 through #18). Just as at a racetrack, the Gailes clubhouse looks out over the finish line. There's no stopping at the ninth hole; that's way off on the other side of the track!

With Glasgow Gailes just across the road, there's a powerful attraction to spend a full day playing golf at the Gailes. Certainly these two courses make one of the strongest one-two punches in Scottish golf

See also: Glasgow Gailes, Kilmarnock, and Royal Troon.

68. Whitekirk Golf and Country Club (1995)

Region #: 3   **Category:** parkland
Architect(s): Cameron Sinclair
Length: 6225-6526   **SSS:** 72   **Par:** 72

Address: Whitekirk nr N Berwick, E Lothian EH395PR
Directions: 5 mi SE of N Berwick off A198

Reservations phone: 01620-870-300   **Fax:** 01620-870-330
Email: countryclub@whitekirk.com
Website: whitekirk.com
Booking Contact(s): club mgr   **Professional:** Paul Wardell

Club Mgr: David Brodie
Fee(s) (2005): wkday £25, day tkt £35; wkend £35, day tkt £50
Deposit (2005): £10
Visitor Policies: all wk   **Buggies:** 15 - general hire

Surrounded by rolling farmland, Whitekirk Golf and Country Club perches on and around a high, graceful hill that dominates the terrain near Whitekirk hamlet midway between North Berwick and Dunbar. This place reminds me of the movie *Field of Dreams:* "Build it and they will come." Landowner-developer George Tuer built it in 1995 and they are coming. It's a popular place with locals for miles around.

Americans will feel right at home at Whitekirk. Visitors are welcome at all times. Indeed, the whole idea of Whitekirk is daily-fee visitor appeal. To that end, the facility features a comfortable, classy clubhouse with good food service and a full-blown leisure club (unfortunately, *not* available to visitors). Outside, golf carts are lined up just like at home and a 300-yard, American-style practice range encourages a proper warm-up (a rarity in Scottish golf). Plans are on the drawing board for a sixty-to-seventy room hotel and an additional eighteen holes of golf.

So, Mr. Tuer has not missed a beat when it comes to marketing. Furthermore, the course itself happens to be a worthy addition to Scottish golf.

A young Scottish designer, Cameron Sinclair, did the work here and he did a good job of it. Four sets of tees accommodate golfers of all abilities. Strong par 3s and several long par 4s put a lot of starch in this golf experience. Elevated teeing grounds provide outstanding views over the rolling Lothian countryside—to nearby Tantallon Castle and out to the sea five miles away. This is a good bargain in Scottish golf and ideal for a buggy candidate.

Most Frequently-Called Reservations Telephone Numbers

From outside the United Kingdom, dial 011-44, then the following:

Brora 1408-621-417
Carnoustie 1241-853-789
Crail Golfing Society 1333-450-686
Cruden Bay 1779-812-285
Dunbar 1368-862-317
Gleneagles 1764-694-469
Golf House Club - Elie 1333-330-301
Kingsbarns 1334-460-861
Leven Links 1333-428-859
Lundin Links 1333-320-202
Montrose 1674-672-932
Nairn 1667-453-208
North Berwick 1620-892-135
Prestwick 1292-671-020
Royal Aberdeen 1224-702-571
Royal Dornoch 1862-810-219
Royal Troon 1292-311-555
St. Andrews Bay 1334-837-412
St. Andrews Links Management 1334-466-666
Scotscraig 1382-552-515
Turnberry 1655-334-135
Western Gailes 1294-311-649

Notes

APPENDICES

APPENDIX A

Golf-Readiness Checklist

❏ Golf bag with rain hood

❏ Golf balls: at least 3 per round - or buy them there

❏ Tees; divot repair tool; ball markers; pencils

❏ Two pairs of shoes (metal spikes are ok)　　❏ or rubber overshoes

❏ Hat (preferably waterproofed)　　❏ stocking cap or earmuffs

❏ Umbrella

❏ Waterproof rain suit　　❏ Windbreaker

❏ Sweater(s) (dress in layers)

❏ Two towels and/or washcloths (for cleaning ball, glasses in the rain)

❏ Winter gloves (yes, even in summer it can get cold)

❏ Sunscreen

❏ First-aid kit: tape/bandaids/ibuprofen or aspirin/lanolin

❏ Water bottle (there won't be any drinking water on most courses)

❏ Ziploc bags (to keep food, etc., separated/dry)

❏ One or two 2 to 3-foot *bungee cords* (to secure bag to trolley)

Nongolf items
❏ USGA handicap card

❏ Allan Ferguson's *Golf in Scotland*

❏ Passport　　❏ Driver's licence

APPENDIX B

Useful Internet Sites

Following is a list of websites of general interest and of many lodgings mentioned in the text. Sites of individual golf courses can be found in "Part III, The Directory of Courses."

General Interest

aboutscotland.com - general, incl lodging
bta.org.uk - British Tourist Authority
www.dcs.ed.ac.uk - malt whisky information
eif.co.uk - Edinburgh International Festival
electricscotland.com - general interest and history
historic-scotland.gov.uk - Historic Scotland
islaywhiskysociety.com - Islay Whisky Society
houseofbruar.com - House of Bruar nr Pitlochry - gift emporium
news.bbc.co.uk - British Broadcasting Co.
nationalgalleries.org - National Galleries of Scotland
nms.ac.uk - National Museums of Scotland
nts.org.uk - National Trust for Scotland
walking.visitscotland.com - hiking
scotch-whisky.org.uk - association of whisky distillers
scotchwhisky.net - all things whisky
scotland-info.co.uk - general
scotsman.com - Edinburgh, national newspaper
smws.com - Scotch Malt Whisky Society
visitscotland.net - VisitScotland (formerly the Scottish Tourist Board)

Transportation and Communication

arnoldclarkrental.co.uk - Arnold Clark rental cars
ba.com - British Airways *(other airlines - see, p. xx)*
britrail.com - rail transportation
calmac.co.uk - Caledonian-MacBrayne ferries
firstscotrail.co.uk - rail transportation
inter800.com - toll-free telephone numbers
multimap.com - online mapping service
poirishsea.com -- P & O Irish Sea ferries
rental car companies - see p. xx
streetmap.co.uk - mapping service

Scottish Golf

oldcourse-experience.com - The Old Course Experience
opengolf.com - official site of the British Open
randa.org - The Royal and Ancient Golf Club
scottishgolf.com - Scottish Golf Union

scottishgolfhistory.net - Neil Laird, golf historian
scottishgolfsociety.com - Scottish Golf Society
teetimescotland.com - fee-based internet booking
uk-golfguide.com - course directory; accommodations; links; info bulletin boards

Golf Discount Cards and Open Competitions
aberdeenshiregolfclassic.com - Aberdeenshire Golf Classic
carnoustiecountry.com - Carnoustie Classic and Carnoustie Dream Ticket
gallowaygolfclassic.co.uk - Galloway Golf Classic
golfeastlothian.com - Golf East Lothian Passport
greensavers.co.uk - Bunkered Magazine's 2-for-1 program
openfairways.co.uk - UK-wide offers (4 for 3, 2 for 1)
scottishgolfclassics.com - Drambuie Scottish Golf Classics
2-fore-1golf.com - UK-wide offers
weeyellowbook.com - The Wee Yellow Book (club open competitions)

Fife and St. Andrews
eastneukwide.co.uk - East Neuk Promotional Group
eatingoutinfife.co.uk - Fife restaurants
st-andrews.ac.uk - University of St. Andrews
standrews.org.uk - St. Andrews Links Management
standrews.co.uk - Kingdom of Fife tourist board
saint-andrews.co.uk - Town Council

Other Regions and Towns
agtb.org - Aberdeen and Grampian Highlands
angusanddundee.co.uk - Angus and Dundee
arran.net - Isle of Arran
ayrshirescotland.com - Ayrshire
ayrshire-arran.com - Ayrshire and Isle of Arran
boatofgarten.com - Boat of Garten and Speyside
dufftown.co.uk - Dufftown and whisky country
gael-net.co.uk - West Highlands
grantown.co.uk - Grantown-on-Spey and Speyside
highlandescape.com - Highlands
isle-of-islay.com - Islay
north-berwick.co.uk - North Berwick
peterhead.org.uk - Peterhead
pitlochry.org.uk - Pitlochry Festival Theatre
scot-borders.co.uk - Borders tourist board (southeast)
scotland-inverness.co.uk - Inverness
visitarran.net - Isle of Arran
visitdornoch.com - Dornoch
visithighlands.co.uk - Highlands tourist board
visitnairn.com - Nairn

LODGING

$ = under £30 per person per night (most 3-star B & Bs and some 4-star B & Bs)
$$ = £30 - 45 (most 4-star B & Bs and many 3-star hotels)
$$$ = £45 - 70 (some 3-star hotels and most 4-star hotels)
$$$$ = over £70 (some 4-star hotels and all 5-star resort hotels)

General
aasc.co.uk - Association of Scotland Self Caterers
aboutscotland.com - private promotional service
hotels-scotland.co.uk - private promotional service
scotlandsbestbandbs.co.uk - B & Bs promotional service
smoothhound.co.uk - private promotional service
theaa.com - UK Automobile Association
visitscotland.com - VisitScotland (formerly the Scottish Tourist Board)

Lodging - Region #1 (Fife)
aboutscotland.com/fife/queensterrace.html - 18 Queens Terrace, B & B, St. Andrews $$
ardgowanhotel.co.uk - Ardgowan Hotel, St. Andrews $$$
aslar.com - Aslar Guest House, St. Andrews $$
balbirnie.co.uk - nr Glenrothes $$$
balgeddiehouse.com - nr Glenrothes $$
bestwestern.com - Scores Hotel, St. Andrews $$$$
crawsnesthotel.co.uk - Craw's Nest Hotel, Anstruther $$
dunvegan-hotel.com - Dunvegan Hotel, St. Andrews $$$
edenhousehotel.com - Eden House Hotel, Cupar $$
hazelbank.com - St. Andrews $$$
lundin-links-hotel.co.uk - Largo $$
macdonaldhotels.co.uk - Rusacks, St. Andrews $$$$
monarchshouse.com - Monarchs House, St. Andrews $$$$
oldcoursehotel.co.uk - St. Andrews $$$$
oldmanorhotel.co.uk - Lundin Links $$$
rufflets.co.uk - Rufflets, nr St. Andrews $$$$
russellhotelstandrews.co.uk - St. Andrews $$$
standrewsbandbs.com - private association of B & Bs
standrewsbay.com - St. Andrews Bay Resort Hotel, nr St. Andrews $$$$
standrews-golf.co.uk - St. Andrews Golf Hotel, St. Andrews $$$$
st-andrews-golf-lodge.com - St. Andrews Golfing Lodge, St. Andrews $$$$
sandilandsfife.co.uk - Sandilands B & B, Lundin Links $$
stayinstandrews.co.uk - local promotional association
standrewsalbany.co.uk - Albany Hotel, St. Andrews $$$
thegolfhotelcrail.com - Golf Hotel, Crail $$
thehazelton.co.uk - The Hazelton B & B, Crail $$
theinn.co.uk - Inn at Lathones, nr St. Andrews $$$
theinnonnorthstreet.com - The Inn on North Street, St. Andrews $$$
thespindrift.co.uk - The Spindrift Hotel, Anstruther $

Lodging - Region #2 (Ayrshire)

anchoragehoteltroon.co.uk - Anchorage Hotel, Troon $$
copperbeechtroon.com - Copper Beech B & B $$
costley-hotels.co.uk - Lochgreen House, Highgrove House, Troon $$$
gemmelldunduff.co.uk - Dunduff Farm B & B, Dunure $$
lochwoodfarm.co.uk - Lochwood Farm B & B, Saltcoats $$
paramounthotels.co.uk - Marine Hotel, Troon $$$$
parkstonehotel.co.uk - Parkstone Hotel, Prestwick $$
piersland.co.uk - Piersland House Hotel, Troon $$$
southbeach.co.uk - South Beach Hotel, Troon $$$
thorncrofthouse.com - Thorncroft House B & B, Troon $$
turnberry.co.uk - Turnberry Hotel $$$$

Lodging - Region #3 (E. Lothian)

belhavenhotel.co.uk - North Berwick $$
glebehouse-nb.co.uk - Glebe House B & B, North Berwick $$
golfinn.co.uk - Golf Inn, Gullane $$
greywalls.co.uk - Gullane, country house hotel $$$$
hopefieldhouse.co.uk - Gullane B & B $
kilspindie.co.uk - Kilspindie House Hotel, Aberlady $$
*macdonaldhotels.co.u*k - Marine Hotel, North Berwick $$$
openarmshotel.com - Open Arms Hotel, Dirleton $$$
thegolfhotel.net - The Golf Hotel, North Berwick $$

Lodging - Region #4 (Angus)

carnoustie-hotel.com - Carnoustie Golf Course Hotel & Resort $$$$
carlogie-house-hotel.com - Carnoustie, mid-size hotel $$
links-hotel.com - Carnoustie Links Hotel $$
lochlorian.co.uk - Carnoustie, small hotel $$
oldmanorcarnoustie.com - Old Manor B & B, Carnoustie $$

Lodging - Region #5 (Inverness/Dornoch)

ballifhotel.btinternet.co.uk - Ballifeary Guest House, Inverness $$
carnegieclub.co.uk - Skibo Castle, Dornoch $$$$
claymorehousehotel.com -- Claymore House Hotel, Nairn $$$
cullodenhouse.co.uk - nr Inverness $$$
dunainparkhotel.co.uk - nr Inverness $$$
eagle-dornoch.co.uk - The Eagle Hotel, Dornoch $$
highfieldhouse.co.uk - Dornoch B & B $$
golf-view.co.uk - Golf View B & B, Tain $$
invernessbedandbreakfast.co.uk - Inverness Assoc. of B & Bs
lyndale.dircon.co.uk/guest - Lyndale Guest House, Inverness $$
mansfieldcastle.co.uk - Mansfield Castle Hotel, Tain $$$
morangiehotel.com - Tain $$$
swallow-hotels.com - Royal Golf Hotel, Dornoch; Newton Hotel, Golf View - Nairn $$$
moyness.co.uk - Moyness House B & B, Inverness $$
scotland2000.com/dornochcastle - Dornoch Castle Hotel $$
silverwells-inverness.co.uk - Silverwells Guest House $$

Lodging - Region #6 (North/Northeast)

aboutscotland.com/aberdeen/savock.html - Savock B & B, Foveran $$

macdonaldhotels.co.uk - Ardoe House, Aberdeen $$$

marcliffe.com - Marcliffe at Pitfodels, Aberdeen $$$$

kilmarnockarms.com - Kilmarnock Arms, Cruden Bay $$

udny.co.uk - Udny Arms, Newburgh $$

redhousehotel.com - Red House Hotel, Cruden Bay $$

stolafhotel.co.uk - St. Olaf Hotel, Cruden Bay $$

the-queens-hotel.com - Queens Hotel, Aberdeen $$$

Lodging - Region #7 (Perthshire/Central)

beinnbhracaigh.com - Beinn Bhracaigh B & B, Pitlochry $$

dunmurray.co.uk - Dunmurray B & B, Pitlochry $$

gleneagles.com - Gleneagles Resort Hotel $$$$

moulinhotel.co.uk - Moulin Hotel, Pitlochry $$

rosemountgolf.co.uk - Rosemount Golf Hotel, Blairgowrie $$

Lodging - Region #8 (Arran/Kintyre/Islay)

bridgend-hotel.com - Bridgend Hotel, Islay $$

craigard-house.co.uk - Campbeltown $$

glenmachrie.com - Glenmachrie B & B, Islay $$

machrie.com - Machrie Hotel & Golf Club nr Port Ellen $$$

thehuntinglodgehotel.com - The Hunting Lodge, nr Machrihanish, Kintyre $$

kilmichael.com --- Kilmichael Country House Hotel, Arran $$$$

APPENDIX C

Tourist Information Offices

Aberdeen
St. Nicholas House
Broad Street
01224-620-415

North Berwick
1 Quality Street
01620-892-197

Arbroath (nr Carnoustie)
Market Place
01241-872-609

Pitlochry
22 Atholl Road
01796-472-215

Ayr (nr Troon-Prestwick)
Burns Statue Square
01292-288-688

St. Andrews
70 Market Street
01334-472-021

Edinburgh
Waverly Market
Princes Street
0131-557-1700

Airport Information
Aberdeen 01224-722-2331
Edinburgh 0131-333-1000
Glasgow 0141-887-1111
Inverness 01667-464-000

Girvan (nr Turnberry)
Bridge Street
01465-714-950

Glasgow
35 St. Vincent Place
0141-204-4400

Inverness
23 Church Street
01463-234-353

APPENDIX D

Daylight Hours, April - October

(Glasgow; for comparison, daylight-saving time observed throughout)

Date	Sunrise	Sunset
April 1	6:49 a.m.	7:54 p.m.
April 15	6:13 a.m.	8:22 p.m.
May 1	5:35 a.m.	8:55 p.m.
May 15	5:06 a.m.	9:22 p.m.
June 1	4:41 a.m.	9:50 p.m.
June 15	4:31 a.m.	10:04 p.m.
July 1	4:36 a.m.	10:05 p.m.
July 15	4:52 a.m.	9:53 p.m.
August 1	5:21 a.m.	9:25 p.m.
August 15	5:47 a.m.	8:54 p.m.
September 1	6:20 a.m.	8:12 p.m.
September 15	6:48 a.m.	7:36 p.m.
October 1	7:19 a.m.	6:54 p.m.
October 15	7:47 a.m.	6:18 p.m.

APPENDIX E

Annotated Bibliography

General

Begley, Eve. *Of Scottish Ways*. Minneapolis: Dillon Press, 1977. A chatty overview of Scots history and socio-political culture for the layman.

Blundell, Nigel. *Scotland*. London: PRC Publishing, Ltd., 1998. A big, beautiful coffee table book with the requisite fabulous pictures, but without fear of substantive history or literature. A chapter on single-malt whiskys is first-rate.

Fisher, Andrew. *A Traveller's History of Scotland*. Gloucestershire UK: The Windrush Press, 1990. Weak on twentieth century, but otherwise thorough review of Scottish history from Roman times.

Fraser, Elisabeth. *An Illustrated History of Scotland*. Norwich UK: Jarrold Publishing, 1997. Lives up to its title; lavishly illustrated and well-written. In a word, excellent.

Herman, Arthur. *How the Scots Invented the Modern World*. New York: Crown Publishers, 2001. The subtitle of this book is "The True Story of How Western Europe's Poorest Nation Created Our World & Everything In It." The publisher may be guilty of hyperbole, but that does not diminish the value of this impressive work of intellectual history. The focus is on the 18th century's vibrant Scottish Enlightenment.

Sawyer, June Skinner (ed). *The Road North: 300 Years of Classic Scottish Travel Writing*. Glasgow: Neil Wilson Publishing, 2000. A compilation of essays and book excerpts organized chronologically by region and period. This book gives the reader a feel for the uniquely northern qualities of Scotland.

Taylor, Nicola. *Live and Work in Scotland*. Oxford: Vacation Work, 2001. Part of a series. You don't need to move to Scotland to benefit from this book.. A section of special interest, "Daily Lives," comprises about one-third of the text. Lots of information on everything from phones to schools.

Tranter, Nigel. *The Story of Scotland*. Moffat, Scotland: Lochar Publishing, 1987. The author tries to avoid the catalog approach to history but, frankly, with Scots history that's a tough assignment. Tranter was one of twentieth-century Scotland's most prolific writers, penning dozens of books about Scotland, both fiction and non-fiction.

Fiction: Catherine Coulter, Antonia Fraser, Diana Gabaldon, Margaret George, Neil Gunn, Margot Livesey, Jenifer Roberson, Sir Walter Scott, Jessica Stirling, Nigel Tranter.

Guidebooks

Baxter, John, et. al. *Scotland: Highlands and Islands.* Lincolnwood, IL: Passport Books, 1997. Excellent for detailed planning. Divides the Highlands into eight regions and highlights with photographs, maps, and sidebars. A focus on walks will please hikers.

McNeeley, Scott, ed. *Fodor's Scotland.* NY: Random House (Fodor's Travel Publications), revised periodically. The usual Fodor stew including chapters on history and golf. Regional presentation with tour recommendations; two chapters dedicated specifically to Edinburgh and Glasgow. A good index and two dozen stylized maps are helpful. Fodor's is fine, but food/lodging choices are limited in the extreme.

Ramsay, Alex. *Scotland.* London: HarperCollins, 1996. Beautifully-produced paper volume (112pp) features the author's photography. Eleven chapters focus on the regions of Scotland plus Edinburgh and Glasgow. Good maps with evocative text highlight features/attractions of each region.

Smallman, Tom, and Cornwallis, Graeme. *Scotland.* Melbourne, Australia: Lonely Planet Publications, 1999. The best of the general guidebooks—packed with useful and esoteric information. Major weakness: Lonely Planet's aggravating habit of citing lodging/restaurants at opposite poles on the expense spectrum. Best combined with a good specialty book on accommodations.

Williams, David. *Scotland's Best-Loved Driving Tours.* NY: Macmillan Travel, 1996. Part of a Frommer series produced by the Automobile Association and updated periodically. Twenty-five itineraries are organized under four broad geographic headings. Each tour includes directions, distances between recommended stops/ highlights, and an approximation of drive time. Sidebars highlight special attractions to walkers, history buffs, families, etc. Excellent photographs and glossy stock make this a first-rate planning guide and travel companion.

Lodging

Brown, Karen and June. *Karen Brown's England, Wales & Scotland: Charming Hotels & Itineraries.* San Mateo, CA: Karen Brown's Guides, latest revision. The subtitle of this volume really should be "Charming and *Unrelentingly Expensive Hotels.*" If your taste runs to the high-end, then these selections are right down your alley; Scotland has some of the most expensive hotels in the world.

Sawday, Alastair. *Alastair Sawday's Special Places to Stay in Britain.* Bristol, UK: Alastair Sawday Publishing, revised periodically. A selective book that celebrates "variety, individuality, good taste and high standards." The accent is on B & Bs, small hotels, and country inns. Each entry is pictured and described on a half-page, then located with good directions and a flag on regional maps in the front of the book. But watch out! Innkeepers pay to get into this book.

VisitScotland. *Where to Stay: Bed & Breakfast.* Revised annually. This and the following entry for hotels and guest houses combine a wealth of information on lodging. The books divide the country into eight regions. Introduction explains the tourist board's rating and classification schemes. A location index is organized by town. Double bogie: no size, price, or star-rating indices.

VisitScotland. *Where to Stay:Hotels and Guest Houses.* Revised annually. Visit Scotland also publishes self-catering and camping guides.

Golf

Bamberger, Michael. *To the Linksland: a Golfing Adventure.* NY: Penguin Books, 1992. Written by a Philadelphia sports reporter who spent a year as a caddie on the European professional tour. This is a hymn to the mystery and romance of golf in Scotland. A contemporary classic.

Browning, Robert. *A History of Golf: The Royal and Ancient Game.* NY: E.P. Dutton & Company, Inc., 1955. A veddy, veddy British (and delightful) look at the history of the great game from the longtime editor of Britain's *Golfing Magazine*, with lavish attention to arcane detail—all of course before the modern era ushered in by Palmer, Nicklaus, et. al.

Callander, Colin (ed.). *Golfing Gems: The Connoisseurs' Guide to Golf Courses in Scotland.* Laddingford, England: Beacon Books, 1997. A guide to the editor's favorite sixty courses in five regions of Scotland. Detailed descriptions of courses include color photos, course cards, restrictions, and travel directions.

Campbell, Malcolm. *The Scottish Golf Book.* Edinburgh: Lomond Books, 1999. Probably the best-selling book ever produced on Scottish golf. Ubiquitous in Scotland at phenomenally low prices for such a lavish production. Photographs by Glyn Satterley. Sketches, drawings, and photographs on virtually every page. Seven chapters cover the history of the game and its outstanding players, followed by descriptions of 48 courses organized under three headings—historic courses, classic courses, and hidden gems. A parade of "most fearsome holes," a review of great events, memorable British Opens, and a chronology close out this great contribution to the bookshelf on Scottish golf.

Cornish, Geoffrey S. & Whitten, Ronald E. *The Architects of Golf: A Survey of Golf Course Design from Its Beginnings to the Present, with an Encyclopedic Listing of Golf Course Architects and Their Courses.* rev. ed. NY: HarperCollins Publishers, 1993. First published in 1981, the title says it all. Chapters 1-4 survey the origins of golf in Scotland and, most important, the relationships between the land and the evolution of the game. An encyclopedic listing of architects and their courses allows the traveler to identify the courses of, for example, James Braid and Tom Morris. An index by course name is helpful.

Dodson, James. *Final Rounds: A Father, a Son, the Golf Journey of a Lifetime.* New York: Bantam Books, 1996. This is a moving tribute to the life of a cancer-ridden father with only a few months to live. Someone once said, "Sports writing gets better as the ball gets smaller." Dodson's prose is exhibit #1. This one will bring a tear to the eye, a lump to the throat, and joy to the heart.

Edmund, Nick (ed.) *Following the Fairways.* Northumberland, England: Kensington West Productions, Ltd., 1997. Comprehensive guide to UK golf courses. Informative thumbnail sketches of courses, but contact information, fees, and other data are outdated. Color photographs of signature holes and clubhouses. Schematics of many of the courses. Organized by region.

Finegan, James W. *Blasted Heaths and Blessed Greens: A Golfer's Pilgrimage to the Courses of Scotland.* New York: Simon & Schuster, 1996. This charming and informative volume by the dean of American golf writers is the result of twenty golf expeditions taken to Scotland since 1971. Finegan reviews some sixty courses in twelve chapters organized by proximity. Careful course descriptions are augmented by the author's evocative portraits of surrounding towns and countryside. Until you go, this is "armchair travel" at its best (unfortunately out of print). Finegan has written similar reviews of courses in Ireland, England and Wales.

Gillespie, Curtis. *Playing Through: A Year of Life and Links Along the Scottish Coast.* NY: Scribner, 2003. The best of the recent spate of books combining reportage with personal reflections. The locus of Gillespie's work is Gullane village where, over the course of a year, the writer comes to terms with the ghost of his deceased father while celebrating golf on Gullane Hill and the crotchety camaraderie of Archie Baird and green-grocer Jack Marston.

Hamilton, David. *Golf: Scotland's Game.* Kilmacolm, Scotland: The Partick Press, 1998. A penetrating history from one of the most widely-quoted and respected contemporary students of the game. From primary sources, Hamilton develops a clear and persuasive argument that golf was (a) a winter game; (b) played in a "short" version and a "long" version; and (c) nurtured and organized in Scotland (not imported from Holland). Hamilton's prose is surrounded by oodles of fascinating illustrations and photos. This one's a "must have"—unfortunately, out of print and soon to be a collector's item.

_____. *Scottish Golf Guide.* Edinburgh: Canongate Books, Ltd., 1995. Revised edition of a small book first printed in 1984. Brief descriptions of eighty-four courses are organized alphabetically. A forward by Sean Connery and essays by a native on weather, dress, and the history of golf in Scotland round out the presentation.

Konik, Michael. *In Search of Burningbush: a Story of Golf, Friendship, and the Meaning of Irons.* New York: McGraw-Hill, 2004. The ultimate "golf buddy" book. The foils here are a friend with a bone disease and a two-week pilgrimage to Fife in search of Michael Murphy's mystical golf club, "Burningbush," with the story coming to rest at MacDuff's Cave near the 15th green at Crail's Balcomie Links. A great companion volume to take traveling with *Golf in the Kingdom.* As they say in Scotland, "Well done."

Mackenzie, Richard. *A Wee Nip at the 19th Hole.* NY: Bantam Books, 1998. A wee nip of a book about the caddies of St. Andrews by the current caddie master of the Old Course. Nicely-produced with atmospheric photographs, this one will not win any literary prizes but makes for a good bedside read.

McGuire, Brenda and John. *Golf at the Water's Edge: Scotland's Seaside Links.* NY: Abbeville Press, 1997. A small book, lovingly produced, with sketches by John McGuire. Twenty-one courses are profiled. The watercolor renditions of course layouts are helpful and each short essay does a good job of capturing the history and character of the courses treated. An enjoyable if only moderately-useful little volume.

Murphy, Michael. *Golf in the Kingdom.* New York: Viking, 1972. After playing a round of golf on a misty Scottish links, imagine yourself sitting in the clubhouse, looking out over the 18th hole, with a bowl of hot soup and a dram of local elixir, reading this cult classic—the top-selling golf book in publishing history. As you commune with Shivas Irons and contemplate the "mystery of the hole" and the "whiteness of the ball," it just doesn't get any better than this. For literary diversion, this is still the best book to take along on your golf trip.

_____. *The Kingdom of Shivas Irons.* NY: Broadway Books, 1997. The long-awaited sequel to *Golf in the Kingdom,* this one wanders a bit farther afield—some would say a little too far. Be that as it may, every fan of Michael Murphy will love it (and that's all of us, isn't it?).

Rubenstein, Lorne. *A Season in Dornoch: Golf and Life in the Scottish Highlands.* NY: Simon & Schuster, 2001. Lots of golfers read this book in 2002 and flocked to Dornoch over the next couple of years to see the slice of heaven Rubenstein enjoyed with his wife one idyllic summer. An entertaining, evocative portrait of a small village and the central place of golf in the life of that small village.

Stewart, Tanner. *Hallowed Ground: A Golf Trip to Scotland.* Baltimore: PublishAmerica, 2004. Eight well-heeled, middle-age guys make a trip to Scotland to play the Open rota courses and stay in expensive hotels. Despite the once-in-a-lifetime approach and high-end orientation, the author and his pals are a reasonably sensitive lot who appreciate Scotland and occasionally escape the reservation. Stewart could have used a ruthless editor, but his book is still useful and informative for those making a first and perhaps only trip to the auld sod.

Tobert, Michael. *Pilgrims in the Rough: St. Andrews Beyond the 19th Hole.* Edinburgh: Luath Press Ltd., 2000. A delightful perspective on the history of the town by a resident San Andrean. Parallels are drawn between the early pilgrims to St. Andrews and the pilgrims who flock to the links today.

Whyte, David J. *Golfer's Guide: Scotland - 150 Courses and Facilities.* London: New Holland Publishers, 2001. Part of the Globetrotter series, this book features dozens of stunning pictures taken by Scotland's leading golf photo-journalist. Organized by eight regions, short but informed course descriptions are augmented by an introductory essay on each region and two pages on food, lodging, and nongolf options.

INDEX

Golf in Scotland can be purchased either in whole or in part in electronic format from Ferguson Golf (1-800-835-6692) or at *www.fergusongolf.com*.

Updates and corrections to critical information in *Golf in Scotland* will be posted on the Ferguson Golf website.

Wholesale buyers: contact Baker & Taylor, Unique Books, or Ferguson Golf.

The Author

Allan McAllister Ferguson was born in Decatur, Illinois, in 1944. As president, chief cook, and bottlewasher of Ferguson Golf since 1999, he personally works with golfers to create memorable trips to Scotland. He typically makes two trips annually to refresh contacts and conduct research. Mr. Ferguson is retired from other businesses. During the 1980s, he and his wife, Ruth Wimmer, changed the look of commercial baby toys with their line of black and white developmental products still sold under the trade name, "Wimmer-Ferguson Child Products." Mr. Ferguson lives in Denver, Colorado, with his wife and a dog named Jezebel.